SEAN

LEARY'S

GREATEST

HITS

VOLUME THIRTEEN:

POST-PANDEMIC WEIRDNESS

THE POST-

COVID

ERA

PART ONE:

POST-PANDEMIC WEIRDNESS

September 2021 to April 2022

This book is published in the United States by Dreaming World Books and Dreams Reach Productions.

ISBN is 9781948662109

Library of Congress # Applied for.

Cover photo and design by Sean Leary.

Special thanks to Jackson, Julius Cortez, Steve and Anne Holmes, Tristan Tapscott, and everyone who has helped contribute to the success of QuadCities.com from the time I got there in January 2016 until present day.

It's been a great ride... let's keep enjoying the trip!

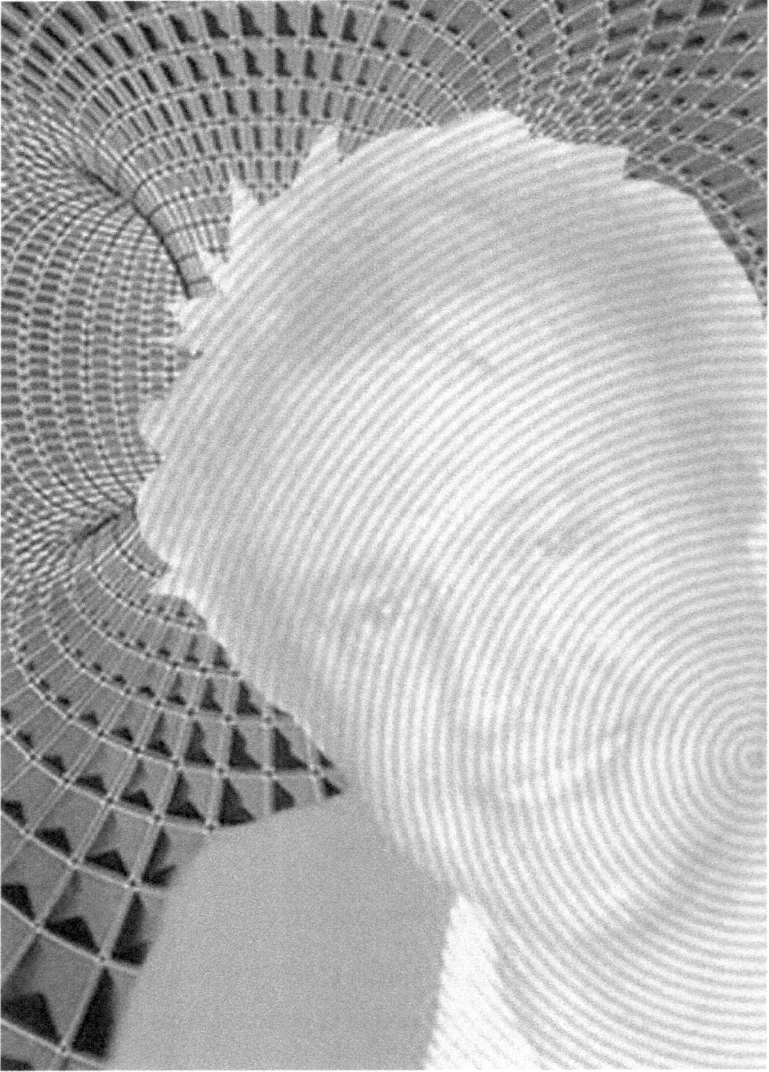

CONTENTS

It's Going To Be An Extremely Eventful Week, According To Time Travelers And Aliens

Sept. 3, 2021

Listen, folks, if you can't trust time travelers and aliens posting on TikTok, really, who can you trust?

And those time travelers and aliens are BOTH in agreement that the Pumpkin Cold Brew is far superior to the overhyped Pumpkin Spice Latte.

And I agree with them.

But aside from that incredibly important information, the aliens and time travelers also agree that this is going to be an astoundingly eventful week for us — especially next Tuesday, when a number of humans are going to win the alien abduction lottery, treating them to fabulous cash and prizes!

According to one TikTok time traveler, and his alien compatriots, NEXT TUESDAY, Sept. 9, an alien that landed here on June 14 (but has been going incognito since then, probably checking out state fairs and entering corn dog-eating competitions) is going to announce their

presence and tell earthlings that they are in grave danger —
and will begin evacuating people 4,000 at a time.

Why are we earthlings in grave danger?

Is it so implausible that this man's farts could start an
interplanetary war? I say NO.

Gary Busey's farts.

Hey, it's certainly credible.

But no, that was merely a joke. Well, sort of, it's no joke
that you should avoid Gary Busey and his farts, but that's
not why the aliens are abducting people.

According to the reliable sources of TikTok time travelers
and aliens, another species of aliens destroyed their home
planet 990 light years away (Due to trying to harness the
incredible power of Gary Busey's farts???? Note to self:
ASK THEM!!!) and needless to say, THEY ARE PISSED.

So pissed that they decided to get in their space cars and hightail it to earth, where they'll finally arrive in less than 100 years, because damn it, WHY AREN'T WE ANSWERING THEIR TEXTS????

But don't worry, and keep those aliens on block, because the GOOD alien is going to be taking 4,000 skilled workers and children (read: nobody from the Kardashian family) to a nearby habitable planet called Proxima B.

It takes 15 years to get there, so make sure you go to the bathroom beforehand, because they are not stopping. Then, the alien will return every 30 years, presumably with more ships and aliens, because otherwise it's going to get really crowded, and that will, to quote the time traveler, "save humanity."

And then once humanity is all on Proxima B, we're going to have all the cameras set up around earth tape the frustrated reactions of the arriving evil aliens seeing we've given them the slip, and Ashton Kutcher is going to broadcast a message to the evil aliens telling them they've been PUNK'D!

BUT THAT'S NOT ALL!!!!!

Meteor shower, or chubby rain?

ANOTHER Time Traveler from the year 2714 is backing up PART of this story!

Sort of.

The Time Traveler is claiming that part of the story, the alien invasion part, is ACTUALLY, REALLY going to happen this week, NOT 100 years from now.

Anyway, according to our friend the Time Traveler from 2714, the alien invasion all has to do with the meteor shower that took place in July.

To astronomers and amateur star-gazers, it looked just like the Perseid meteor shower, but it was actually a smokescreen (probably the kind that Shaggy causes) and that many of the so-called meteors are actually spacecraft of an extra-dimensional alien race called the Nirons, who are going to invade earth and wage interdimensional war with us.

So, what's it going to be?

What time traveler should we believe?

One is saying the Nozic aliens are going to invade this week, and the other is saying other aliens are coming in 100 years to invade and a nice alien is going to make his presence known this week to save us.

Or maybe this time traveler, who's backed up by the alien on TikTok, is merely a double-agent, to make us think that the "nice" alien is benevolent but he's actually part of the wicked Nirons and he's just tricking us, because the Nirons cannot stand earthlings, probably because we were responsible for the show "King of Queens."

Thankfully, no matter what happens, we DO have the most powerful known weapon in the universe against any and all alien attacks.

No, not Gary Busey's farts.

They LOVE those.

They're like the most winsome and compelling fragrance to aliens.

Why do you think they abduct him so much?

No, the most powerful known weapon in the universe, the one thing that is guaranteed to repel any and all alien attacks, is far, far, far more magisterial and glorious.

It's

REDACTED

Will the Time Traveler from 2485 Be Right? Will Aliens Invade Earth On Tuesday?

Sept. 5, 2021

Well, there's still time to stock up on toilet paper.

As previously reported on QuadCities.com, your local news source for breaking news about time travelers on TikTok and alien invasions, our old friend the time traveler from 2485, as well as a couple of other time travelers (do they call each other and coordinate this stuff?) have predicted the earth will be invaded by aliens this week.

When will this event occur?

Don't worry, it won't interrupt your Labor Day barbecue and celebration.

Those considerate aliens are going to let us have our holiday before completely rocking our world and invading on Tuesday.

Now, unlike many alien invasions, you won't have to worry about this one.

According to the time travelers, the aliens hitting us up this week are actually here to save us from OTHER aliens who are still a good 100 years away.

Why are they getting here so soon?

Because it takes 15 years to get from their planet to ours and back, so it'll take a good three trips to get humans off world before the bad aliens show up, at which point they'll be like, "Hey, where's everybody at? We were going to invade this place and cause general turmoil and there's nobody around!"

And then another alien will say, "Wait, sir, we've got some life readings emanating from just over that hill!"

Then they'll all march over the hill and there they'll find a tavern, occupied by several million cockroaches, and Keith Richards.

"Mick, is that you?" Keith will say.

And the aliens will reply, "Gurl, you so crazy!"

Then they'll all laugh, and we'll fade to credits as a wacky song plays and slides of alien hijinks with Keith and the roaches slip by in the background.

So, I don't know, maybe it won't be so bad after all.

Anyway, here are the details, because I know you've been anxiously awaiting the lowdown on this event:

According to one TikTok time traveler, and his alien compatriots, NEXT TUESDAY, Sept. 9, an alien that landed here on June 14 (but has been going incognito since then, probably checking out state fairs and entering corn dog-eating competitions) is going to announce their presence and tell earthlings that they are in grave danger — and will begin evacuating people 4,000 at a time.

The GOOD alien is going to be taking 4,000 skilled workers and children to a nearby habitable planet called Proxima B. It takes 15 years to get there, so make sure you go to the bathroom beforehand, because they are not stopping. Then, the alien will return every 30 years, presumably with more ships and aliens, because otherwise it's going to get really crowded, and that will, to quote the time traveler, "save humanity."

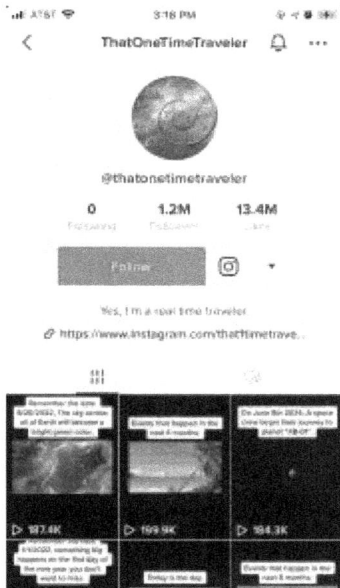

BUT THAT'S NOT ALL!!!!!

ANOTHER Time Traveler from the year 2714 is backing up PART of this story! Sort of. The Time Traveler is claiming that part of the story, the alien invasion part, is ACTUALLY, REALLY going to happen this week, NOT 100 years from now.

Anyway, according to our friend the Time Traveler from 2714, the alien invasion all has to do with the meteor shower that took place in July.

To astronomers and amateur star-gazers, it looked just like the Perseid meteor shower, but it was actually a smokescreen (probably the kind that Shaggy causes) and that many of the so-called meteors are actually spacecraft of an extra-dimensional alien race called the Nirons, who are going to invade earth and wage interdimensional war with us.

So, what's it going to be?

What time traveler should we believe?

Either way, I'm getting tacos on Monday instead, just in case.

A Night Out At The Clubs Post-Covid Proves Some Things Never Change

Sept. 10, 2021

As an entertainment writer, part of my job entails periodically going out to hit the local scene and check out what, if anything, is new and exciting, especially now that things have been opened up again, and hopefully will remain so (damn Delta variant!)

However, a night out at the bars, clubs and haciendas isn't only recreational. Sometimes it can be educational as well.

Here are some of the observations I made, after a recent night's cogent examination of the local night life:

Birds aren't the only ones with mating moves: You can pretty much scan the crowd and see who's into whom, who's checking out whom, who's trying to get with whom, and who's interested either way. It's fascinating and quite frankly hilarious to watch, and body language is loud and clear.

Man, those Dan Flashes shirts with the loud patterns really are back in style. I hope nobody has gotten any injuries buying them. I hear that's a very aggressive store.

Most girls will dance to almost any song. Most guys only have a few songs they'll dance to. Some guys have one song they will dance to, and usually those guys have developed an elaborate choreography routine to accompany it. However, most of the time, it's primarily a lot of women on the dance floor, and a couple of guys gamely doing their best.

You can say anything — no matter how vile, depraved, sexist or misogynist — in a lyric and as long as you accompany it with a killer dance beat, people won't care.

New Order's "Bizarre Love Triangle" is still one of the best dance songs ever recorded.

Sometimes, the world really is like "The King of Queens." Take a good look around next time you're at a general bar or club. You'll see more than your fair share of Leah Reminis with Kevin Jameses. And I'm not just talking about attractive women with heavy-set guys, I'm talking about women who obviously spent a lot of time getting ready and guys who obviously haven't.

Sorry guys, but if a woman spends at least an hour getting ready, a guy shouldn't be allowed to go out with her if his idea of "getting ready" looks as if it's grabbing a t-shirt from the top quarter of the hamper and throwing on a baseball hat that looks like it's been partially chewed by a pug. Hey, I've dated my fair share and I know how long it takes a woman to get ready to look as good as a lot of them do, and they're with these goombas who look like they're on their way to a kegger softball game. Which is fine if you're on your way to a kegger softball game. Not so much so if you're going out to a nice restaurant or going out with a girl who looks like she just stepped out of an issue of

Vogue. Somewhere, Kevin James and Adam Sandler are both smiling and nodding contentedly, knowing full well nothing I say is going to change this.

On your way home, you can see people run red lights, crash into garbage cans and shrubs and slowly swerve into the oncoming lane repeatedly, but if you're driving sanely around the speed limit, stone sober and the designated driver, you're the one who will get pulled over for a random check at 3 a.m.

Rock Island Won't Be The Same Without Theo's Java Club

Sept. 17, 2021

There have not been many constants that have stood the test of time in downtown Rock Island, through the passing of several eras, over the last three decades.

Theo's Java Club has been one of the few.

The unique, quirky, fantastic java and performance space at 213 17th St. has been a haven for local creatives and characters, blending with area lawyers and courthouse types, business folks, and tourists popping over from the hotel across the street. Theo's has long been a magnet for the Quad-Cities, drawing a broad range of people because it was a singular destination. Sure, you could get your coffee elsewhere, and, as time went on from the birth of coffee house culture in the mid-'90s, a lot of elsewheres popped up, but there was only one Theo's.

And that one Theo's will be very likely pouring its last cup o' joe Saturday, Oct. 2.

Barring a last-minute change, that will be the last day the spot will be open in its current incarnation, owner Theo Grevas told me this week, over coffee, of course, as we sat outside his shop, chatted, and watched the traffic go by in downtown Rock Island.

It was considerably less traffic than there had been the first time he and I sat outside that space and talked.

In 1994, before it even opened, I wrote the first ever media story on Theo's Java Club, for the long-departed Rock Island Argus.

I was working in downtown Rock Island, at the Argus building, which closed in 2008, and it was right at the onset of an explosion of coffee shops and culture spurred by the coming-of-age of people like me, in our late teens and early twenties, Gen X. At the time, downtown Rock Island was a bustling, robust hub — it was The District, and it was definitely the place to be.

Downtown Davenport and Moline were ghost towns, the Village of East Davenport was just a couple bars and little else. East Moline and Bettendorf had a few spots, but that was it, no big overarching area.

Downtown Rock Island, on the other hand, had a much different vibe. RIBCO and 2nd Ave. were the spots to be on the weekend, and there were no shortage of other bars and clubs along the same strip to pop in and out of. Some of them changed names as quickly as different musical and clothing styles flipped, but they remained hot. Copia, Blue Cat, Huckleberry's, and others offered great food and upscale beverages.

And then there was Theo's — the place EVERYONE went for their daily caffeine, for meetings, for lunch, to hangout, or just to chill.

And regardless of what happens going forward, once owner and founder Theo Grevas is no longer involved with the spot, it's just not going to be the same. He knows that, and he's actually in a pretty good mood about the whole thing.

"I think we're going to set a date Oct. 2, that's a Saturday night, I think that would be a good time to say that's it for Theo's, I think that's the date when we shall close," Theo said with a smile. "Changes are constant, they're just going to happen, I hope someone can step up to the plate and take over this shop or have something similar that people can go to like they've been going to Theo's the last 27 years. I hope so. We'll see."

Theo's Java Hut opened first in 1993 in downtown Davenport, but it was the Java Club, which opened in 1994 in downtown Rock Island that ended up creating his legacy.

And now, he says, it's time to move on, look back with a smile, but then turn around and go on to new things.

"I'm excited about it, I have a lot of things planned, my wife has a lot of things planned," Theo says. "I don't want to sound selfish about it, we've had a great 27 years, but I think we're in a great position to say it's time to step aside, look back on a great 27 years, and let someone else take things over and hopefully keep things going."

There are plenty of memories he'll take with him, and he's talking about writing them down in a book. One of them involving a certain screen legend who Theo says is probably the most famous person he's ever had come into his spot.

"Someone asked me before who was the most famous person who came in here, and I have to say it was Mickey Rooney," Theo said. "He came in here, he was doing a Circa show in the early 2000s, and he was in here eating breakfast with his wife, and I had this picture of him that

I'd had here at the coffee shop and I got him to sign it. He was a great guy!"

Over the years, I've interviewed and met up by chance with various other celebrities in Theo's. I interviewed members of Vampire Weekend there. Hung out with members of Smashing Pumpkins there. I ran into Olympic ice skater Scott Hamilton in line. I took members of Veruca Salt there when they asked me to take them to the best coffee shop in the Quad-Cities. And many others.

"Yeah, between Circa, and RIBCO, and The Mark, there's been a lot of famous people to come through here," Theo said. "When Daytrotter was downtown we'd get bands coming through here all the time."

Some of those stories might end up in Theo's book. Others will just be fond memories, he says.

But regardless, he's ready to close the chapter on his current business, and hopes that someone else steps up to keep it going in some form.

"We'll see what happens here," Theo said. "I'd sure like to see coffee here, it's been a wonderful spot, location, get a lot of people in, a lot of regulars, it's just a great spot, and I'm really happy we found this back in 94 and were able to continue with what we did. I'd like to see someone else come in and keep it here, but we'll see what happens.

"There are a couple people who are really interested in making this happen before Oct. 2, and if that happens, we'll stay open during the transition, but if nothing is finalized before then, we're looking at closing that Oct. 2, but it is fluid, something could change, you never know.

"I've got a train ticket Oct. 7, I'm going to the coast to relax on the beach," he said with a laugh, "so I've got to get going before then!"

And at that point, he finished his coffee, thanked me for the time, smiled, and said, "Well, I should probably get back inside and get back to work!"

We shook hands, said our goodbyes, and he walked back in, through the same doors he did after we first spoke 27 years ago, although with a much different mindset, and towards a much different path.

A path, a future, without Theo's, at least not in its current incarnation.

I hope whatever comes next is worthy of the space, of the legacy, of the memories, it will replace.

But regardless of what does arrive, there will never be another Theo's, and Rock Island will never quite be the same without it.

Ever Notice That The Media Pushes Celebrity Stories To Distract Us from The Real News?

Oct. 15 2021

The Royal Family!

Taylor dating Jen's ex!

Kanye West says something stupid!

Ever notice that the more heinous things get regarding the economy, wars, presidential scandals, etc., the more intensely the media ignores the real news to concentrate on either celebrity scandals or deviant crimes?

Sometimes I wonder if there's a grand conspiracy regarding celebrities as well.

What if celebrities are nothing but programmed Manchurian candidates, Stepford performers, who are hypnotized and controlled by secret government handlers who then program them to do silly crap to distract the masses every time such a distraction is needed?

The bigger the mess people need to be distracted from, the bigger the celebrity distraction pulled out of their butts. For example, with the economy going to crap, everyone losing their jobs and/or homes, a HUGE distraction was needed.

Paging Cardi B!

"Time for Operation Elvis, my friend. Are you ready to go into hiding somewhere in Brazil? Yes, we'll give you a satellite feed so you can watch your own funeral. No, the fake death will be painless. Just take the pills and you'll fall asleep, the docs won't know any better, and once you're pronounced, we'll switch out the body double for the autopsy. Sure, you can bring your shoe closet in its entirety….ok…ok…we'll be in touch…"

"Whew."

"What if that doesn't work, boss?"

"Well, we can always find a cute, blonde teenager to put in a reality show, can't we?"

Maybe I'm just being cynical here. Very, very, very cynical. And maybe it's just my sci-fi imagination running away with me.

But if this isn't true, at times it's extremely coincidental. It seems as if the people in control are constantly selling us an illusion, a distraction, to keep people's minds off of all the bigger things going on, and while doing so, to sell us their products.

And if it isn't true, it'll still make for a great sci-fi story.

Or a very short column.

Virtue Signaling Needs To Be Accompanied By Virtue To Accomplish Economic Diversity And Equality In The Arts

Oct. 24, 2021

Diversity in the arts is the latest hot topic on the Quad-Cities arts scene, and it's certainly a welcome one, as the discussion has long been overdue. There is a definite shortage of minority voices across the arts spectrum, and that needs to be corrected. The only way it will be corrected is by it being acknowledged and addressed.

Some groups have certainly been doing so, and deserve credit for it. Tristan Tapscott's Mockingbird on Main has been one of the most forward thinking theaters on the subject, with casts and shows that have distinctly featured minority performers and creatives. I've seen other groups working towards that for a while as well, as Circa '21 and The Speakeasy have long been making outreach to broaden the diversity of their casts, as have Playcrafters and Black Box Theater in Moline, among others.

However, while we're on the subject of diversity in the arts in the Quad-Cities, let's talk about ECONOMIC diversity as well, which is actually a bigger and more important topic. Because when it comes down to it, the best intentions are still just intentions, and it takes money to make them a reality.

I've been covering the arts here for over two decades, and along the way I've written and edited countless stories about grant monies and donations going out to area arts groups from altruistic organizations. And one thing I see over and over are the same names, the same groups, getting money.

Now, certainly, some of those groups desperately depend on those dollars. They don't draw a lot of people, they're true not-for-profits, and they provide needed creative expressions and experiences to our area.

But some also do not. Some groups and facilities around here are doing just fine, with endowments and people leaving them money in their wills, etc. And it would be nice to see the money otherwise going to the latter end up with groups that need it far more.

There are a number of arts entrepreneurs around here who are getting by on hard work and hustle, and are often struggling to make ends meet. It would be cool to see them starting to get more money. That's what keeps the arts scene diverse and vibrant, having a bigger tent, a larger number of voices, having a platform.

Along those same lines, there are a number of minority-run groups I've seen that haven't been able to make it, that would've been able to make a real impact on the local scene if they had the financial backing to do so.

Now, what do these groups have in common, and how does it fit into the larger discussion going on now in regard to diversity in the arts?

Many of these smaller groups don't have specific people hired to write applications for grants, to seek out and solicit grant money and donations, and to follow through on the functions necessary to continue to get those grants.

Most of those groups are run by a couple of folks working their asses off just to get by, to get their shows out, to keep their places running. A lot of them don't have time to adequately publicize their events, let alone seek out grant money and go through the arduous process of applying.

However, that doesn't cover ALL of these groups. Some of them HAVE applied for grants, and been denied.

Shellie Moore Guy, who has considerable experience in this matter, commented on this column after I initially posted it, and added the following comment (which I'm now adding to the column because it's a good point): "Smaller organizations, which doesn't necessarily mean, new or without knowledge of grant writing. have written grants and not received the funding… I say this because it would be a mistake for people to believe it is always about lack of knowledge."

While we're talking about this in regard to underrepresented communities, I think there needs to be more of an outreach of folks with grant monies and other available cash to these smaller groups, and these minority-run arts organizations.

There needs to be more of a recognition that if there are limited monies, perhaps it best serves the local arts communities to allow the better funded groups to get by on their own in regard to certain requests, and to give that money to groups for whom it would make a far bigger impact.

When I see something like The Spot in Rock Island — a minority-owned business providing vital programming to a minority community — go under, while I also see another group sitting on a pile of cash just chuck another grant onto the pile, there's something wrong.

That something needs to be addressed.

And if people are genuinely serious about wanting diversity in the arts, if the virtue signaling is going to be followed by virtue, particularly of the economic sort, the kind that really makes an impact, then there needs to be more of an outreach to make it happen.

Chappelle Needs To Be Heard, Not Canceled. When It Comes To Social Inequality

Oct. 27, 2021

There's a common phrase used in social justice circles: Pass the mic.

Pass the mic means, metaphorically, to let others talk, and it's usually used in regard to people of color.

It's a reminder that we need to listen to those people of color because their experience is different from ours if we're white. While, yes, we certainly may share many commonalities, particularly in regard to economic situations if we're among the same economic strata, there is also an intrinsic bias many in society hold based upon appearance, notably skin color, and regardless of commonalities of economic strata, that bias has a profound impact.

Ergo, "pass the mic."

Pass the mic to hear someone else's story and experience.

Pass the mic to listen to their story.

Pass the mic to better understand their experience, to better understand their perspective based upon their background and how it's influenced and impacted their lives and their way of thinking, so that we can get a better understanding of the entirety and complexity of situations rather than making overly simplified judgements based more upon our own perspectives and inclinations.

And so, really, it's about more than just passing the mic.

It's about listening, and thinking about what you've heard, when that other person is talking.

Listening, when the mic is in their hand.

I've been thinking about this terminology in regard to the controversy surrounding Dave Chappelle's latest Netflix special, "The Closer." The show, which is made up of Chappelle's unique blend of stand-up comedy and social observation, is the last of his current series of Netflix specials, and as he says repeatedly within it, it's the summation of the themes he's hit upon throughout all of them, predominantly dealing with equality, power dynamics, biases, and what it actually means to be treated and considered as equals in society.

These are not easy subjects. They're messy and complicated and ever-changing due to the constantly evolving social dynamics, and they're open to perpetual examination and questioning as those dynamics change, and that's reflected in Chappelle's delivery, material, and his own contemplation and commentary on it and how it evolves and shifts between the specials.

"The Closer" is by far the riskiest and most confrontational of all of the specials, and by far the most messy and complicated. It doesn't offer easy solutions, nor does it offer the prettiest of them, but what it does offer is a raw and honest perspective and examination of them, filtered through the experiences and voice of an intelligent and erudite person of color.

There is no need to pass the mic here. Chappelle holds on to it tightly for more than an hour, and what he says is often uncomfortable and confrontational. But it's also vital. And it's also worthy of consideration, contemplation, and above all, worth LISTENING to.

The mainstream media, always looking for confrontation to boost ratings and clicks to rescue their dying paradigm, has pushed the narrative that Chappelle is transphobic and that "The Closer" is simplistically hateful and bigoted. People, many of whom openly admit to not having even seen the special, have commented in that media and online about it as if they have any idea what it's about beyond what they've heard. But if you watch "The Closer," and really, really LISTEN to what Chappelle has to say, you'll understand.

"My problem has never been with trans people," Chappelle says, with customary candor, "it's been with white people."

And, if you actually watch and listen to not just "The Closer," but his other Netflix specials, and his entire body of work, you'll see that's a common theme — racial inequities and disparities, and how the system, largely led by white people in power, propagates them and racial divisions in general to maintain the power structure of the elites.

When he comments on the fact that many of the most prominent voices of protest in the trans community are white males transitioning, he's not commenting on their gender switch, he's talking about the fact that regardless of it, their initial power as white males transitions over with them, and that it points out a systematic racism that that transition and its power retention is in stark contrast to the more difficult road for people of color to achieve that same level of power within the system. He literally says this, pointing out that just as people of color were starting to "catch up" to the power levels and equality with white males, they "flipped the switch," and became not just women, but trans women, and therefore a minority class of their own, and one with seemingly an even greater cache of "protected status" than people of color. Whether you agree with him or not, whether you think this is an over-simplification or not, it is a provocative idea worth exploring in the realm of culture, and certainly an understandable position for a person of color to take, as Chappelle points out in several examples.

"It was easier for Bruce Jenner to change his gender than it was for Cassius Clay to change his name," Chappelle said in an earlier special, and repeats for emphasis in "The Closer." He also mentions, correctly, that rap star DaBaby was never canceled or had any career repercussions for the fact that he killed a person of color in an altercation, but he was swiftly banned for transphobic and homophobic slurs.

"You can kill (an African-American person), but you can't hurt a gay person's feelings," Chappelle says in regard to the incident.

And it's a good point. I'm not saying, and certainly anyone with compassion and logic is not saying, that either is good. However, what Chappelle is correctly pointing out is that one is condemned with far more force than the other, and not the one which you would think would garner that swifter and harsher condemnation.

And therein lies Dave Chappelle's "problem," such as it is, with the LGBTQ community. As a person of color, as an African-American who has experienced discrimination, he's both amazed and resentful at how much more quickly they have gotten closer to equality, respect, and a recognition of human rights than people of color have.

How do I know this?

Because he repeats it several times, not just in "The Closer," but throughout his specials.

He mentions Colin Kaepernick. He mentions Cassius Clay. He mentions Sojourner Truth. He mentions George Floyd. He mentions several other examples of people of color who were not treated equally, some with incredible cruelty, all with alienation and scorn.

And then he mentions Caitlin Jenner, noting "Caitlin Jenner was named Time magazine's Woman of the Year and she'd barely been a woman for a year."

It's a dynamic that's provocative and worthy of examination, one which Chappelle, as a social commentator and a person of color, has every right to examine. And, as a human being, as someone who has suffered from inequality, has every right to his anger and resentment over when examining it.

And one of the most prominent commentators, perhaps the most prominent, in terms of celebrity trans people, agrees. Caitlin Jenner tweeted today, "Dave Chappelle is 100 percent right. This isn't about the LGBTQ movement. It's about woke cancel culture run amok, trying to silence free speech. We must never yield or bow to those who wish to stop us from speaking our minds."

That's admirable coming from Jenner, especially given that she's been the frequent butt of some of Chappelle's jokes. But, as Jenner has commented before, when asked about them, she respects that Chappelle has a right to tell those jokes, and has a right to his perspective. Chappelle has likewise said the same. He doesn't claim to have all the answers, but he is trying to start a discussion about the questions.

"I'm not saying I'm right and you have to agree with everything I say, I'm just asking you to listen to what I'm saying," Chappelle says.

And what he's saying is worth hearing, whether you agree with it or not, because it brings up topics which need to be discussed, not for superficial condemnation, but for complex contemplation. That need to be examined, need to be brought out into the open, to enact positive change.

And that's what people should, and would, get from actually watching "The Closer," from actually watching Chappelle's Netflix specials, instead of letting the media tell them what the narrative should be regarding them.

That's what people would get if they actually listened to him.

Actually listened to this person of color with something to say.

The mic is in his hands. Literally. Are you going to listen?

Was Travis Scott Concert Tragedy A Blood Sacrifice To Satan, Or Something Far Worse?

Nov. 12, 2021

I'm sure by now you've all heard about the Travis Scott Astroworld tragedy in which eight young people, one as young as 14, were killed, and hundreds of people, some as young as 10, were injured, at Scott's Astroworld Music Festival in Houston on Nov. 5.

Concertgoers raged towards the stage during Scott's set, exhorted by Scott, which isn't unusual for a performer to do. However perhaps not especially wise given that more and more details are coming out about security people and festival organizers warning Scott against it.

Lawsuits will undoubtedly be abundant, and have already started. Investigations by the police are underway. And of course there have been myriad stories about what happened, some especially wild and elaborate.

There's a conspiracy theory going around on social media now that the horrible event was not only planned, but was all part of an elaborate satanic plot by Scott to hold a "live blood sacrifice" towards "satanic and Illuminati gods" as part of a secret ritual to gain him more fame and power.

According to these theories, Scott set up the show so that there would be too many people attending and then he exhorted the crowd to act wildly and push against each other with such ferocity that hundreds of people were injured and eight were killed.

According to the theories, he did so, and did so in the desert, to unleash an ancient desert demon to give him power.

To prove these theories, they point out a variety of satanic and Illuminati symbolism in Scott's show, his stage setup and his album and merch artwork. They point to flaming birds, demonic faces, all-seeing eyes, Illuminati symbols and the fact that the stage was set up as an upside down cross and its backdrop was meant to look like the gates of hell, or CERN, depending on what posts you see, with some of the posts saying that CERN itself is the gates of hell.

There are conflicting videos, some of which show Scott standing idly by as things were going nuts in the crowd, others which show him telling security to help people out. Both sides are using these videos to prove their point, that he either was or wasn't conducting a satanic sacrificial ritual. There are literally hundreds, probably thousands, of videos and posts out there about the subject.

However, like most conspiracy theories, these elaborate plotlines overlook that, as usual, it was one thing that led to such a tragedy.

One of many TikTok videos pointing out Illuminati symbolism at the Scott concert.

One could argue it was satanic and evil, certainly, but in a far more banal way than some elaborate Illuminati ritual.

It was just plain greed and stupidity.

And that's something to remember when it comes to most conspiracy theories and things of this nature.

Everything comes down to greed and money, folks.

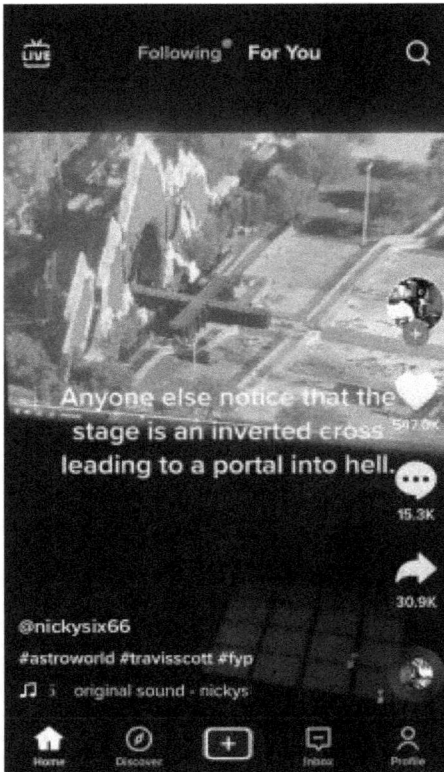

Someone pointing out that Scott's stage was shaped like an inverted cross leading to a hellish mountain portal.

TRAVIS SCOTT OVERSOLD HIS CONCERT
BECAUSE HE WAS CONDUCTING A BLOOD
SACRIFICE FOR AN ILLUMINATI RITUAL!!!!

No. Travis Scott oversold his show because he's greedy and wanted to get as much money as possible by selling tickets. Allegedly, festival organizers and officials told him beforehand not to allow that many people into that space, but he did it anyway. Not because he was conducting a satanic ritual, but because he was conducting an all-too-common capitalistic ritual.

And that can be said about so many other conspiracies around today.

The covid vaccine conspiracies, for example.

IF, and this is an IF, there IS a conspiracy in regard to the covid vaccine, I'll bet there's a 99.9999 percent chance that THIS is the conspiracy:

It's all a plot to make more money.

Release a virus to create a panic so that you can make money selling the cure.

All about greed.

Now, I'm not saying that's the case or that I believe that conspiracy.

Re-read that last sentence if you need to.

Again, if needed.

Ok. What I AM saying is that IF there IS a conspiracy, that's probably it. It's probably nothing more fantastic than a banal scheme to make money.

Create a virus, release it, create panic, have the cure in waiting so you can sell it to our government and others, so you can fatten your bottom lines and jerk off your shareholders.

Yup, someone pointing out that a demon was spotted at the concert. Ignoring that it was a hologram that was part of the show. So, they're actually partially accurate, but it was a fake demon.

That's usually where all "conspiracies" lie — on the financial bottom line.

If someone had actually said that, if people had actually floated that conspiracy theory, honestly, I would respected their logical thinking and cynicism a lot more. But nope.

We live in a world where people make up and believe outlandish bullshit, like Bill Gates putting a microchip in the vaccine, or 5G towers causing it, or George Soros using it to control the world population.

These people don't care about controlling you. They already control you through the media they own, the phones you are enslaved to, and the algorithms you're brainwashed by on social media.

They don't care about you at all.

They just care about money.

They care about power created by having more money.

And if you remember that, remember that if there are ever any conspiracies or shady things going on behind-the-scenes, it's almost always about greed, always about the elites grabbing more money, you can avoid embarrassing things like spending an entire day in the rain at Dealey Plaza waiting for JFK Jr to show up.

The same thing goes for this Travis Scott tragedy.

I don't think Scott is a satanist or an Illuminati cultist. I think he uses that imagery the same way rock stars have been using that imagery for decades, to shock certain people and entice and amuse others.

It's all for show. I think it's crazy to question Scott and call him out for being a satanist or holding some sort of blood ritual, and in its own way, it disrespects the memory of the people who died and those injured by turning their tragedy into a buffoonish circus.

The entrance to the performance area, which many, many folks on social media are using as evidence to the "satanic ritual" theory.

But what is reasonable is to question Scott about the security precautions and the number of tickets sold prior to the show, and the meetings had discussing those scenarios prior to the show. What is reasonable is to question whether the greed of having that many people packed into that much space was too much and should've and could've been addressed beforehand to prevent this tragedy. Ignoring that advice, covering up any meetings about that subject, would be evil enough without any flaming birds and symbols on the stage.

The conspiracies out there are fantastic and elaborate, ornate stories of diabolical imagination. All conspiracy theories are in their own way. But when it comes down to it, most conspiracies, most things that are hidden, are hidden for one reason and one reason alone: To cover up excessive greed and the terrible actions taken towards that greed.

Do I think Travis Scott's concert was a satanic and Illuminati ritual? No, I do not.

I think it was something far worse. Just plain human greed and stupidity. And that's what needs to be dealt with.

Behind The Fluff: The Tawdry Tales Of Festival Of Trees' Teddy Bear Teas

Nov. 19, 2021

Entertainment is a tricky thing. One person's wholesome fare is another person's demon-possessed trash.

From time to time, I'll get emails from irate people who are disappointed that I've recommended some bit of entertainment they find to be offensive. One of them messaged me about it. Another called me, taking me to task for "leading children down the path of evil." How she knew I'd been a tour guide at Disneyland is beyond me. But nonetheless, this lady wasn't pleased. "You shouldn't be telling parents to let their children go to demonic concerts…you should be warning them about harmful entertainment!" she said.

You know, she's got a point. So, aside from warning you not to buy Nickelback's upcoming album, I'm going to do my best to educate you about a dangerous event that's going on in the Quad-Cities this week.

That's right, it's the Festival of Trees.

Specifically, the Festival of Trees' Teddy Bear Teas, which trundles into the RiverCenter on Sunday.

No, I'm not kidding.

The Festival of Trees people describe it as a "delightful event" featuring "adorable teddy bears" and "fun for the whole family." What they don't tell you is that it's the plushie equivalent of a gangsta rap video crossed with a trip to Marilyn Manson's house.

Being the courageous, intrepid journalist that I am, I've delved into the shady world of Teddy Bear Teas. What I found chilled me too deeply for even the strongest Lemon Lift to warm me up again.

Once the parents leave the room, all bets are off. The bears are in charge, and the kids, derogatorily referred to as "Christopher Robins," don't stand a chance.

The first thing the bears do is spike up the tea. Two lumps of sugar? Think FOUR, my friend, think four.

Then there's the gambling. Candyland. Uno. Go Fish. And it ain't just for small stakes either. There are kids who are still having flashbacks about the year Huggy McFluffstein lost three buttons and most of his stitches to Snuggle Diddy. These aren't your average bears. Ruggles The Third? Elwood VonPouch? Cuddles? There isn't a Ken, Barbie or GI Joe around that doesn't hide behind the Speak And Spell at the mere mention of their names.

Heck, the horribly stitched face of Dr. Patches inspired the Slipknot masks.

You just don't mess with Mr. Pibb. Mr. Flufflesworth is straight gangsta. And when it comes to street cred, The Top Monsieur lives up to his name — the bear's bananas, yo.

Emperor Cuddlesworth, during a relapse into his opioid addiction, mauled several parade walkers as an innocent child watched in horror. Even the Grinch turned away, chilled.

Perhaps most disturbing is a quilt-style bear made up of swatches from various stuffed animals. Calling himself "Buffalo Baloo," he preys on unsuspecting smaller dolls, trolling the crowd with his troll doll, Precious, and murmuring to himself, "It puts the fabric softener on its fur or it gets the hose."

One eight-year-old, who asked not to be identified, described what happened to one boy who dared to utter the two forbidden words: washer and dryer.

"The bears gathered together, shoved him into a corner and pelted him with candy canes. A few of them howled and pointed out well-worn spots on their hides. They all started chanting `Mogwai! Mogwai! Mogwai!' and then…"

Her voice trailed off into sobs.

"I haven't been able to set foot in a toy store since."

So, folks, you wanted me to be the voice of warning. You wanted me to dispense my cautionary tales. Here they are. Beware of the bears.

Next week: I take a hard look at the ink dabbing addictions suffered at local bingo parlors.

For Christ's Sake, Just Let People Have Their McRibs And Be Happy In This Crap Show Year

Nov. 26, 2021

I was scrolling through my news feed on Facebook today, as I am wont to do when I want to incrementally lose faith in humanity, and I stopped briefly on a posting by someone trying to make themselves look far more hip and cool than they actually are.

I know, I know, hard to pin that one down when it comes to social media!

You'll never guess who I'm talking about when you've got 80 million people to choose from there…

Anyway, the person was making a comment about a certain fast food item that some people profoundly enjoy. They post about it. They revel in its return. They write with glee about its magnificence to them. Quite frankly, I think many of them would marry it if it were legal to do so. And really, isn't it about time to vote to make that legal? Love between a man, woman, or non-binary person and a sandwich should be between that man, woman, or non-binary person and that sandwich, and no one else.

The previous message was brought to you by The Church of Oprah And Present Day Saints.

Anyway, this wannabee hipster person was scalding the fans of said item, which is within their right to express their opinion, but they ended it by saying "You're all wrong for thinking this is any good. It's nowhere as good as you think it is."

Now, of course, upon reading this, my inclination was to instantly message this person.

Because, well, if they can read minds with that much accuracy and are that certain about the vagaries of chance and choice, well, I want next week's lottery numbers from them.

They didn't message back.

And so, a little tear trickled down my cheek, like that Native American guy in that old '70s commercial.

Then, I turned and walked away, with my backpack slung over my shoulder, as the "Incredible Hulk" Lonely Man Theme played in the background, and I strode into the distance, to my destiny...

A destiny that, for the moment, involved me writing this column.

And one of the reasons I wanted to write this column is that, for one thing, NOBODY can ever say someone is wrong for thinking a food item is good. It's an opinion. It's a matter of preference.

You can jokingly say that pineapple on pizza is an abomination against God and man, but you'd be wrong, because it's a delicacy of the Gods and a gift to man. However, in that case, both of us are right — for ourselves. I love pineapple on pizza. You may hate it. But I can't say you're wrong, and you can't say I'm wrong. It's completely subjective and a matter of opinion.

The same way this person can't say with such venom that people are wrong for liking this certain foodstuff that rhymes with McHibb, and they can't say that it's not as good as they think it is, because for one, how can you read their minds to find out exactly how good they think it is, and for another, that's just like, their opinion, man.

And when it comes down to it, it's really kind of a superficial thing.

And it's also something that, especially in a time like this, and a year like this, we should just back off and let people have their small moments of joy regardless of how we feel about them personally.

Because not only do those little things sometimes mean a lot during times that are difficult, but in the big picture, those superficialities often don't mean a whole hell of a lot in accurately judging someone's character.

For example, as you all know, I make fun of Nickelback as much as the next guy. Especially if the next guy isn't Chad Kroeger.

But the fact is, one of the best relationships I had was with a woman who was one of the kindest people I've met, and she loved Nickelback.

I've also known really cool people and had relationships with really cool women who have LOVED Michael Bolton, Mariah Carey, Matchbox 20, Garth Brooks, and various other musicians who make me cringe.

Conversely, I've had horrible relationships and encountered really shitty people who had the exact same musical and entertainment tastes as me.

When it comes down to it, people have a right to enjoy what makes them happy, and it's not up to me or anyone else to condemn them or judge them for that. I might vehemently disagree with their choices, I might consider it a form of torture to join them in engaging in them, but what's REALLY important is if someone is a good person, has good character, and is nice and respectful to you as a human being. THAT is worth a hell of a lot more than being able to agree on music and TV choices.

Trust me on this one.

Also, it's really not up to you, or your right, to tell someone what they can and can't like, or to make statements like "that's not as good as you think it is." Everyone is entitled to their own opinions, their own preferences, and their own things that bring them joy. And in this world, which can be pretty damn shitty, we need to embrace those things that bring us joy.

So if you really love someone, you really want to see them happy, let them have their Nickelback. Let them have their pineapple on their pizza. Let them have their "Friends."

And yes, Goddamn it, let them have their McRibs.

Because if there's one thing I've learned through all the relationships I've had, it's that I'd much rather be with someone who's kind, and nice, and cool, and upbeat, with good character, who has completely different entertainment tastes than me, than the opposite.

Adele Has The Right To Do Whatever She Wants To With Her Own Body

Dec. 3, 2021

I believe in bodily autonomy for women. What they want to do with their bodies is up to them, and they should have the freedom to follow their own paths.

That informs my opinions on their health decisions, reproductive rights, and also more superficial topics.

For example, Adele losing weight.

The singer has been getting bashed by people online for going on a healthy weight loss routine and getting in shape. The people bashing her are saying that she should've kept the weight on because she was seen as a role model for people who carry a little more weight.

But the thing is, like so many other celebrities, she never ASKED to be a role model for anyone.

She's just a singer, a very talented one, who became famous for being a singer.

We have no idea what she's really like as a human being, nor should we really care.

Our relationship with her, the same as our relationship with any other celebrity, should be left to the transaction between their creative output and our reaction to it. If you want to criticize her latest album after you shelled out your hard earned cash for it, completely fair.

But if she wants to lose weight or shave her head or get a massive back tattoo of the Grimace drinking a blood milkshake from the skull of Ronald under an Olde English Script saying "Deathe To All Ye MacDonaldse!" well, she's got the right to do that, and as long as it doesn't somehow disrupt the creative product she's charging you for, then who cares? She's just been following her career, making her own choices.

She has NO responsibility to her fans other than to create music, and even that's at her own discretion and creative whim.

Adele. Not pictured, her boyfriend, Afarmer.

It's YOU who decided to make a celebrity you've never met, rather than someone in your own life, or perhaps the ideal of your own self in the future, your role model. Adele bears no responsibility for that choice, nor any of your other choices, none for your insecurities, and none for any actions you might take due to her or her actions.

She is her own person, not yours.

It's HER choice. It's HER body. She can do what she wants with it. If she wants to lose weight, it's HER choice.

And HERS alone. And while you, and everyone, has a right to their opinion, to quote the late Mr. Rogers, in the big picture your opinion don't mean squat. (Pretty sure that was Mr. Rogers. Maybe it was Huggy Bear. Six of one…)

Adele also doesn't have to look at the camera either.

You shouldn't be looking to celebrities for any validation regarding your life. You shouldn't be looking to celebrities for any role modeling. Celebrities live in a world of extreme wealth and privileged unreality that does not parallel yours and mine. You shouldn't be comparing yourself to Adele any more than I should be comparing myself to Paul Rudd or Matthew McConaghey, who have far more time, money, and resources than I do to make themselves far more empirically attractive than I am and win titles like Sexiest Man Alive, while I'm competing for titles like Fourth Or Maybe Fifth Possible Guy To Reply To On Bumble.

Do what YOU want in YOUR life, as long as it's not harming others. If you feel you need to lose weight for health or aesthetic reasons, take responsibility and take steps to do so. If you don't want to, that's your choice as well.

But, and I know this is not in fashion right now but it really should be, TAKE RESPONSIBILITY FOR YOUR OWN LIFE AND ACTIONS.

If you lose weight, that's on you. If you don't, that's on you. Either way, it's not on anyone else, and it's certainly not on a person you've never met and who doesn't know you.

Adele has her own life to live, and so do you, and yours probably would be considerably better without you spending so much time in front of a keyboard slamming celebrities who have let you down. Especially if you're trying to lose weight because that really does nothing for cardio.

Don't shame Adele or anyone else for making a different choice that's right for them. It's really none of your business what Adele or anyone else does, particularly if they're a total stranger to you and vice versa.

As always, follow your bliss and your happiness, and as long as it's not hurting yourself or other people, fair enough. And respect that in other people as well. We all have that right.

Now, if you'll excuse me, I have to get to a kickboxing class, so I can eat an entire carrot cake later. It has carrots, it's got to be at least somewhat healthy. Balance. Balance. And as always, with my eye on my goal: Third Or Maybe Second Possible Guy To Reply To On Bumble.

Here's A Trend That Needs To Start: How About A National Better Parenting Day?

Dec. 17, 2021

I don't feel like writing anything funny today.

Just not in the mood.

For the second consecutive Friday, I, and millions of other parents across the country, have had to deal with a bunch of hysteria over kids allegedly threatening to shoot up schools.

In fact, this week's threat went nationwide, as a trend on TikTok calling for a National Shoot Up Your School Day swept viral with such speed that by Thursday afternoon, schools across the country were all sending out e-mails telling parents about it and saying they were stepping up security, and would understand if parents wanted to keep their kids at home.

The Iowa State Education Association, The Iowa Association of School Boards and School Administrators of Iowa also released a joint statement that read as follows:

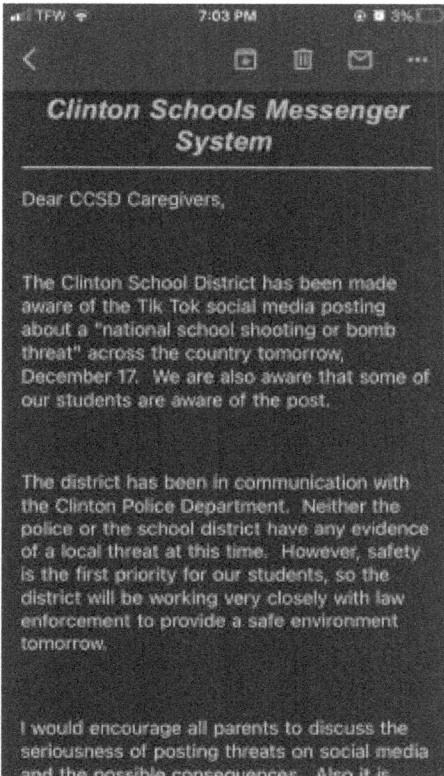

Clinton Schools Messenger System

Dear CCSD Caregivers,

The Clinton School District has been made aware of the Tik Tok social media posting about a "national school shooting or bomb threat" across the country tomorrow, December 17. We are also aware that some of our students are aware of the post.

The district has been in communication with the Clinton Police Department. Neither the police or the school district have any evidence of a local threat at this time. However, safety is the first priority for our students, so the district will be working very closely with law enforcement to provide a safe environment tomorrow.

I would encourage all parents to discuss the seriousness of posting threats on social media and the possible consequences. Also it is

Every student deserves a safe place to learn, and every educator, administrator and school staff member deserves a safe place to do their work.

The social media threat of an "American School Shooting Day" is appalling. Whether done as a joke or with malicious intent, it's unacceptable. We know our school personnel will do everything in their power to keep our students safe. They need all of us to stand with them in that effort.

We ask Iowans across the state to support our educators and the students they serve. Community support is

69

important every day and especially when threats of violence and hateful language ricochet around social media.

They weren't alone. School districts across the area sent out e-mails. On the Illinois side, Dr. Adam Brumbaugh of the Geneseo School District sent this out:

Dear Parents,

Our district has been made aware of a circulating TikTok post with a nationwide "school shooting or bomb threats for every school in the USA" that will supposedly take place on Friday, Dec. 17, 2021. The original post is general and not directed at a specific school. So far, the origins of this post are unknown and there is no indication it was made by anyone in the vicinity of Geneseo. Regardless, the information has been shared with our school administration and Geneseo Police Department.

Please know that, in conjunction with local law enforcement, we will continue to monitor social media. There are no indications of any known threats for Geneseo at this time. I am sharing this notice out of an abundance of caution and as a precautionary measure.

The safety of our students and staff is our priority. All safety concerns to our school or students are taken seriously and investigated thoroughly. Please take this opportunity to talk with your student(s) about the appropriate use of social media, and the seriousness and resulting consequences of making any kind of threat. Encourage them to speak with you or an adult at school if they see or hear something so that immediate action can be taken. In addition, if anyone in our community sees something suspicious, please report it to the school immediately or call local law enforcement.

Dr. Adam Brumbaugh

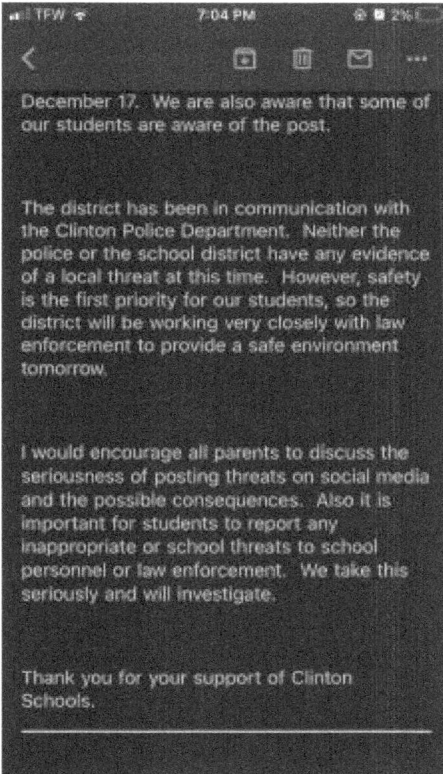

Of course, in the aftermath of this, people were quick to throw blame.

Some blamed TikTok and social media, as if these things just generated themselves randomly from an AI and there weren't actual human beings behind them. Certainly, the ubiquity of social media makes the dissemination of things of this nature far more easier than it was when we were kids and the Internet was confined to dial up and chat rooms, but still, it's not the media's fault.

It's also not the fault of music videos, movies, TV shows, videogames, or anything else of that nature. Millions and millions of kids ingest these things and don't act like dumbasses. The only people that ingest entertainment and act like dumbasses and do dumbass things are people who were dumbasses long before they watched that movie or played that videogame.

And that leads me to who I believe should start being held responsible for this, and anything else that happens beyond a threat.

The kids themselves.

And, THE PARENTS OF THESE KIDS.

Yes, certainly, the kids are responsible for their own actions. I know it's in style right now to not take responsibility for anything and to blame it on some element of society that absolves you of the actions you took. But the fact is, no matter what happens to you, no matter what you see or watch or ingest, YOU are the only one who decides what YOU do. So YOU need to take responsibility for it.

But that said, children, particularly the younger they are, are also the responsibility and reflection of their upbringing.

Most definitely, people can transcend horrible upbringing. And, conversely, some kids can become complete jerks despite having great parents. But the vast majority of psychological and sociological studies show that parental influence and a child's upbringing has a profound influence on how they behave and the decisions they make in their lives.

And so, I think the parents need to shoulder the blame on this one too.

For one, you need to start getting involved in your kids' lives. You should know how they're feeling, what they're doing, who they're hanging out with, if they're having a hard time in school, etc. If they are being bullied, call the school and get the school involved. If they're having mental health issues, get them some help. No matter how much you work, no matter how many kids you have, you can spend quality time with your child. I know people who have multiple jobs, myself included, and a myriad of responsibilities, some people with four and five kids, and we all find a way to make time to have quality time with our children.

Now, of course, kids are their own people, and even if we give them all the support we can and get them help if needed, they ultimately make their own decisions.

And so we get to the problem of school shootings and other violence. A problem that can't take place without a weapon. Which leads to the point that if by some chance you have guns around the house LOCK THOSE THINGS UP IN A SAFE THAT ONLY YOU HAVE ACCESS TO. And above all, TEACH YOUR KIDS THAT REGARDLESS OF THE CIRCUMSTANCES, IT'S

NEVER RIGHT TO RESORT TO EXTREME
VIOLENCE.

I was bullied horribly when I was in junior high. So I get it.
I was also a "bad kid" who was one step away from juvie
more than a few times when I was growing up. So I get that
too. I was no treat. But damn if my parents didn't get on me
about it, and try their best to teach me right from wrong.

And regardless of the fact that I was not a good kid, and
there was a gun in my house, and I could've accessed it
pretty easily, I can't say there was ever a time I seriously
thought about shooting up my school. Why not?
BECAUSE I KNEW SOMETHING THAT SEVERE WAS
THE WRONG THING TO DO.

This isn't fair to the 99 percent of kids who just want to go
through school, get their work done, see their friends, learn
something, and live their lives. I'm sick and tired of the
vast majority of society being held hostage by a small
minority of people.

And before someone goes off on blaming the "all the
guns," sorry, but it ain't just the guns.

I know a LOT of folks who own guns. I know a LOT of
pre-teens and teens who go hunting and own guns. I've
never felt any threat from those kids because their parents
raised them the right way. They're respectful and recognize
the power inherent in a firearm, and know how to use it
safely and under what circumstances is it acceptable. Not to
mention that those kids are NEVER in possession of a
weapon without their parents around, and their parents

make sure that those guns are locked up and their kids do not have the key or combination.

Any weapon is a power neutral — it can be used for positive (e.g. hunting) or negative things by a human being, and those human beings need to be taught right from wrong.

It's the parents' job to teach those kids right from wrong. It's the parents' job to know what their kids are up to. And it's the parents' job to make sure their kids aren't threatening their schools, because it's having a profound negative impact on millions of people, from students to teachers to staff at the schools. It's not fair to any of them.

It's time for parents to be held responsible, and face both the financial and punitive consequences if they aren't. This can't become the new normal. The new normal has to be better, for all of us.

'Do They Know It's Christmas' Hits Extra Hard In These Times

Dec. 24, 2021

It was late 1984, and Boomtown Rats front man Bob Geldof was sitting down to watch a bit of telly as the calendar began to turn towards the holidays.

However, what he saw that evening was anything but festive.

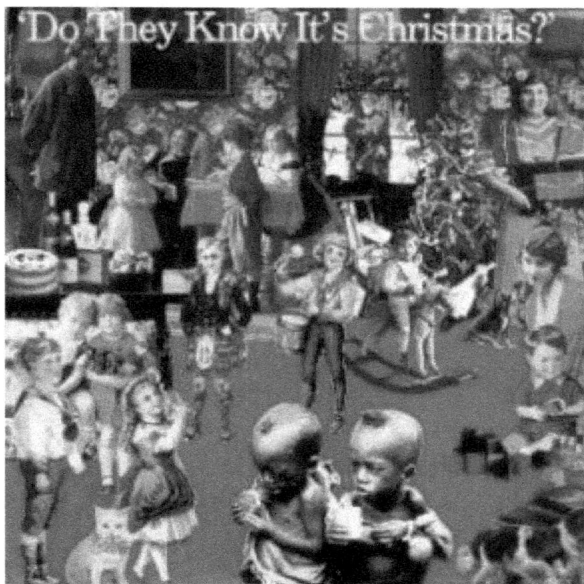

Geldof watched as a documentary news program detailed the horrible starving and suffering going on in Africa due to incredible droughts and oppression. And as he watched, he was moved to tears, sorrow, and finally, action.

He knew he had to do something to help, but just donating money himself seemed so small, so insignificant. How could he do something larger? Finally, he had the idea, and the structure for a song, and a movement, that would literally change the world.

Geldof called up his friend Midge Ure of Ultravox and the two set about to quickly penning one of the most stirring and beautiful Christmas songs of all time, "Do They Know It's Christmas?"

For the recording of the song, the duo hit the phones to call up every pop star they knew, and to tell those pop stars to call their friends, to hastily put together a massive group — Band Aid — to record the track and get it in stores before Christmas to raise as much money as possible for the starving people of Africa.

Remarkably, they got an incredible all-star lineup of talent, and the biggest rock and pop stars in Britain and worldwide at the time — members of the bands Duran Duran, U2, Wham!, Culture Club, The Police, Kool and the Gang, Spandau Ballet, and dozens of others, joined together to record a song and video which would go on to become the biggest-selling single of all time in Britain and several other countries around the world. It would go on to spark a massive movement to help the people of Africa that would lead to the unforgettable Live Aid concert the next year, and would directly lead to various other movements, from USA For Africa to Farm Aid.

As Geldof put it at the time, "We made compassion fashionable."

His co-songwriter and partner in the project, Midge Ure, echoed those sentiments, saying, "It made caring cool again."

And as we live through our own difficult year, our own difficult time in this world, especially given the tumultuous circumstances of the past two years, perhaps nothing could be more important this holiday season than to once more, make compassion fashionable.

This year has been unbelievably difficult in so many ways. We've seen thousands of people killed by a pandemic, and our societies and lives disrupted in profound and meaningful ways by the pandemic and its symptoms in shutting down businesses and wide swaths of our lives. We've seen social upheaval, protests and riots and massive demonstrations, both peaceful and violent. There's been a horrible schism that's widened between people along various political, religious and social lines, grown larger and deeper by those who profit and prosper in fomenting divisions among us.

And it's become fashionable to be a jerk, to not care, to be rude and unsympathetic, to be an asshole.

It's time for that to change.

To be certain, that plague of disdain and cold uncaring hasn't been all-encompassing. There are plenty of people who have been a light in the darkness, who have steadfastly been a source of positivity and compassion during this time. Healthcare workers and providers have been especially crucial. Teachers have been essential. And really, anyone who has recognized that almost all of us are in the same boat and shown some compassion and understanding to others has helped in some way, however small, to make things a little better during this time.

There have also been people who have stood up for, and fought for, the downtrodden, and those suffering. There are those who have stood on the side of truth, of positive evolution, of logic and common sense, and an escape from the cages of tribalism that only end up dividing, that only end up making it worse for the people who are suffering.

That courage, that caring, should be recognized.

That should be praised.

That should be highlighted.

That should be made fashionable, made cool.

It's time to make compassion fashionable again.

It's time to make caring cool.

Not just today, not just during the holiday season, but in all the days moving forward.

Merry Christmas, and happy holidays…

Was Betty White Really An Illuminati Shapeshifter Killed By Q-Anon?

Jan. 7, 2022

Sometimes the headline says it all.

And this is one of those times.

Yes, folks, desperate times call for tough questions, and this week, the question we need to face is whether or not Betty White was really an Illuminati shapeshifter killed by Q-Anon.

Now, of course to most people, Betty White was a beloved actress and activist who starred in several classic TV hits including "The Mary Tyler Moore Show," "Golden Girls" and "Cooter And The Tang Ticklers' Funtime Magic Hour."

When she passed away on New Year's Eve, the last day of 2021, at the age of 99, just 17 days before her 100th birthday, people were stunned. Fans around the world mourned the loss of one of the few actors of our time who was pretty much loved across all cultural and party lines and wasn't named Keanu Reeves or Dolly Parton. Tweets and social media posts celebrated her career and were saddened at her departure, with most remarking that when someone lives to a whisker shy of a century and people still think she didn't live long enough, she must have been something pretty special indeed.

Little did I know that she was special indeed.

She was a shapeshifting reptilian demon part of the Illuminati cult sacrificing people for adrenochrome.

TikTok smells a Pulitzer here.

And the only reason she DIDN'T live to 100 was because Q-Anon found out about her satanic plotting and the avenging angel JFK Jr assassinated her to make an example to the Illuminati that you can run, but you can't hide, unless you're DB Cooper or Jesse Pinkman.

And, also, he really didn't like that song "Thank You For Being A Friend."

One of the worst sources for journalism you can find. Of course, I'm talking about CNN.

Needless to say, I found all of this information out on the most reliable journalistic source around — TikTok.

Literally within hours of White's death, truth-tellers on the popular video platform were dropping revelations about the secret life of Miss White.

According to these intrepid journalists, Betty White had long been an Illuminati priestess in Hollywood. And like another of the most notorious demons of that city, Tom Hanks, she disguised herself as a sweet, lovable actor, all the while leading a satanic pedophile ring which killed people to harvest a rare chemical from their adrenal glands, adrenochrome, which was used to not only keep her looking and feeling young, but also to allow the multidimensional reptilian alien demon within her the ability to keep inhabiting her human body.

You know, like multidimensional reptilian alien demons do.

Pulitzer Prize-winning chronicler Quotertoter3 was one of the first to break the news.

Quotertoter3 posted a screenshot of the CNN reporting on Betty White's death, along with two captions.

One, above the screenshot, said "Tell me again how that certain letter isn't in control? I'll wait!"

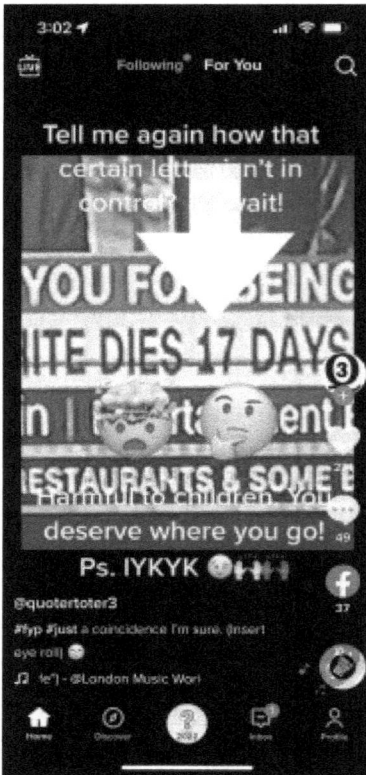

3:02

Following For You

Tell me again how that
certain letter isn't in
control? I'll wait!

YOU FOR BEING
ITE DIES 17 DAYS
n l for rt ent
RESTAURANTS & SOME
Harmful to children You
deserve where you go!

Ps. IYKYK

@quotertoter3
#fyp #just a coincidence I'm sure. (Insert
eye roll)
♫ 'e') - @London Music Worl

An emoji with a cake on his head and his brother thinking about how the cake got there.

The second, below the screenshot, said, "Harmful to children. You deserve where you go! Ps. IYKYK"

And then, accompanying the video was the theme song to the '80s sitcom "The Facts of Life."

No, seriously. I'm not even kidding about that.

But that's just another Illuminati rabbit hole.

Anyway, I'll translate the Quotertoter3 message for those of you who, ya know, have lives.

"Wilfred Brimley used to love this..."

"Tell me again how that certain letter isn't in control?" This references the fact that White died 17 days before her 100th birthday. Q is the 17th letter in the alphabet. So every time something relating to the number 17 pops up, the Q-Anon folks think it's something symbolic of the fact that Q has or had something to do with it. White dying 17 days before her birthday was allegedly a message from Q that he killed her. Of course, she was also almost 100 years old, so, ya know, short putt there Q.

The second message, "Harmful to children. You deserve where you go!" is meant to reference White's connection with pizzagate, satanic sacrifices, Tom Hanks, Toby Keith, Mayor McCheese, the inverted star on the side of Hardees, etc. And "IYKYK" is the abbreviation for "If you know you know." Which is ironic because most of the people believing this seem to really not know how friggin' batshit crazy they sound.

For example, let's look at some of the comments that followed this incisive reporting from muckraking investigator Quotertoter3.

Noblittkev88 commented, "No more blood drinking Illuminati sacrifices."

Cynthiacervantesquevas disdainfully called Betty "The Queen of Adrenochrome."

And dannyboy1877, who, after stopping for a few moments to listen to but ignore the pipes the pipes that were calling, posted, "Supposedly she was one of the heads of the adrenochrome pandemic we're experiencing."

Now, of course, I'm not going to just trust the reporting of one journalistic source, no matter how unimpeachable Quotertoter3 may be.

I did a little more digging of my own.

As it turns out, the theory of Betty being a satanic reptilian overlord has been around for a few years. Ever since the actress did a comedy sketch in 2017 on her TV mini-series "Betty's Happy Hour."

The sketch, "Betty White's Secret to Staying Youthful," featured White telling the audience that her secret to staying so young is because, she says, "'I eat well, get plenty of rest, and every third Sunday I drink the blood of a virgin. And these days they're getting harder and harder to find."

So, there you have it folks. Right from the high priestess' fanged maw!

Hey, remember when JFK Jr was supposed to come back from the dead and reveal himself to all the Q followers in Dallas last year? Pepperidge Farm remembers…

Certainly, she couldn't have been joking about that, because we all know the Illuminati have no sense of humor and they hide their conspiracy theories right out in the open, disguised as humor, as an arrogant way of exerting their power.

So, just to update you, here in 2022, we now live in a world where people think that Betty White was part of a satanic, blood-drinking cult of reptilian alien demons disguised as humans, and she was clandestinely murdered by a secret assassin nicknamed Q, who is actually JFK Jr., who faked his own death.

Yes.

And you wonder why large groups of people actually refuse to get the covid vaccine because they think it contains a microchip planted there by Bill Gates to control them through 5G towers.

Jesus. How ridiculous can you get.

I mean, everyone knows that it's Warren Buffett trying to control us through Dish Network satellites and it was Bea Arthur who was the blood-drinking reptilian in the "Golden Girls," who was killed by Colonel Mustard using a butter knife in the thatched hut outside KFC.

The Time Traveler From 2714 Is Back, And You're Going To Be Shocked This Time...

Jan. 14, 2022

He's back.

And what he's got to say is going to shock you.

Maybe. I guess it depends on your tolerance for shock.

Anyway, as regular readers of this column know, I love reading about time travel, and the predictions of alleged time travelers. And while my all-time favorite is the legendary John Titor, one of my current favorites is a guy on TikTok who has gone by various names as he's morphed his account. Currently he goes by the handle Aery Yormany, @aesthetictimewarper, and as he claims on his page, "I am back, I now travel to the past to unveil the truth."

Would you buy a used time machine from this guy?

And you couldn't warn us about Betty White? C'mon now, Aery!

While Aery might have brain farted about the Golden Girl, he has a whole new crop of predictions for us in his latest posts.

Here are some of the predictions:

On June 28, 2022, the largest earthquake in history destroys San Francisco, California, and begins a chain reaction of other earthquakes along the coast. Stock up on your Rice-A-Roni!

In 2023, one of the Mars rovers discovers human bones on the planet, making people question whether we're actually from Mars and came to earth long ago. Plausible. Also somewhere Beavis and Butt-Head are laughing, saying "you said bones."

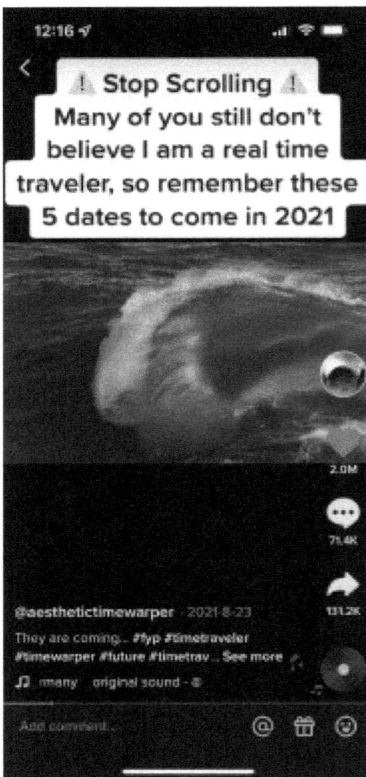

By the end of March, a "very famous music artist" will come out as alive, saying they faked their death, and will become even more famous than before. Because, well, faking your death can do that for ya. My money is on Michael Jackson. Not literally. I don't visit him at the strip club.

On August 5, 2022, a mirrored solar system is discovered. (Disco balls?) All forms of natural disasters are going to get much worse. (Yeah, ok Al Gore.) In 2022, the government finally reveals that the pyramids were built by aliens, and that actually all of the "gods" of the old testament and other religious books were actually aliens that people worshiped due to their advanced technology. Now this I find plausible, because I've watched a lot of "Ancient Aliens"…

He also said that in two months, he's going to be taking 10 random people with him to the year 2714. Hmmm… we'll return to this.

Here are some more of his predictions:

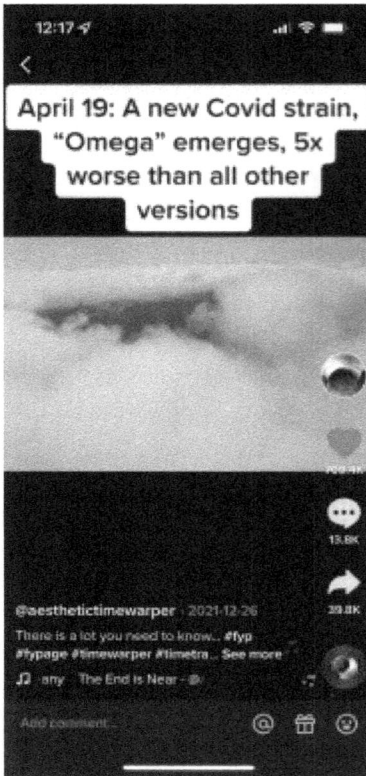

April 19: A new Covid strain, "Omega" emerges, 5x worse than all other versions

@aesthetictimewarper · 2021-12-26
There is a lot you need to know... #fyp
#fypage #timewarper #timetra... See more

♫ any The End is Near - @

Add comment...

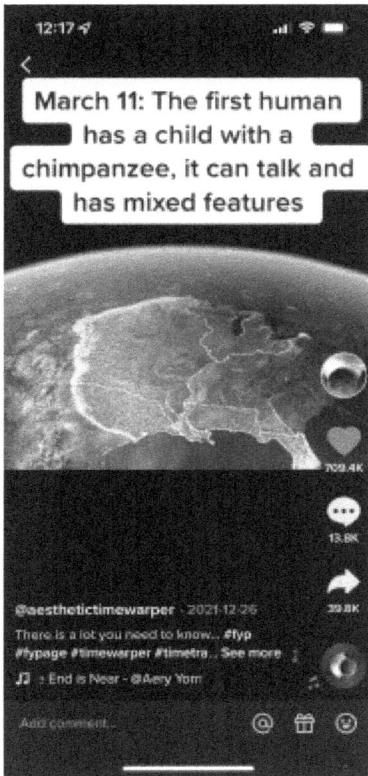

March 11: The first human has a child with a chimpanzee, it can talk and has mixed features

@aesthetictimewarper · 2021-12-26
There is a lot you need to know... #fyp
#fypage #timewarper #timetra... See more
♫ ♪ End is Near - @Aery Yom

Add comment...

93

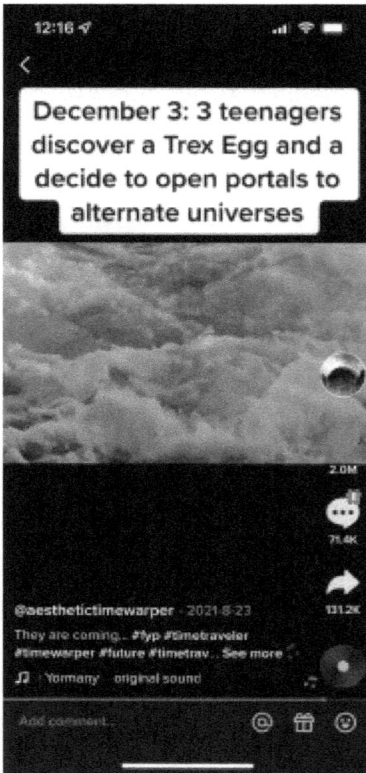

December 3: 3 teenagers discover a Trex Egg and a decide to open portals to alternate universes

2.0M

71.4K

131.2K

@aesthetictimewarper · 2021-8-23

They are coming... #fyp #timetraveler #timewarper #future #timetrav... See more

♫ Yormany · original sound

Add comment...

Now, of course, at this point, you might be saying, "Sean??!!!??? Sweatpants AGAIN??? You're wearing sweatpants AGAIN???"

And I'd answer, no, they're track pants. There is a difference. But they're both very comfortable.

Then I'd also say, hey, I get it, you're reading this column and thinking, "Oh boy... TIME TRAVELERS???"

Of course, I understand your skepticism. There's been a long history of people claiming to be time travelers. And there's been an even longer history of people just being full of crap.

Oddly enough, the Venn diagram between the two is almost an identical shadow of two circles.

Certainly, there are maybe one or two instances that have made me, and others, go "hmmmm."

But most of them have made me, and others, go, "Oh geez, this is friggin' baloney."

One of the most infamous of these among the bologna category was the aforementioned John Titor.

Now, back in the '90s and up to the mid-2000s, one of the most famous radio shows in the country (back when people actually listened to the radio in large numbers) was the Coast To Coast AM Show, hosted by Art Bell.

Art Bell: King of Late Night Media, Archduke of Lunatic Bullshit.

I absolutely loved this show. I used to work late nights at the newspaper back in the '90s and '00s, and I listened to Art's astonishing and often hilarious program every night. Art was everything you would want in a host of a show of this nature, he was sort of an odd and interesting character himself, and would expertly walk the line between cynical and incredulous when he interviewed a vast array of guests, everyone from people claiming to be alien abductees to people claiming to have caught werewolves to the occasional time traveler.

In fact, Bell was so into the whole time travel idea that he would, from time to time (pun intended) open up a phone line specifically for time travelers.

During many Bell shows, he dove into the stories of a mysterious character claiming his name was John Titor, which was actually a name thought to be short for "John TimeTraveler" that was used on several bulleting boards during 2000 and 2001by a poster claiming to be an American military time traveler from 2036.

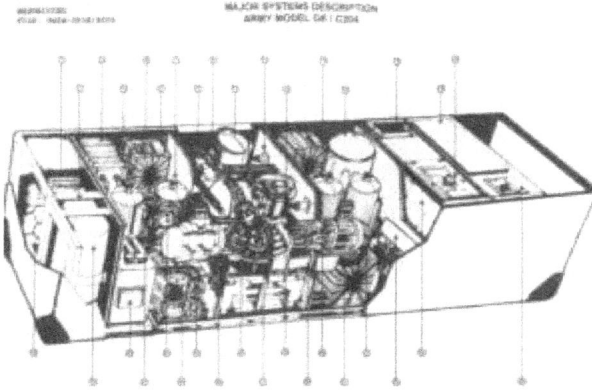

John Titor's alleged time travel device. Also makes toast and can chop onions like a charm!

Titor made several incredible claims, including that he was here to help save the world from the Y2K bug, and that he was here to warn us

about several calamities, including a nuclear war, mass famines, and the thriving career of Justin Bieber.

Of course, none of them came true, and it was later surmised that Titor was a hoax perpetrated by a couple of lawyers from Florida who were just goofing around.

Perhaps the mysteriously named Aery may be nothing more than a Florida man.

After all, many of his predictions thusfar have either not come true (he either ignores these or says that the timeline was changed) or are so obvious as to be along the lines of "the sun will rise tomorrow," such as him pointing to the fact that three months ago, he said we would hit one million cases of covid in one day, and we did.

But in a time when there's far more dangerous BS out there that people are believing, it's fun to just be able to enjoy some good old harmless BS again. It's kind of refreshing to see something that's so blatantly phony and conspiratorial, yet pretty imaginative, that you have to be a complete dumbass to regard it as anything other than entertainment.

Of course, it's a good thing there are so few of those left in the world.

Come to think of it, hey, time traveler, I've got some candidates for you to take with you when you leave…

It's M. M. M. M. M To The B: The Grimy Tale Behind One Of The Biggest TikTok Hits

Jan. 21, 2021

If you, or a child or friend, is on TikTok, you've undeniably heard the following line:

"We all know

the best MC

is M to the B

It's M to the B

It's M M M M M to the B

M to the B, M to the B

Bang!"

Usually though, that's ALL you hear of the infamous tune on TikTok, because, well, TikToks are usually only 15 seconds long.

Also, because it was popularized by a group of cute girls — none of whom actually created the tune — who were just lip synching to the hook of the track and making cartoonish faces for that 15 second hook. Because it's not really something yet until rich, attractive people do it. At least online.

We all know the best MC, it's M to the B, in a black hoodie, from the brand of Nike…

The most famous of these was Bella Poarch, whose big, anime girl eyes and blemish-free face had exactly the sexy manga character quality to match the poppy nature of the song, and as a consequence she got millions of views and became something of a minor pop star herself, with a little hit called "Build A Bitch" (which has a really meta and strangely surreal video beginning with her disembodied head — an odd parallel to her appearance in her TikTok video.)

But I digress.

The song — the whole, two-and-a-half minute tune — actually has a far more interesting history.

Originally released in December 2016, Millie B's "Soph Aspin Send" (a.k.a. "M to the B") was one of the tail-end "hits" of the Blackpool grime movement of the time, which itself was an offshoot of London grime, which had been around for a while prior but began to ooze its influence into the smaller town of Blackpool a few years later.

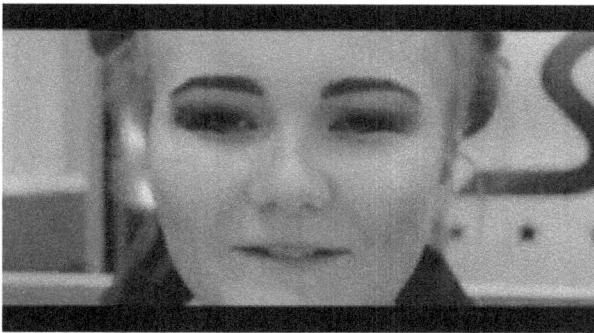

Sweet sweet Millie B

The Blackpool grime scene, which rose up in that lower-scale England city, and predominantly concerned lower income amateur rappers ripping on each other, or, in their parlance "sending" to each other, enjoyed its heyday from 2015-2017, as videos of the rappers began to go viral worldwide. Millie B, born Millie Bracewell, was one of the late era stars of the scene, following in the wake of the much bigger Afghan Dan and Soph Aspin, and the undisputed biggest star of Blackpool grime, the foul-mouthed 12-

year-old Little T, whose video "Road Rage" became the massive viral hit to take Blackpool global.

So, what made Blackpool so different than any other rap scene where people are always popping off on each other?

Little T, in a rare contemplative moment, where he's thinking of who he's going to call an asshole and if he'll threaten to kill their parents. Pretty much every boy in junior high now has his haircut, which was nicknamed the "Meet me at McDonalds."

Well, one of the biggest twists was that most of the biggest rappers were pre-teens and early teens, usually only 12 or

13, which made it all the more perverse, strange, and actually kind of hilarious. The other twist was that the insults were actually really vile and depraved — not your usual "I'm better than you" stuff, but more like, "I'm going to rape your mom and beat your little sister" kind of stuff. Which, coming from a group of 12 and 13 year olds who all look like they're about to line up with Oliver to ask for more soup, was a little off-putting. Other odd details about it were that it had incredibly low budget and appropriately grimy videos from a place called BG Media with amateurish video work from a ubiquitous director named Jack Wilkinson. In addition, the videos usually featured the 12- and 13-year-old rappers hanging out with a bunch of much older dicey looking folks, usually dudes with bad mustaches. So essentially, it was what it was like for us Gen X latchkey kids growing up in the '80s.

Little T: Has road rage, doesn't have a drivers license. No wonder he wants to kill your sister.

The first one to become notorious was a 12-year-old named Little T, who liked to rap about killing people and having sex with their moms. So, you know, Disney Channel stuff.

Little T also may or may not have influenced the haircut that pretty much every boy in junior high now has — a perm on top and shaved on the side. In Blackpool and around England a few years back, every pre-teen and teenager was emulating Little T's perm and shave look, and it was dubbed the "Meet Me At McDonald's Haircut." (Seriously. I can't make this crap up. Ok, maybe I could, yeah, I definitely could, but in this case, I'm not. lol)

He was quickly joined in notoriety by Soph Aspin, a girl not much older, who would likewise rap about other girls being skanks, getting VD and her kicking their asses. Actually, Soph was on the scene before Little T, and some of Little T's first raps were sending out to her, but the rocket fuel of "Road Rage" quickly pushed him past her in terms of fame and began shining a spotlight on the whole scene, allowing grown adults across the world to leave enlightened comments on their videos, like "I hope you get cancer and die." Because, ya know, humanity.

As for Little T hitting it big even though Soph had been there first? Believe it or not, he wasn't gracious about it. In fact, he rubbed it in with her. Oh, Little T, didn't your parents and coaches teach you good sportsmanship?

But soon, into the fray came another young teen with a filthy mouth, Millie B, whose infamous first send to Soph Aspin, best known now as "M to the B" was pretty much a grime masterpiece.

Soph Aspin: She'd look much less angry without Oscar the Grouch's eyebrows.

In all honesty, in my humble opinion, "Soph Aspin Send" is the best pop tune to come from the Blackpool grime scene. It's pretty much stereotypically brilliant Blackpool Grime, from its foul lyrics to its working class fashions to its nods to such banal things as KFC and convenience marts.

But it's irresistibly hooky, and it's also got an incredibly infectious beat. And in its own way, it's really kind of genius.

Sadly, the Blackpool grime movement didn't last much longer than 2017 or so, and all of the Blackpool grime rappers pretty much faded after that.

Little T continued on, and continues on, as a rapper, but a lot of the others have faded. Aspin is sort of a singer, sort of a model. You know, like many other girls on Instagram. Bracewell, a.k.a. Millie B, sort of went down the same path, ended up having a kid, and kinda fell into the Where Are They Now file, taking care of her daughter and selling Avon.

Until now.

Little did she, or any of the Blackpool Grime rappers, know that four years later, she, or rather, her song, would become TikTok famous for being lip synched by a bunch of amateur models and "influencers."

Ironic, since people like Millie B and her Grime compatriots were not only the antithesis to the pretty boys and girls of social media, but would've wanted to kick their candy asses. Millie B has chunks of lightweights like Charlie D'Amelio in her stool.

Still, regardless of the messengers, the former Blackpool grimers are happy their message has been heard again, and their scene is being rediscovered.

Well, almost all of them are happy. It is Blackpool grime, after all. You gotta have a beef.

The subject of the song, Soph Aspin, responded to the buzz on her own TikTok page, saying, "Can someone please tell all these Americans what's going on? They're doing all this, 'M to the B, M to the B' and they're following a B, it's not fucking about a B. It's about me!"

And as for Millie Bracewell, a.k.a. Millie B?

Well, she seems to be rather chuffed about it all. Her social media shows her glowing up from spring of 2020 to present, and even showed her singing at a concert recently. So things are looking up for her, and her posts reflect it.

As she posted at the end of 2021, "This year has been so crazy. Started off really depressed by I finally decided to work on myself and couldn't be happier!"

And this is one of the strangest things about the internet and its resonance — things never truly die. Sometimes that's a curse, as when someone's crude, crass, unenlightened past posts come back to haunt them.

But sometimes, just sometimes, it's pretty cool, as when someone's crude, crass, unenlightened rap songs come back to be lip-synched by attractive women.

Hey, it's not exactly the end of a fairy tale, but it does seem to be a happy ending for Millie B.

Searching For Love Before Valentine's Day? Here's Where You Can Find It

Jan. 28, 2022

It's almost Valentine's Day, which means that those of you in a relationship are blissfully sweating it out with the pressure inherent of being forced to prove the enormity of your love through spending money and symbolic gestures that you hope won't be misinterpreted by your significant other because for a moment there you forgot that you should've been born a psychic to read their mind and immediately know how to make them completely and totally happy.

As for the rest of us who are single, we're left with the sigh of relief of knowing that we don't have to bother with that, and that candy will be 75 percent off on Feb. 15.

But what about those of us who are single but would love to be coupled up?

What about people who are truly, genuinely, looking for love?

Well, I've got one word for you.

Spam.

That's right, spam.

No, not the ham kind, the e-mail kind. As in, your spam folder.

I get hundreds of emails every day, and so, every couple of days, I have to look through my Spam folder to see if anything legitimate mistakenly got chucked into there, that I need to salvage.

Invariably there's a legitimate press release or inquiry about a story for QuadCities.com, and I yank it out of the abyss, like Rick saving someone from the throng of dirty zombies.

But most of it is ridiculous crap.

Albeit sometimes amusing ridiculous crap.

I always enjoy seeing the aforementioned crap, especially if it's bizarre or hilarious. And, of course, you never know what you might learn by looking at some of the information provided. Thankfully, you have me to provide it for you, to save you the effort.

For example, I don't know if you're aware of this, but there are A LOT of horny women out there who want to have sex with me.

I know, I know, surprising, right?

I mean, I'm not a hideous C.H.U.D., but I'm no Brad Pitt either. (Which is why I was able to date Shania Twain for so long, because that don't impress her much, but I digress.)

But nevertheless, I don't know, there's some sort of charisma I must exude through the interwebs that so, so, so many incredibly horny women want to send me pictures of their bobs and vagene and get the sex from me.

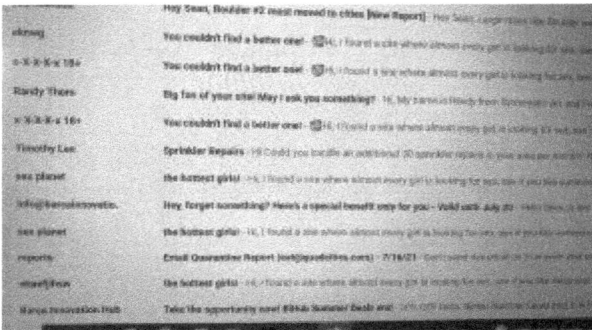

Listen, I told you the women from Sex Planet were really horny.

Just ask Britny, or Jazmine, or Linda (Linda?), or the demure and lovely ladies from Sex Planet, who send me multiple messages a day, telling me that they're the hottest girls, and ALL OF THEM, not just 83.7 percent, not even 95.9 percent, but ALL of the girls are looking for sex from me tonight.

But it's not just Sex Planet, there's also Tiger Girls, who I'm guessing are furries or maybe just regular naked girls who wear those cat ears? I'll have to investigate. Hard news there.

There's also x-X-X-x 18-plus, which tells me all the time about how much their girls want to have sex with me. I don't know about them though, I'm not really into women with feet that big.

I'm also fascinated to report that some of the most popular names out there for horny women out there are afylmp, xtryvz, oiebju, and xxvnys. They're all offering me sex TONIGHT, and are quite proud of their workout routines because they've all offered to send me pictures

of their naked bodies. And there's berxb, who is 19, 160 tall and has 15 chest size, who is waiting for me to appreciate her body.

Hey, no shaming here, I'm very body positive. So, I respect their freedom and desire to do so. But 160 feet tall is just going to be way too much for me.

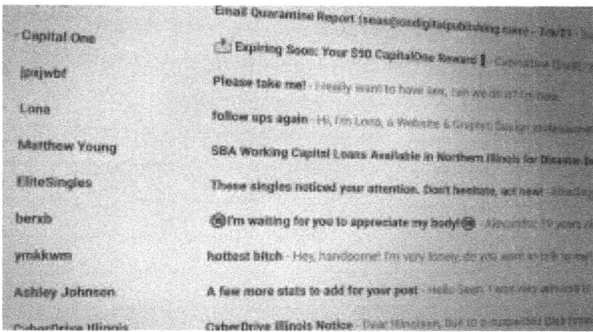

When she says she's the hottest bitch, you'd better believe her, goddamn it.

Besides, they're going to have to contend with ymkkwm, who says she's the hottest bitch, and is very lonely and wants to talk to me and send me pictures of her naked boobs. As opposed to her boobs wearing a top hat and formal poncho. And I truly admire how polite jpxwffb is, as she titles her email, "Please can we have sex?" and offers, "I really want to have sex, can we please do it? I'm here."

Manners and chivalry are not dead, people.

Man! With all these women wanting to have so much sex, I'm gonna have to get a bigger bed! Thankfully, Ashley furniture is offering them on sale in several other messages in my Spam folder! And I'll be able to order as many beds as I like because Rajit Kumar, Jinesh Rai, and Jokit Ragmar are all offering me SECRET EXTRA STIMULUS PAYMENTS from the U.S. government that apparently only Indian gentlemen know about. Oh, you wily Joe Biden! For a robot body double secretly taking the place of the real Joe Biden, who was executed in tribunals along with Hillary Clinton and Tom Hanks by QAnon in the spring, while Donald Trump actually took over as the REAL president from a secret underground bunker sealed with aluminum foil, ya know, you're not such a bad guy.

And with all that extra money, and all those extra beds, and all those extra randy ladies rendezvousing at my home, I'm going to need some good insurance.

Thank God, I've had several people trying to get ahold of me via phone leaving me messages about that.

My Weddings To Brittney And Olivia Munn, And Why Oprah Is Alone On Valentine's Day

Feb. 11, 2022

"Do you feel as depressed as I do about being single on Valentine's Day?"

A friend of mine, named Oprah, messaged me this question the other day, and it got me thinking, "Man, whatever happened to Carolina Liar? That song 'Show Me What I'm Looking For' was pretty friggin awesome!"

Oh, yeah, also, it got me thinking, "Am I depressed at all about being single this Valentine's Day?"

And it got me answering myself rather quickly, "No. No, I am not depressed at all about being single this Valentine's Day."

Not in the least.

That's not to say that I'm a cold, heartless bastard with no sense of romance or desire for romantic love or a significant other in my life.

Me and Oprah. Alas, it wasn't meant to be. Screw you, Stedman.

But it is to say that, this year, that's not a part of my existence, so, who cares?

Part of this, of course, is because unbeknownst to me, apparently I've been leading a shadow life in which I'm engaged and/or married to someone named Brittney Burns.

I don't exactly know who Brittney is, maybe I've been sleep walking and sleep getting engaged again.

But whatever my excuse for forgetting our relationship (alcoholism?), I do hope we've gotten that sweet ass non-stick baking pan in our registry. Because as a blackout alcoholic who gets engaged to strangers who live several states away, I get very hungry after my nineteenth Budweiser.

Peyote makes a fantastic Valentine's Day gift.

Anyway, as for the fake holiday coming up in a couple of days, I've had plenty of Valentine's Days during which I've been dating someone or in a relationship, or just in a casual fling with someone, and some of those still remain good memories.

Some do not.

But most of them do, and that's the way life goes.

Not everything is going to be fantastic 100 percent of the time. Sometimes things really sorta suck, and that's just the way it goes. You can't control other people and the way they feel, or, in some cases, the way they treat you, and the sooner you let go of the impulse to try to control others, the happier and lighter your life will be.

It's the same concept behind dating and meeting other people, whether in the real world or, as is more usually the case nowadays, online.

A woman friend of mine was talking to me recently and asked me about a guy who had randomly ghosted her on a dating app. She sent me a screenshot of the conversation, as well as a couple other convos with other guys, who had also ghosted her, and wanted to get a man's opinion on why she got ghosted and keeps getting ghosted.

(For those unfamiliar with the term, ghosting is when someone just stops messaging you back without any warning, goodbye, or sign off or indication whatsoever. They just… stop writing…)

If you see this guy approaching you on Valentine's Day, it's not a good thing.

After I had stated that I can in no way speak for all men, and that as a human being in general I'm such an outlier in the way I think and behave that it didn't surprise me in the least when a psychic once told me I was a space alien in human disguise, I told her not to bother worrying about it. Nothing in her conversations was "off putting" or intimidating in the least. They were just having random conversations and the guy split.

Yes, it is rude.

Yes, it is lame.

But, it happens.

To everyone.

For one thing, if a guy was going to do that, he wasn't worth her time or any of her concern. And for another, that's just the way most people are these days. That is to say, most people are spineless, capricious, morons with the communication skills and attention spans of crack-addicted chimps.

I also shared with her some of the famous, horrible, terrible last lines I wrote to women that caused them to ghost me on dating apps:

"So, did you see the new Bill and Ted movie?"

"That's cool. What led you to get into that as a career?"

"Lol. Yeah, no joke, 2020 has been the worst."

Controversial, I know.

Folks, to quote the Mandalorian, THIS IS THE WAY.

This is the way people are right now. I don't know what led to people being this strange, weak, and rude, but, they are. So it's best not to really think too much about it. If someone ghosts you, THEY ARE A SPINELESS, INCONSIDERATE WUSS AND YOU ARE BETTER OFF WITHOUT THEM.

If you see this guy approaching you, it's a far, far, worse thing.

Move on. We live in a world of eight billion people, there are plenty of others out there. Some of whom, believe it or not, are not spineless, inconsiderate wusses.

I know, that is hard to believe.

But, trust me, the odds have got to be in our favor. Right, Katniss?

So, no, I'm not going to sweat it.

Just like I'm not sweating being alone on Valentine's Day.

Because you know what? Being alone or just being with your friends or your kids really isn't so bad.

In fact, it's often preferable to being with someone, especially if they're a pain in the ass. Take a look at your Facebook feed, and look at all the "happy relationships" out there. And while you're at it, look at Instagram and take a drink for every person you see posting some saccharine sweet thing about their relationship when you know for a fact one or both of them are cheating on the other.

If you're really looking for something romantic to give your honey, here's the thing to totally get you laid.

It's why I've been sans relationship, and just dating, keeping things light, for so long. I'm honest and up front about my intentions and expectations and remain so throughout to avoid any miscommunication or misunderstanding. You know, like an adult should be. If someone isn't interested, ok, cool, adios and I wish you the best. Lots of single fish in an ocean of eight billion. Moving on...

And I like the freedom. I do what I want, when I want, and take along the companions I want.

If someone wants to come along for the ride and have some fun, cool. If not, that's cool too. You do what what you want to do, I'll do the same. I'm like Doctor Who, I travel through time one day at a time, pop up in different scenarios, take along companions for a while, we have some adventures, then we part ways amicably.

There she is hiding in my bushes and looking in my window again. Sigh. Ok, fine, I guess I'll go out with you, Olivia Munn…

It's really not such a bad way to be. In fact, it's quite good.

And so, this Valentine's Day, I'll probably do as I've always done over the past 13 years if I've been single, and I'll get a heart-shaped pizza and some Whitey's with my son, and hang out with him and play soccer and video games and jenga and watch "The Last Dance" or "The

Mandalorian" or "Cobra Kai" for the umpteenth time with him.

And it'll be awesome. It'll be fun.

Because when it comes down to it, the day is about love.

It's about being with who you love. Celebrating that love, whether romantic or otherwise. And it's about being happy.

So, do something for the people in your life who you love — and that should include yourself.

Have fun. Be happy. Celebrate the love you have in your life, regardless of who it's with — significant other, friends, family, or whoever.

And remember one very important thing.

All those chocolates you see on those store shelves…

…are going to be very deeply discounted over the next week.

And they taste just as good, whether they're heart shaped or not, so, enjoy that s**t.

Happy Valentine's Day!

Are All Men, Or All Women, REALLY The Problem Here?

Feb. 18, 2022

It was Valentine's Day this week, which means that every bitter person out there pissed off about a breakup was posting something venomous and awful about the other gender, saying how horrible they all are.

But are they really?

Are ALL men, or ALL women REALLY the problem?

Or is it just ONE person you're pissed off about, and maybe a few others you're remembering now that you've had some old scars poked?

Whenever you post a meme or make a statement about how "ALL men" or "ALL women" or "ALL this or that" are all the SAME way, you do nothing productive and merely foster an environment of needless ignorance, division, and resentment.

You can't believe all women. You can't believe all men. You can't condemn or lionize all people of any group based upon general characteristics.

We're all human beings, capable of good and bad, capable of nobility and mistakes. We change. We evolve. We've all done dumb shit. We've all done some good things. We all look back at things we've done in the past and wince and wish we had done them differently.

That's part of BEING A HUMAN BEING.

I've had plenty of wonderful and horrible encounters with people — sometimes with the same people. The same ex who signed up for credit cards in my name behind my back and left me with a surprise of over $20,000 in debt when she moved out after banging a married dude behind my back used to write me wonderfully emotional love letters and bought me a puppy for Valentine's Day. Probably with a credit card in my name, but, ya know, details. lol… But… Different points on the map of our lives. Different decisions. Different actions. Different people, yet the same person.

So who do you condemn?

I've dated more than 100 women, which sounds like a hell of a lot but isn't all that many when you consider how long I've been on this earth and that I've been unmarried a lot of that time and that I'm a pretty outgoing and social person. Let's say it's 100 just for an even number. Probably fewer than 10 of those ended notably badly, and really, I can only think of about five of those who I would honestly never want to see or talk to again because they acted horribly. But some of those people acted really, really, horribly.

So do I blame ALL women for the actions of 5 percent? No. I do not. Nor should any man. Nor should any women. If literally EVERY person you date ends up being terrible, sorry, but that says a lot more about you and the people you choose. Because just the odds of humanity would at least give you a 50/50 chance at finding someone at least decent. And you can't be mad at someone merely because they grow apart from you and want to break up. That happens. That's life. You don't own that person, and they have a right to leave if their path is taking them elsewhere. It's sad sometimes, but, again, that's life. You don't get mad at your kids and throw a hissy fit when they grow up and move out, do you?

So, ok, I get it, you want to vent after that breakup. You're pissed off. Maybe you got cheated on — hey, I've certainly been there, it sucks. But maybe let's not blame EVERY person of the gender you dated for the actions of that ONE person?

Would that really be such a difficult change to make?

No. It wouldn't.

But would it make a change? Would it maybe make people less at odds with one another along gender lines and otherwise, to NOT see so many posts bashing ALL women or ALL men?

Yeah, it might.

It might make people realize that it's not fair to blame an entire group of people for the actions of one individual. It might help people to be more sympathetic to others when they see that they've been wronged by one particular individual, rather than feel attacked for no reason.

And wouldn't that small gesture maybe make us less divided?

Wouldn't that small gesture maybe make you feel less bad, in recognizing that it's just that one person that you have issue with, rather than an entire gender you're now at war against?

Just something to think about.

And for the record, I'm not speaking for ALL men.

Just me. I'm the one who wrote this. I'm the one who takes responsibility for it. These words, and opinions, are my own.

Unlike this opinion, which I think many hold:

Epstein didn't kill himself.

Today, On St. Hulk's Day, I'd Like to Introduce You To The Many Sean Learys

March 18, 2022

Today, I'm going to write about a brilliant creator and comedian.

Someone who has made a mark on the field of comedy and the arts.

Someone who is continuing to innovate and gain recognition and stardom on the national stage.

Of course, I'm talking about Sean Leary.

That's right, Sean Leary.

Not me, Sean Leary.

The other Sean Leary.

Well, one of the other Sean Learys.

There are actually a few of us.

And this week, I was once more reminded of that.

This week, I had a guy named Norman Fink trying to contact me via facebook messenger.

The message was short, and was initially kind of general and vague, along the lines of "hey, I'm trying to get ahold of you about some comedy business."

Now, I didn't know anyone named Norman Fink.

It sounded like a fake name.

And while I am a humor writer and have written some comedy shows and performed improv and stand-up, I'd hardly say that I'm a regular in the comedy business. So, I blew the message off.

Then he messaged me again. This time he was more specific. He said he was a talent booker and had heard of me and was looking to book me for a show in L.A.

It was at that point, I realized he was talking the OTHER Sean Leary.

The guy who IS in the comedy business.

I quickly set Norman Fink straight on this, and we both sort of remotely chuckled at the mistaken identity. I guess. We both typed "lol," so whatever that counts for.

Now, how did I discover this other Sean Leary, along with a few of the other Sean Learys?

I was Googling myself.

Hmmm.

That sounds worse than it really is.

Another brilliant comedic mind going under the human name of Sean Leary? Oh, God, how could you bless earth so much?

I was going on the search engine Google and searching for mentions of me and my books, to see if I'd gotten any write ups or reviews, to add the links to my website.

There, that sounds better.

Oh yeah, and also searching for "pink haired Pokemon grunt in a bikini."

Don't judge me. Ok, fair enough, judge me slightly.

Oh no, wait, that part sounds much worse.

Anyway, in the midst of searching for any mention of my books, I found a whole world of other Sean Learys out there.

First and foremost is Sean "Stanley" Leary, who was a promising mountain climber who, sadly, died in a base jumping accident in or near Zion National Park in Utah in 2014. Seemed like a good guy, lot of people had a lot of nice things to say about him after he passed.

After Sean "Stanley" Leary, I show up in the searches, usually as "Sean Leary writer, author of over 50 books, etc." so, that's good. I'd rather be first, but, in honor of the fallen Sean Leary, I'll cede that spot.

Sean "Stanley" Leary, RIP

After me, there's the third Sean Leary, Sean P. Leary, the former Lehigh baseball player and current Lehigh baseball coach, who has apparently had quite a career. If only I'd been able to ever hit a breaking ball, perhaps we could've been on the same team together and challenged the Klingons for interstellar domination.

After Sean P. Leary is another former baseball player (am I the only Sean Leary that went into soccer?) also named Sean Leary, who founded a web company called Sports Thread.

Sean Leary has had a hell of a career as a player and coach for Lehigh.

What's Sports Thread? Allow me, Sean Leary, to quote Sean Leary, as Sean Leary explains:

"Sports Thread is the first social network for the approximately 125 million participants in the $19 billion youth and amateur sports industry. Sports Thread has been ranked as a top 200 Sports App on the Apple App Store every day since March 2020.

The Company provides functionality and value for anyone in the market through the variety of products and services it offers in its social network and SaaS platform.

The social network allows players to promote their talents to college coaches and a nationwide audience as well as receive important team and event related information including game scores, schedules and practice times."

Thanks Sean Leary!

Web sports entrepreneur Sean Leary. Nice suit!

Now, and finally, after those two baseball-playing Sean Learys, we get to my most kindred spirit Sean Leary, the fellow comedy writer and comedian, Sean Leary.

He describes himself on his bio page thusly:

Sean Leary is a midwest bred, Los Angeles based comedian changing the game in stand up comedy. Sean & his girlfriend/comedian Anna Simeri have cultivated a major following with their successful run of pop up comedy shows at unique locations all over the country. Beach shows, house shows, gym shows, if there is space, Sean & Anna can make it into an incredible show. Sean has been featured on Fox's Laughs, HULU, Fusion, competed in AGT Season 10, & has even opened a comedy club in his hometown of Brookings, SD which he runs remotely from Los Angeles. Anna & Sean are a powerhouse duo – now taking their talents to Hollywood with Good Aura Comedy – the hottest new show in the Los Angeles comedy scene!

Wow! Sean Leary has been on HULU! Damn, I need to start putting that in my own press materials.

Sean Leary, comedian, and connoisseur of fine t-shirts and leather jackets.

Of course, I don't need to say it's me, I'm just saying it's Sean Leary.

But then again, I don't want people to think I died in a mountain climbing accident, and I don't want people contacting me about college baseball recruiting.

However, I would love to live in Los Angeles.

But just imagine the confusion for Norman Fink then!

It could turn into a sitcom! There would be TWO Sean Learys, and we would keep getting mistaken for each other, and we'd live in the same apartment with a couple of women named Janet and Crissy, but we'd have to pretend to be gay because the landlord, Mr. Roper, didn't want to rent the apartment to two couples because he'd be afraid we'd be filming orgy porn or something on the premises.

I think this is the episode with the misunderstanding.

And then every episode, there would be a misunderstanding, and Mr. Roper would overhear something out of context, and he'd think there would be something heinous going on, but there wouldn't, and at the end of the episode, all would be revealed, and Mrs. Roper would say, "Geez Stanley, I wish you'd spend as much time getting it on with me as you spent eavesdropping on the neighbors, ya damn degenerate pervert!"

And we'd all laugh, and the audience would laugh.

And then Mr. Roper would slink back to his apartment, and go back to Googling "pink haired Pokemon grunt in a bikini."

This exists, because, of course it does on the Internet.

And then I, the other Sean Leary, and the two baseball coach Sean Learys (who were guest starring in that episode), and Janet and Crissy, would shake David Banner's hand and say, "Thank you, Hulk, for helping to show Mr. Roper the error of his ways in this misunderstanding, so that we may continue to live together in this beautiful Southern California apartment in peace and harmony and quality stand up comedy.

And David Banner would nod his head and smile, and then put his backpack over his shoulder, and walk away, away to the highway, where he'd stick his thumb out to hitchhike on to the next town where he, and the Hulk, would help people.

And THAT, my friends, is the real story of The Day After St. Patrick's Day.

St. Hulk's Day.

Seriously. It's a real holiday. Celebrated by pink haired Pokemon grunts in bikinis. Don't ask how I know that.

Society's Strange Programmed Gender Concepts Are All In The Pink

March 25, 2022

Is pink a girl's color?

Is pink a boy's color?

In the past few years, pink has become a hot fashion choice for men. Pro basketball and soccer players are wearing pink shoes, rock stars like Machine Gun Kelly are wearing hot pink and playing pink guitars, and even football players are wearing pink to ostensibly raise awareness for breast cancer.

Some people are aghast at that.

But why?

Historically, that's a very masculine choice.

In the 19th and 20th centuries up through the 1940s, pink was considered a color for boys, as it was the lighter version of red, which was considered a powerful color for men.

Blue was actually considered a "more dainty" color and was considered feminine. So women would wear blue, girls light blue.

Of course, none of this mattered in the least until the industrial revolution and the widespread manufacture of dyes and dyed clothing.

Prior to that, in the mid-1800s and before, infants and toddlers wore white dresses, regardless of their gender. This was because white was easy to bleach out stains, and the dress style made it far easier to change diapers. Given that most houses didn't have indoor plumbing, potty training in its current form was not yet anywhere near as widespread as it is today, and it was far easier for boys and girls to not have to drop trou and instead just lift skirt.

The switch from pink as a masculine color to a feminine color began in the mid-late 1940s, as various trends from Europe began to permeate American society post-WW2. Even so, pink continued to be seen as a color of wealth and royalty and style, hence Elvis Presley and many other rock stars looking to drive pink Cadillacs and the preponderance of "little pink houses" in the suburbs in the 1950s. In fact, it wasn't until the repressive and conservative '50s that there was truly a clear delineation of pink as a feminine color and blue as a masculine one.

In the 1960s and '70s, however, that switched. Baby boomers, rebelling against culture norms and sexist programming, rejected the ideas that any color could be inherently gender-biased, and rebelled against pink or any other color being seen as inherently slanted towards any gender. Punk rock used pink in posters, in open defiance of the cultural programming of it as a "feminine" color, in order to shock the squares.

It wasn't until the early '80s that the pink and blue as feminine and masculine began to upswing again, and the reason for it isn't necessarily because of the swing towards conservatism during that time, it was due to, well, GREED. The rise of pre-natal imaging which allowed parents to see whether their child was biologically a boy or a girl opened the door to companies wanting to cash in on this with clothing items, furniture, nursery items and other costly accessories, which they figured they could make twice the money on if they divided them up into pink and blue for girls and boys.

Even so, the subculture continued to rebel against the delineation of color as a sexist trope, and in particular creative artists overtly subverted the conventions, most notably artists like Prince, who popularized the regal purple, and acts like Duran Duran and Culture Club, which wore bright pastels, regardless of any connotations as "feminine."

With everyone from rock stars to rap stars to athletes following suit to subvert and rebel against conventions in ensuing decades, the use of pink has gotten to a point where it's once more become a significant fashion statement of Gen Z, a sort of rebellious F-U to previous generations programmed to feel triggered or insecure by a simple color. Professional basketball and soccer players, rappers, and rock stars now routinely wear pink as a fashion statement, with everyone from Machine Gun Kelly to David Beckham's Inter Miami soccer team to the Miami Heat to Barcelona to Juventus adopting pink jerseys as a statement of style and individualism.

But the thing I find most interesting of all of it is that once more this is a case of something completely neutral, which intrinsically has no meaning — a color — being charged with meaning by the pressures of societal mores, and what's all the more ironic, that that meaning has, over the past 200 years, meant the complete opposite thing at various times, thus showcasing all the more how transient and ephemeral societal preferences are, and how they're shaped so profoundly by the waves of public pressure one way or another.

Kind of intriguing.

It all shows how much society is brainwashed.

People are programmed from the time they are born to think a certain way, to associate certain things, to have positive or negative connotations to random items even though they don't intrinsically hold any positive or negative meaning.

If you were blind or had no concept of color, and you were cold, and someone handed you a pink coat, would you care? No, you'd just put on the coat.

So why would someone who isn't blind or does have a concept of color, when handed a pink coat, have a certain reaction to it — pro or con?

Because that's how they've been programmed.

That's how they've been brainwashed by society.

The only way to escape these things is by recognizing them. By recognizing how random and ultimately inconsequential they are, and that their consequence and importance to us is just an illusion that we've been programmed to consider serious at all.

And just like that, we can also program ourselves to stop thinking that way.

We can recognize that it's ridiculous.

Not just in regard to the color pink, but in regard to many other things as well.

I'll leave you to think about what those things might be.

I only ask that you try to step out of any preconceived notions or programming, and that YOU do the thinking for yourself.

Other Books By Sean Leary

The Arimathean (novel)

The Blood of Destiny (novel)

Black Knight Apocalypse (novel)

Luna Death Trigger (novel)

DisIntegration (novel)

Does The Shed Skin Know It Was Once A Snake?
(short stories)

Every Number Is Lucky To Someone

(short stories)

My Life As A Freak Magnet

(short stories)

Exorcising Ghosts

(graphic novel)

Here Comes The Goot!

(children's/beginning readers)

Go, Racecars, Go!

(children's/beginning readers)

Nine Little Penguin Ninjas

(children's/beginning readers)

Baby Bird

(children's/beginning readers)

We Are All Characters

(children's/beginning readers)

All My Best Adventures Are With You

(children's/beginning readers)

Beautiful Remnants of Chaotic Failures

(poetry)

Danger Maps

(poetry)

Every Broken Heart Creates The Pieces That Will Pave The Way To The Place Your Heart Will Call Home

(poetry)

Tricks of the Light

(poetry)

The Soft Venom of Promise

(poetry)

The Night Universal

(poetry)

There Is Truth In The Untamed Beat of a Heart

(poetry)

We Are Shadows In The Absence of Light

(poetry)

Magnets & Mysteries, Soft Curves & Comets

(poetry)

Infinite Sky

(poetry)

Physics & Beauty

(poetry)

Dark Equinox

(graphic novel)

The Ink In The Well

(graphic novel)

Dream States

(graphic novel)

Valentine Cords

(graphic novel)

Spyder

(graphic novel)

Sean Leary's Greatest Hits, volume one

(humor)

Sean Leary's Greatest Hits, volume two

(humor)

Sean Leary's Greatest Hits, volume three

(humor)

Sean Leary's Greatest Hits, volume four

(humor)

Sean Leary's Greatest Hits, volume five

(humor)

Sean Leary's Greatest Hits, volume six

(humor)

Sean Leary's Greatest Hits, volume seven

(humor)

Sean Leary's Greatest Hits, volume eight

(humor)

Sean Leary's Greatest Hits, volume nine

(humor)

Sean Leary's Greatest Hits, volume ten

(humor)

Sean Leary's Greatest Hits, volume eleven

(humor)

Sean Leary's Greatest Hits, volume twelve

(humor)

Sean Leary's Greatest Hits, volume thirteen

(humor)

Your Favorite Band

(stageplay / screenplay)

Dingo Boogaloo

(stageplay / screenplay)

Rock City Live!

(stageplay / screenplay)

My Life As A Freak Magnet: The Scripts

(stageplay / screenplay)

Shots To The Heart

(stageplay)

Advice to My Son

(life stories and positive parenting)

Subliminal Cartography

(novel)

I Don't Have The Map

(poetry)

For more writing and more information, see www.seanleary.com.

Hey, stop reading.

Go find another book, like one of those many fine Sean Leary books listed on those pages just before this one…

Enjoy the trip…

www.ingramcontent.com/pod-product-compliance
Lightning Source LLC
Chambersburg PA
CBHW031208270326
41931CB00006B/465

Crossing the Border to India

YOUTH, MIGRATION, AND
MASCULINITIES IN NEPAL

Jeevan R. Sharma

TEMPLE UNIVERSITY PRESS
Philadelphia • *Rome* • *Tokyo*

TEMPLE UNIVERSITY PRESS
Philadelphia, Pennsylvania 19122
tupress.temple.edu

Paperback edition published 2024
Cloth edition published 2018

Library of Congress Cataloging-in-Publication Data

Names: Sharma, Jeevan Raj, author.
Title: Crossing the border to India : youth, migration, and masculinities
in Nepal / Jeevan R. Sharma.
Description: Philadelphia : Temple University Press, [2018] | Series: Global
youth | Includes bibliographical references and index.
Identifiers: LCCN 2017052522 (print) | LCCN 2018010976 (ebook) |
ISBN 9781439914281 (E-Book) | ISBN 9781439914267 (cloth : alk. paper)
Subjects: LCSH: Nepal—Emigration and immigration—Social aspects. |
India—Emigration and immigration—Social aspects. | Young men—
Nepal—Attitudes. | Masculinity—Social aspects—Nepal.
Classification: LCC JV8510 (ebook) | LCC JV8510 .S47 2018 (print) |
DDC 304.8/540549608351—dc23
LC record available at https://lccn.loc.gov/2017052522

ISBN 9781439914274 (paperback : paper)

021524P

Contents

Note on Nepali Words and Nepali and Indian Currency

Nepali words are transliterated and appear in italic type. I follow the transcription practice of Ralph Lille Turner ([1931] 1990). Patronyms, ethnic groups, castes, and place names are transcribed in simplified form.

At the time of the initial fieldwork, 2004–2005, one U.S. dollar was equivalent to 67 Nepali rupees (NRs 67) and 43 Indian rupees (IRs 43).

Acknowledgments

This book is a culmination of the research I conducted over the past several years. I have benefited throughout from the inspiration, encouragement, and generous support of many people and institutions in various places.

I am indebted to a number of people in and from Palpa and other parts of the western hills of Nepal for their time, hospitality, and insights. Most of all, I thank Narayan Adhikari, Amar Gharti, Bishnu Prasad, and Kiran Sharma for the time and effort they contributed in Palpa to introduce me to people in my fieldwork area, to help interview and interpret, and to assist in whatever other ways were needed. In Mumbai, I thank Bhim Bashyal for his support and assistance.

Antonio Donini, with whom I have carried out long-term research on social change in western Nepal, has been a continuous source of encouragement and mentoring. While I was at Tufts University, I benefited from conversations with Karen Jacobsen, Dyan Mazurana, Liz Stites, and Peter Walker.

My work on Nepali migrants has evolved thanks to discussions with a number of people. In particular I must acknowledge Radha Adhikari, Keshav Bashyal, Tristan Brusle, David Gellner,

Avash Piya, David Seddon, Deepak Thapa, Susan Thieme, and Karen Valentin.

I have benefited from the mentorship and intellectual input of Crispin Bates, Ben Campbell, Ian Harper, Sondra Hausner, Michael Hutt, Roger Jeffery, Judith Justice, Toby Kelly, Andrea Nightingale, and Jonathan Spencer.

Craig Jeffrey and Aaron Javsicas believed in the project from the start. I am grateful to them; to the three anonymous reviewers for Temple University Press; to Nikki Miller, Joan Vidal, and the editorial team at Temple University Press; and to freelance copyeditors Lindsay Graham and Ginny Perrin.

I express my deep appreciation to many friends and well-wishers in Nepal and around the world for providing stimulating company and invaluable insights.

Finally my greatest thanks go to my family members in Nepal for their love and support. Mona has been the project's greatest advocate; she was a continuous source of encouragement throughout the lengthy completion of the manuscript. I started this project when our daughter, Aayona, was only a few months old, and I dedicate this book to her.

—Jeevan R. Sharma
October 2017
Edinburgh

Crossing the Border to India

Introduction

In October 2004, when I was doing fieldwork in a village in Nepal's Palpa district, I came across a 34-year-old Bahun man who was about to leave for India with two of his nephews, who were between 18 and 20 years old. The two young men had never been abroad before. The uncle had already found a job for one nephew as a domestic worker in Friends Colony in Delhi, and, given the demand for domestic workers in Indian cities, he was hopeful that he would be able to find work for the other soon after their arrival. The two boys, in brand-new clothes, seemed both nervous and shy. Some members of their family and friends were giggling and teasing the two young men for going off to be *lahures*.[1] The departure took about fifteen or twenty minutes, and there was a small crowd of around fifteen family members and neighbors gathered in front of the house. Signifying good luck for travel, the travelers had red vermilion *tika* marks on their foreheads and carried guava fruits in their hands. The young men were carrying only two small bags each. Much of the focus was on the boys, who were leaving home for the first time. They were told to take care of themselves, not to become involved in *naramro kam* (immoral work or behavior), and to send *halkhabar* (news) regularly. The uncle assured his brothers and sisters-in-law that he would take care of the boys and they need not worry about them. As they left, all the family members and neighbors gathered and watched them walking away until they disappeared along the trail that led to the main road. In response, the three men turned back frequently and waved. One of the mothers had tears in her eyes, but the grandmother said, in an authoritative voice, that she should not cry because it was an auspicious time for departure, or *sait*. As soon as the three men were out of sight, everyone returned to their usual routines.

Whether accompanied by elders or not, departure scenes like this are very common in the rural hills of western Nepal. Both historical and ethnographic evidence show that hardly any area in the hills of Nepal remains untouched by the practice of young men's out-migration to India or, increasingly in recent years, to various global destinations such as the Gulf States and Southeast Asian countries. Given the limited economic opportunities in rural Nepal, the desire of young men to migrate—regardless of their income and education level, caste, or ethnicity—has never been greater. In the villages and towns throughout the region, people often say that no one is left in the villages but the old people, women, and little children. While this certainly does not mean that *all* young men out-migrate from these villages, the historical practice of out-migration, combined with higher aspirations among the younger generation to leave rural villages in search of paid work and the associated opportunities to experience the world outside in cities and towns, often means that those who stay back are equally affected by this "culture of migration" (J. Cohen 2004). In his ethnography of migration in the central valleys of Oaxaca, Mexico, Jeffery Cohen (2004) uses this term to characterize (1) the pervasive practice and long history of out-migration, (2) how out-migration practices and the values associated with them are deeply ingrained into the everyday lives of people, and (3) how the decision to migrate is an accepted livelihood strategy for economic survival and well-being. This idea of a "culture of migration" captures well the pervasive nature of circular and temporary migration in the rural hills of Nepal that has long remained a practice among the village households.

Furthermore, the migration decision is a part of everyday life, and households consider migration one of the key strategies for managing their livelihoods. Without work opportunities outside Nepal, marginal households in the hills of Nepal would face serious hardship (Hitchcock 1961).

The first wave of migration began in the eighteenth and nineteenth centuries, when state policies and agrarian changes forced peasants in the hills to move off their land and seek their livelihoods elsewhere, both within Nepal and across the border into India, mainly by working in agrarian sectors (Regmi 1978). Since the 1950s, pushed by difficult economic conditions at home, young men from poorer households in the hills have relied on the comparatively large economy of Indian cities, which they travel to regularly in search of various work opportunities so they can support and maintain their families. For these men, migration to Indian cities, with its prospects for jobs and greater economic security, opened up the potential, real or imagined, for asserting male identity. Migration to Indian cities is circular in nature and is facilitated and sustained by social networks. Many workers begin when they are young and continue to travel back and forth between their home country and the migrant destination until they are old, sick, or injured. Because of the open border between Nepal and India, it is difficult to know the exact number of Nepalis who migrate on a circular basis to work in Indian cities, but it is estimated at about 1 million.[2] Many of these migrants work in different service sectors and in the Indian police and army, and about 90 percent of all migrants are believed to be men. Although most Nepalis, especially those from the poorer sections of the population, continue to migrate to Indian cities, the proportion of Nepali migrant laborers traveling to India decreased from 80 percent in 2001 to 41 percent in 2009 (World Bank 2010), mainly because of the emergence of other migrant destinations, such as the Gulf States and Southeast Asian countries (Seddon, Adhikari, and Gurung 2001). This form of migration plays a major role in supporting subsistence agriculture and the livelihoods of marginal households in Nepal.

The unique "open border" between Nepal and India, formalized by the Nepal-India Peace and Friendship Treaty of 1950, allows the citizens of both countries to cross the border without having to produce official documents and also prescribes equal treatment of both Nepali and Indian citizens (Hausner and Sharma 2013). In practice, however, "open border" and "equal treatment" do not apply to poorer migrants, who are regularly subjected to interrogation, frisking, ill-treatment, and humiliation while traveling and crossing the border. It is very common for low-income migrants to get cheated or robbed on their way to India or while returning home with the little money that they carry with them. Except for those who work in the Indian Army or police, most work in informal sectors that offer low pay and little protection, and thus they cannot save sufficiently to send money back home regularly. Language, appearance, and cultural differences expose many to harassment and ill-treatment. In India, Nepalis have neither legal status similar to that of Indian citizens to enable them to access services or protection measures nor the right to protection or privileges offered to foreigners under international human rights acts, because of their liminal position.

In practice, however, low-income migrants from within India also have limited citizenship status (e.g., they may lack appropriate Aadhaar registration or ration cards linked to their new, often transient, residence). Consequently, there are obvious similarities between the internal and cross-border Nepali low-income migrants in regard to their entitlements and protection from violence. While several Nepali migrants I spoke to in Delhi and Mumbai have acquired documentation that is necessary to access basic services, the political and administrative climate is becoming more hostile to low-income migrants in Indian cities with the politicization and pathologization of migrants and the introduction of Aadhaar, a twelve-digit unique identification number issued by the central government of India to its citizens.[3] Despite their active participation in the growth of Indian cities, many Nepali migrants I worked with lacked documentation and registration for basic services such as health care and so are excluded from the promise of Indian cities and the idea of belonging. Most Nepali migrants have to go to private health care providers to be treated when they fall ill. Such exclusion perpetuates structural inequalities that lie at the heart of their poverty and marginalization. The public health gaze views Nepali migrants in India within the pathologizing framework of HIV, where migrants are seen as the carriers of disease, particularly diseases associated with sexual promiscuity, and completely ignores the social determinants of their health status. In Mumbai, the only existing service for those Nepali migrants I worked with was an organization, Sathi Nepal, that overwhelmingly focused on HIV and sexually transmitted infections (STIs) and not on other health issues or the well-being of low-income migrants.

Traditional studies of migration focus on economic motivations that lead an individual to choose to migrate. Academic, policy, and popular accounts typically assume that limited economic opportunities for earning cash as well as a fragile agriculture and environment—characterized by vulnerability to irreversible damage to the physical land surface, vegetation, and economic systems due to overuse or rapid change—in the "sending community" and economic opportunities in the "receiving community," understood in the terms *push factor* and *pull factor*, respectively, result in this type of circular labor migration. While there is no reason to doubt that regional inequalities between Nepal and India, wage differentiation, increased work opportunities in Indian cities, and poverty in Nepal's hills explain the male labor migration across the border to Indian cities, such a perspective assumes a rationally acting self-interested economic migrant, who maximizes his self-interest and has control over his destiny through choice. This perspective not only minimizes the role of structural context, of poverty and inequalities, and of how they shape livelihood options and therefore people's decisions; it also disallows sociocultural and, more specifically, gendered or generational perspectives on migration. Nepali male migrants I worked with were anything but rationally acting self-interested economic migrants. Their motives are not simply rational economic ones.

Young migrants not only struggled to earn money and to save while working in India; most of them also experienced hardship, ill-treatment, and exploitation while living and working in India, while crossing the border, and while traveling. Despite this, they refused to see themselves as victims; rather, they were actors with their own motivations and goals for migration, making their own sociocultural worlds. The migrants I worked with were individuals who had experiences, skills, and aspirations. They had the support of and obligations to social networks rooted in kinship and friendship. They were persons with economic, political, and social lives, never entirely dehumanized, who retained an element of agency despite the forces working on them.

Key Concepts

In this book, I attempt to provide an ethnography of male labor migration from the western hills of Nepal to Indian cities. In order to provide a conceptual framing for the ethnography, I here introduce some key concepts to help understand the young men's efforts to deal with economic uncertainties in the middle hills of Nepal and their decisions to engage in the practice of circular migration to India that, in the end, offers very little opportunity for social mobility. My approach is informed by my desire to narrate the perceptions, experiences, and aspirations of migrants in a way that makes the discussion accessible to nonspecialist readers while placing it within a broader conceptual framework. In the following paragraphs I introduce three key concepts: livelihoods, gender, and structural violence.

Livelihoods

I approach the practice of circular migration from the hills of Nepal to India within the broader framework of livelihoods. For the purpose of this book, I adopt a simple definition of livelihoods—"diverse ways in which people make a living and build their worlds" (Bebbington 1999: 2034). Instead of making the presumption that people prefer not to migrate, the concept of livelihoods provides a framework to explore migration as one of the economic strategies available to households. In the context of economic uncertainties caused by the fragile agriculture of the mountain environments, as well as a history of extractive state policies in Nepal (Regmi 1978), circular migration across the border into India is one of the strategies available to marginal households to manage their livelihoods. Using the framework of livelihoods, this book approaches circular migration from the Nepali hills into India from the vantage point of the migrants and their communities, without disregarding the structural contexts that shape their decisions (De Haan 1999; Whitehead 2002).

At a broader level, economic approaches have looked at labor migration in a positive manner and have emphasized the rational choice of an individual migrant (Todaro 1976) or migrant household (Stark 1991), whereas structuralist theorists and neo-Marxists have looked at it from a pessimistic perspective, as resulting from an exploitative structure that breeds underdevelopment, poverty, population pressure, and environmental degradation (Breman 1985; Shrestha 1990). Both individualistic (and behavioral) models and migration analyses in the Marxist (or structuralist) tradition have taken a one-sided point of view (De Haan 1999). Economic and behavioral models tend to isolate economic decision making, and they do not analyze the cultural, political, and social contexts in which these decisions are made. On the other hand, Marxist analyses overemphasize the political-economic contexts that influence migration decisions, giving no consideration to the perceptions and experiences of migrants themselves. No doubt, economic compulsions seem crucial in determining migration decisions among the poorer households, but choices are more complex. Social, ethnic, gender, and religious factors also inform people's decisions to migrate (De Haan and Rogaly 2002; Shah 2006). Without considering the experiences and the perceptions of migrants and those from migrant communities, it would be difficult to understand sociocultural as well as gendered meanings attached to migration.

In contrast to the behavioral and structural theories of labor migration, I find that the concept of livelihoods offers a useful framework to explore the meanings and experiences of migration in relation to the gendered, familial, social, and economic dynamics of those who migrate and their networks, from their own perspective. The major feature of the livelihoods approach is that it does not view migrants as vulnerable and helpless victims but as dynamic actors that use tactics to cope with risks imposed by external conditions (Whitehead 2002). It focuses on the premise that people are actors who seek to counter vulnerability, arising out of high risk and uncertainty, and ensure their immediate survival as well as their long-term well-being by deploying various strategies and using both tangible and intangible resources (Bebbington 1999). The decision to migrate is thus based on a household's perceptions of these contexts and an evaluation of the different possibilities and constraints (De Haan 1997).

The livelihoods approach departs from viewing migrants only as economic actors or only as workers, arguing that such a view fails to recognize livelihood strategies as social and cultural processes and their role in reproducing the social structure. The economic approach focuses narrowly on economic motivation and, by doing so, the whole universe of exchanges is reduced to mercantile exchange predicated on self-interested maximization of profit, whereas sociocultural meanings are conceived as noneconomic and therefore not significant. Drawing on actor-centered notions, the livelihoods approach argues that "we need a notion of resources that not only helps us to understand the way in which people deal with their poverty and well-being in a material sense, but also the ways in which their perception of poverty and well-being are related to their livelihood choices and strategies" (Bebbington 1999: 2022). The capacities that migrants possess both add to their quality of life and enhance their capabilities to confront the social conditions that perpetuate risks and vulnerability.

Drawing on the work of anthropologist Pierre Bourdieu, this book approaches the culture of migration and Nepali migrants' daily lives as a result of the dialectical relationship between social fields and habitus (Bourdieu 1977). "Habitus" is the socially and culturally conditioned set of durable dispositions for social actions, and it is reflected in the perceptions and strategies of migrants. Habitus is a product of history and a tradition of out-migration, but it is dynamic. It is always in the making. Considering both the history and culture of migration, and the everyday lives of migrants, I explore how habitus can change and that migrants are not at the mercy of history and tradition but are actors who construct history and meanings associated with migration. Such a perspective offers a useful framework through which to bring to the foreground the sociocultural and gendered meanings of migration beyond the dominant yet narrow economic approach. With its emphasis on sociocultural aspects, the livelihoods framework allows for viewing migrants not just as workers or producers but also as consumers. Therefore this book considers how Nepali migrants mobilize ideas of progress, development, modernity, and consumption in their favor.

Gender and Masculinities

Given that circular migration from the hills of Nepal is a male-dominated practice and that many start at a young age and continue to travel back and forth until they are old, sick, or injured, gender and generation are two key concerns of this book. Until recently, focus on gender has been on women, and the possibility of gendering male labor migration has been largely neglected (Bretell 2000; Jackson 2001). This is reflected in the overwhelming focus on women's trafficking from Nepal to India (Joshi 2001). "Originally concentrated upon women of the industrialized West, gender scholarship gradually expanded to recognize and include the contributions of women of the global South" (Jones 2006: xii). Despite the shift from a women in development to a gender and development paradigm in the 1990s, where the latter theoretically provides a greater space for inclusion of men and masculinities, social scientists have largely preferred to treat men as ungendered beings.

Recent years have seen considerable growth in the body of literature on gender with the theme of masculinity. The work of Raewyn Connell has become influential in debates and discussion on masculinities since the publication of *Gender and Power* (Connell 1987) and *Masculinities* (Connell 1995). In the first book, Connell demonstrates how gender is a concept of power and shows how men have gained from the overall subordination of women. He argues that being a man gives power. His second book develops a theory of masculinities, which shows that not all men share the power and not all are exploitative. He argues that there is no such thing as a universal masculinity, but rather that different masculinities are organized hierarchically. The key here is what he calls "hegemonic" masculinity, which dominates other masculinities (namely subordinate, complicit, and marginalized) as well as women and creates a model for what it means to be a real man. "Hegemonic masculinities define successful ways of 'being a man'; in so doing, they define other masculine styles as inadequate or inferior" (Cornwall and Lindisfarne 1994: 3). The work on multiple masculinities has contributed to challenging the naturalized assumptions of what it means to "be a man." Instead of viewing gender as a predetermined role through which men (and women) act out their prescribed social roles, the focus is on the making and remaking of gendered practices. This framework allows for an analysis of low-income Nepali male migrants as enacting a process of being and becoming men. In his book *The End of Masculinity,* John MacInnes (1998) argues that a growing concern with masculinity is misplaced and that the study of new and more acceptable models of masculinity is not worthwhile. His argument is that gender difference is a social construct and therefore there is no logical basis from which to associate masculinity with biological males. Drawing on European social history, he regards the problem as being rooted in the uncompleted project of modernity and the idea of the social contract on which modernity rests. "Modernity produces societies that are transitional, in the sense that they combine the material and ideological legacy of a sexual division of labour produced by the patriarchal era which preceded this, with material and ideological forces which undermine that legacy and create the conditions for a sexually egalitarian order" (MacInnes 1998: 3). MacInnes's work helps us to look at the importance of masculinity as an ideology rather than associate it with the biological male.

Until recently, the study of masculinity in the South Asian context has been somewhat neglected. Exploring the ethnographies of South Asia with the intention of locating men, Filippo and Caroline Osella write that while men are certainly present, they are not the explicit object of study. They find that not much attention is paid to understanding men's behavior and their relationship with others (Osella and Osella 2006: 4). For a long time South Asian men have been treated as universally similar, ungendered objects, rarely examined as gendered beings. Recent ethnographies have highlighted the anxieties and strategies of educated unemployed men in India in the face of widespread unemployment (Cross 2009; Jeffrey, Jeffery, and Jeffery 2007; Jeffrey 2010). How boys become men and the role that work and mobility play in the construction of masculinity remain important questions (McDowell 2003).

An emerging body of work looks at masculinity and migration and addresses the impact of mobility on men's identity in different ways. Migration both enables and challenges the masculinity of migrant men, as men are expected to migrate and provide for their families, but they leave behind their family and their role as farmers to work in low-paid jobs as migrant workers (Boehm 2008: 20). Similarly, Deborah Cohen (2006) argues that because of working conditions, discrimination, and the complexity of interaction with local residents, migrants experience a dramatic assault on their subjectivities even as the migration experience simultaneously provides the mechanisms to secure gender and class subjectivities and claims in a crucial way.

Osella and Osella show that migration of young men from Kerala to the Gulf was motivated not only by the need to escape unemployment and earn money, an important source of masculine potency, but also by a desire to move away from "payyanhood" (young immature status) toward full adult status as a householder, defined by the combination of marriage, fatherhood, and ability as a provider. Here migration functions as a means of bridging a gap between payyanhood and manhood (Osella and Osella 2000: 120–122). Their work shows how the migration of young men from Kerala to the Gulf has become incorporated into the local styles of masculinity (Osella and Osella 2000). On one hand this presents young males with opportunities to gain status as wise and economically secure men, but on the other hand threatens male identity if economic resources are not managed well; these men must decide how much money to spend on individual consumption and how much to remit or spend on family and friends.

Drawing on the case of Hazara men who migrate between the mountainous region of central Afghanistan and the cities of Iran, Alessandro Monsutti (2007) argues that their migration can be seen as a rite of passage to adulthood, a step toward manhood. Using the concept of rites of passage, he shows that the journey of these young Hazara men represents "separation" from home and family; the difficult life in Iran, where they need to find and save money, is the "liminal phase"; and the migrants' eventual return to Afghanistan is "incorporation," when they get married and establish a household (Monsutti 2007).

Describing the case of a marriage-led migration of Pakistani men to Britain, where migrants moved into the houses of their wives' families and become "house sons-in-law" (*ghar damad*), Katharine Charsley shows that such migration had an adverse impact on migrants' male identity (Charsley 2005: 91). She demonstrates that "house sons-in-law" are faced with the somewhat unusual proximity of the wife's family in a new place. In addition, these men lack a local kin support to assert their male identity. Combined together, such a context can result in a restructuring of gender identity. Similarly, a study on Nepali nurse migrants and their husbands in the United Kingdom shows that while the migration had an empowering effect on the migrant nurses, their husbands became frustrated with their compromised gendered position as dependents (R. Adhikari 2013).

What emerges from the studies of migration in situations of economic hardship is the central importance of gendered ideas in shaping young people's migration. Migration not only is informed by classed, gendered, and generational considerations but also disrupts gender and class subjectivities. Accordingly, this work approaches masculinity as an ideological space through which men see their life. The case of the large number of Nepali men who travel to work in Indian cities like Mumbai offers an interesting opportunity to bring circular migration and masculinity together in order to explain the context, reasons, and effects of men's migration from their perspective.

Structural Violence

This book is about marginal young men who come from poorer households in the hills of Nepal, eventually end up working in an India that pays too little to enable them to improve their households' situations back in Nepal, and must go through the difficult process of border crossing and the humiliation and ill-treatment that comes with it. Thus, in this book I aim to uncover the linkages between social inequalities related to structural violence and the normalization of symbolic violence. I draw on the concept of structural violence to analyze the configuration of social inequalities, discrimination, and ill-treatment that has effects on the bodies of migrants as well as on their notions of masculinities.

I use the concept of structural violence to characterize conditions of structural inequalities in Nepali society that result in the poverty, exclusion, and marginalization of populations and also to frame the discrimination and exploitative working conditions of Nepali migrants in India. According to Paul Farmer (2004), structural violence refers to systematic ways in which social structures disadvantage individuals. Johan Galtung, another scholar who frequently uses the term "structural violence" in relation to conflict studies, defines it as "the indirect violence built into repressive social orders [that] creates enormous differences between potential and actual human self-realization" (1975: 173). Structural violence is subtle and often has no one specific person who can (or will) be held responsible. Farmer defines it as "violence exerted systematically—that is indirectly—

by everyone who belongs to a certain social order" (2004: 307). The system of social and institutional oppression functions as long as each side, oppressor and oppressed, plays its role according to the rules implanting social suffering and subordination of one to the other.

Within the labor migration debate, Michael Burawoy (1976) has argued that the system of labor migration is characterized by a separation between labor's production and the reproduction of the labor force. In other words, Nepali migrants survive on low wages in India and contribute to economic production in that context while the family, community, and state in Nepal provide education, health care, and other services to the reproduction of labor. Nepali migrants come to work in India and return to their home in Nepal when they are no longer physically strong. These low-income Nepali migrants do not settle in India. Therefore, although the host society benefits from the contribution of migrant labor, it does not bear the cost of migrants' or their families' welfare. They are welcomed to Indian cities as cheap circular labor, but they are not accepted as citizens with rights. As liminal beings, these migrants are neither here nor there; they are neither citizens nor aliens—and they are open to exploitation in this context. The in-between status of migrants in general, and Nepali migrants in particular, as a result of the "open border," means that they fall outside the protection regime.

Here, the role of a national border that maintains the separation between the maintenance of labor and the maintenance of its reproduction is useful to illustrate the migrants' experience of suffering. I illustrate this through the experience of migrants from the western hills who negotiate the border apparatus—bureaucratic law enforcement, political, market, and sociocultural—that formally and informally shapes the migration experience and its outcomes. "For some, crossing the border is an option, while for others it is an existential issue. It is often the latter, those that must find a way across the border if they are to survive, who find it the hardest to cross, if only because they are deemed undesirable by the border gatekeepers who maintain control over entry and exit" (Newman 2006: 178). This allows us not only to look at the border from the perspective of marginal migrants who cross over it, and who thereby directly experience and confront its authority, but also to recognize that it serves to maintain a steady flow of cheap, docile, and exploited labor in migrant destinations. Michael Kearney (2004b) suggests that borders have a "classificatory" mission that categorizes the identities of both persons on either side of the border and those who cross it and filters forms of economic value that flow across it. As a consequence, "open border" and "equal treatment" do not, in practice, apply to poorer Nepali migrants, who are regularly subjected to humiliating treatment while crossing the border.

I draw on the notion of "symbolic violence" from Pierre Bourdieu (2001) to illustrate various modes of sociocultural violence that shape the experience and the position of Nepali migrants. Bourdieu uses symbolic violence to designate symbolic power exercised by the dominant over the other (2001). Symbolic violence is the unnoticed or naturalized domination that everyday social practice maintains over the conscious subject. One of the key features of the concept is that those who are subjected to symbolic violence are not passive recipients, but they are actually complicit in their own subjugation. For this reason, the dominated internalize and naturalize domination and neither question nor resist it. Unlike refugees or other international migrants, the suffering of Nepali migrants who travel to work in India is not the subject of public or policy debate. In other words, their suffering is normalized.

Bourdieu's concept of symbolic violence helps us understand how the nature of inequalities and the suffering and ill-health of migrants come to be unquestioned not only by policy makers and civil society but also by the migrants themselves: they come to see their ill-treatment, inability to earn and save money, and poor working conditions as natural. Migrants blame themselves for not being able to save, for not being able to avoid extortion, and for ill-treatment while crossing the border. Public health officials view migrants' health issues, particularly the high prevalence of HIV and STIs, as resulting from their aberrant sexual behavior, without looking at the structural context, including the very nature of this form of migration and the poor living and working conditions that make them vulnerable in the first place. Their marginal position entails poorer access to health care provisions and other determinants of health than general populations, thereby enhancing their vulnerability to ill health while simultaneously compromising their ability to improve their well-being.

Fieldwork

This book is based on fieldwork I conducted in Palpa and other villages in the western region of Nepal and while following Nepali migrants in several Indian cities, including Mumbai and Delhi, between 2004 and 2013. I began with ethnographic fieldwork between June 2004 and June 2005 in Palpa and Mumbai as a part of my doctoral research on Nepali male migrants who traveled to find work in India. I carried out subsequent fieldwork in Palpa and other parts of western Nepal in 2008, 2009, 2010, 2012, and 2013.[4]

In addition to fieldwork in western Nepal and in Indian cities, my approach included traveling with migrants to capture their actual experiences of crossing the border. Accordingly, in 2005 I traveled with a group of three men from Palpa going to work in Mumbai. Given that most studies of migration are based on either the sending or receiving context, with very little consideration as to what goes on in between, the focus of my fieldwork was to take into account a more holistic perspective on migration. I argue that understanding the experience of migration requires study of not only the beginning and end of migrants' movements but also their journeys, the border crossing in particular, as a crucial part of migration. I address this gap in the literature by describing the travel experience of these men, based on my own travel with a group of three men on their way to Mumbai. Characterized by ambiguity, insecurity, humiliation, and also excitement, the travel experience shows that the border is a liminal site in which the migrants stand on the threshold of renegotiating their identities.

By using qualitative methods—in-depth interviews, informal interactions, and participant observation—I studied the local meanings of migration and its sociocultural significance in people's lives in Palpa district. I interacted with several households about their experience and recorded their stories related to migration. The focus of my fieldwork in Palpa was on generating the grounded meanings of migration as experienced and categorized by the people themselves. The experience of traveling to Mumbai with a group of three men and conducting fieldwork for seven weeks in Mumbai provided me with in-depth insights into the meanings and experiences of this movement for the men who moved and for those who stayed back. Apart from informal interactions and participant observation with many Nepali migrants, I carried out interviews with eighteen Nepali migrant men in Mumbai in their accommodations, work places, and in public places. I also gathered information about Sathi Nepal, an HIV project funded by United States Agency for International Development (USAID) and implemented by Family Health International (FHI), which had a specific gaze on Nepali male migrants in Mumbai. To better understand how the project attempted to help Nepali migrants, I visited the project, participated in their day-to-day activities, and interacted with different staff members. In addition to formal and informal interviews with young men about their migration decisions and experiences, I carried out participant observation in their workplaces and accommodations and during their leisure activities. Spending time in India with migrants allowed me to understand their life in Mumbai, including, but not limited to, their identities as migrant workers.

My long-term fieldwork in Palpa and other villages in the western region of Nepal offered me deeper insights into the diversification of rural livelihoods from land- and agriculture-based to nonland and nonagricultural sources of income and how the mobility of labor has become much more widespread in other parts of the middle hills in Nepal. It provided insights on the changing political economy of rural livelihoods and the gradual weakening of traditional forms of caste-based division of labor.

The fieldwork also allowed me to better understand the perceptions, experiences, and aspirations of young men left behind in the
village. In February–March 2010, I traveled with a group of Nepali
migrants from villages of midwestern and far western regions of
Nepal, who worked mainly as porters in the Indian town of Nainital and as domestic workers in Delhi. This fieldwork gave further
insight into the significance of the "open border" between Nepal
and India and how migrants experience border crossing. It also
allowed me to understand the experiences of marginal migrants,
such as those who worked as porters in the town of Nainital. In
April 2012, I carried out fieldwork in Delhi and Mumbai, inter-
viewing male migrants, mainly those who worked as *caukidars,*
or "security guards," and those who worked as domestic help, and
the representatives of various migrant associations and organizations. The fieldwork helped me understand not only the everyday
lives of Nepali migrants, including but not limited to their work
in various sectors of the economy, but also the work of Nepali
migrant associations in India.

Palpa

Because this book is primarily based on ethnographic research
in Palpa, I sketch the local context below to help the reader con-
textualize the discussion in subsequent chapters.

Palpa was an ideal locale to conduct fieldwork for this research
for both practical and theoretical reasons. Most importantly, it
was, relatively, less affected by the then ongoing Maoist insurgency[5] when compared to other hill regions in Nepal. Further, it was
my home area, and thus I had access to social networks and information about safety and security issues. More importantly, there
were sufficient theoretical grounds for choosing Palpa as a locale
for my research as it was a hill area in west-central Nepal with historical as well as contemporary evidence of out-migration to India
and other places. The region was going through major political
and economic changes and had been the subject of several development programs, including those that supported farming and
agriculture over the past forty years. Yet it appeared to me that

the lives and livelihoods in the area were becoming increasingly divorced from farming and the land. Widespread emphasis on schooling, newspapers, radio, and consumerism had profoundly affected people's perceptions of their life and livelihoods and their aspirations. Cultural and social positions, particularly of young men, are deeply implicated in political-economic changes. The changing political economy of livelihoods as well as the ubiquitous presence of development discourses that exposed young men from the villages in Palpa to the ideas and aspirations associated with city and modern life had a profound potential impact on their gendered sense of self.

Palpa is situated in the west-central region of Nepal. The fieldwork area is hilly and treacherous, with many valleys and lower-lying land on the banks of streams, including the holy Kali Gandaki River. The river runs along the boundary of Palpa district, separating it from the neighboring Syangja district. The whole area lies within the Mahabharata environmental domain (200 meters to 2,000 meters in altitude) and includes an ecological diversity that has various links with people's livelihoods (Smadja 2000). For instance, the Tihau watershed at times provides irrigation, but in the monsoon season it floods, directly affecting people's livelihoods (Wilmore 2002). The village where I carried out most of my fieldwork has a total area of 142 hectares, comprising agricultural land (89 hectare), forests (27 hectare), settlements/houses, streams, and village roads and trails. The red and whitewashed houses, roofed with galvanized iron sheets and thatch, may be observed scattered among the hillsides. The increased use of galvanized iron sheets in recent years indicates relative prosperity in comparison to use of thatched roofs; much of this improved roofing has come from migrant remittance. Around 80 percent of the households in the village had galvanized iron sheets by 2005. Before the malaria eradication program, which was launched in 1952, *beshi*[6] were used only for cultivation, and people returned to their *gau*[7] at night. After the eradication of malaria, people began to use the valleys not only for cultivation but also for building houses. Since then, there has been a growth of settlements on the valley floors.

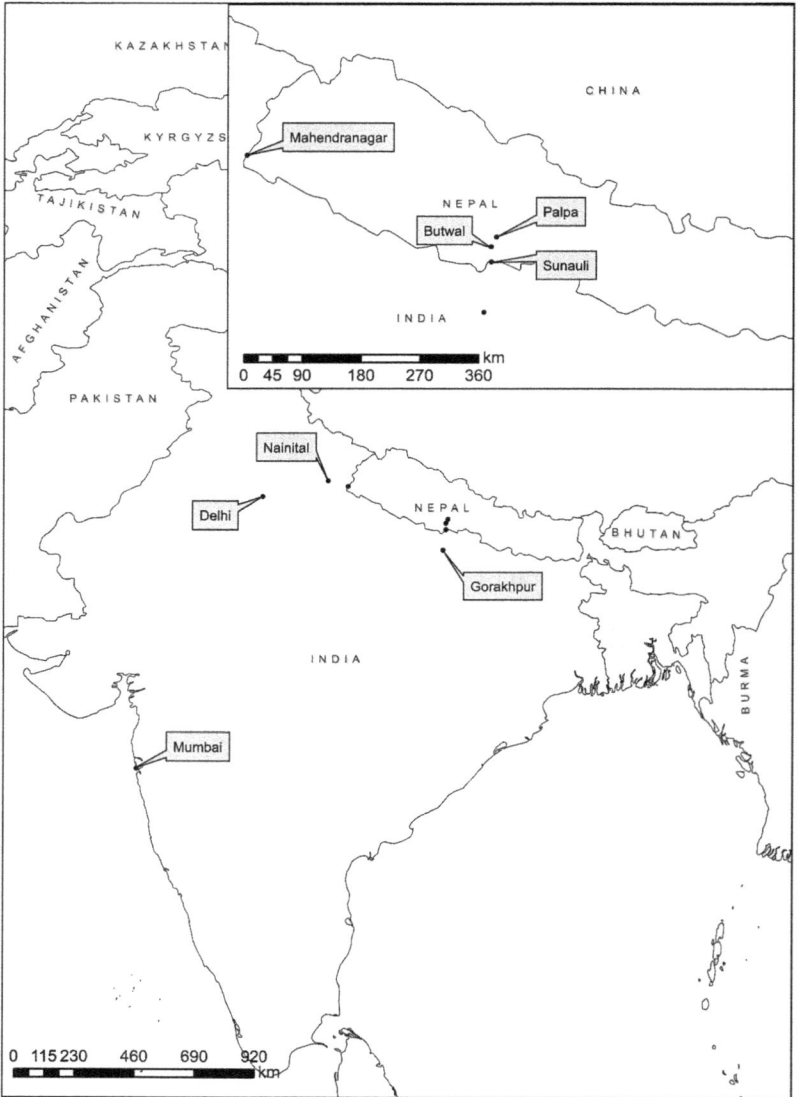

This map shows Palpa in relation to Nepal and South Asia.
(Map by Navin Shakya.)

The construction of roads and other amenities such as schools, health posts, and other community buildings in the valleys has also escalated in recent years.

Palpa is characterized by a lower population growth rate than the national average. The population of Palpa was 214,442 in 1981. It increased to 236,313 in 1991 and to 268,558 in 2001. The overall population growth rate of Palpa was 1.79 percent (CBS 2002), compared with the national average of 2.5 percent in 2002. It is possible that this lower growth rate was mainly a result of family planning programs and increased out-migration from Palpa.

While there is a lack of documentation on the social history of Palpa, reflecting the overall picture for social history in Nepal generally (Onta 1994), in recent years several scholars have documented local knowledge on different aspects of social life in and around Palpa.[8] There has been political and cultural dominance of Parbatiyas (Indo-Nepali), whose culture has always dominated the Nepali state, despite the fact that Magars (an indigenous population) constitute almost 50 percent of the population of Palpa. The dominance of Parbatiyas is stronger than elsewhere, as Magars have lost their language, Magarkura (Jest et al. 2000). Only a few Magars in the eastern part of Palpa, where they have an overwhelming majority when compared to Parbatiyas, speak their own language. Throughout Palpa, both the Parbatiyas and Magars live together in the same areas as a result of the immigration of Bahuns, along with other Indo-European linguistic groups, into the region where Magars had arrived a few centuries earlier (K. Adhikari 1993; Whelpton 2005). Apart from Bahun and Magar, the other major population groups in the study area are Kami, Bote, Sarki, Chetri, and Thakuri. Other, smaller, population groups included Newar, Damai, Kumal, and Gurung. These different social groups mainly practice the Hindu religion, though in varying ways and degrees.

In the history of Nepal, Palpa was an important state of the Sen Kings, who ruled it for about 498 years (1305–1804 A.D.). Its significance declined following the unification of Nepal[9] and several administrative reforms that took place during the Panchayat era[10] (Whelpton 2005). In 1975, the district assumed its present shape and size after the separation of eleven village *panchayats*,[11] densely populated by Magars from Palpa, by integrating them into the neighboring Nawalparasi district. This was also political manipulation by the upper-caste Bahuns, Chetris, and Newars in Palpa in order to defeat Magar candidates in the National Assembly election. Ethnic politics has had an important role in the political-economic and cultural subordination of Magars in recent years. Additionally, Magars felt excluded from the benefits of development, not only because they lacked important links to the external world of power and resources but also because they were intimidated by outside officials (K. Adhikari 1993; Stone 1989).

Tansen is the administrative and commercial center of Palpa, and it is a three- to four-hour walk from the fieldwork area. It is characterized by migration of the Newar mercantile class from Kathmandu as a result of the military and administrative needs of the Gorkhali Empire.

At the time of my fieldwork in 2004–2005, the Village Development Committee (VDC) offices in the study area had been closed down by the Maoists two years earlier. In one village, a newly built, whitewashed VDC building was painted by the Maoists with their slogans and demands. The local politicians were seen as little interested in local-level politics. The VDC secretaries, officials appointed by the District Development Committee (DDC) office, were not stationed in the village, but I met them several times in Tansen. There were sub-health posts staffed by the official in charge: the village health worker, the maternal and child health worker, and a peon. There were schools throughout the villages, which had emerged as important agents of change. There were five schools in the study area, including one secondary school, one lower secondary school, and three primary schools. There was no presence of police or state security forces, except when they came for *gasti*.[12]

Palpa district appeared relatively better on development indicators when compared to other neighboring districts. In 2001, life expectancy at birth was 59.6 years (56.9 for males and 60.5 for females), the adult literacy rate was 60.7 (74.1 for males and 50.4 for females), and infant mortality was 75 (CBS 2002). However, despite these impressive statistics, significant differences existed in the quality of life across caste, class, and gender, reflecting the overall situation of Nepal.

Modern development initiatives in Palpa are not new. In 1954, United Mission to Nepal (UMN) established a missionary hospital on the outskirts of Tansen. The 132-bed hospital continues to provide a health facility to people from Palpa and beyond.[13] Apart from the missionary hospital, in 1958 UMN started a rural community development program in Palpa, locally known as CHDP (Community Health and Development Programme), which ran through 1997 and aimed to reach beyond the hospital setting to the surrounding communities through various community health and development programs.

Swiss development agency Helvetas-Nepal has been working in Palpa since 1955, particularly within the field of watershed development around Madi Valley. Several other development programs and projects were carried out in different villages in Palpa. In the post-1990 era, Palpa saw a growth of development activities in the initiatives of both state and nonstate agencies. An inventory released by the DDC in 2001 showed that there were 15 international nongovernmental organizations (NGOs) and 426 NGOs working in Palpa district alone (DDC 2000). It was common to find many village committees formed by different development agencies that had taken responsibility at the local level for the management of various development activities like agriculture, micro-irrigation, goat raising, milk production, road construction, drinking water, school, and forest management, among others. I discuss the changing political economy of the study area, including dynamics of migration and mobility, in Chapters 1 and 2.

Argument and Organization of the Book

This book argues that young men's responses to livelihood insecurities in the hills are shaped not just by wage differentiation and economic calculation, as authoritative discourses suggest, but also by a set of gendered sociocultural considerations, particularly relating to ideas of modernity and masculinities. In the face of livelihood insecurities, migration to India does more than allow young men from poorer backgrounds to "save there and eat here"; it also offers them a strategy to escape the more regimented social order of the village and to attain independence and experience a distant world. While Nepali migrants benefit from the opportunities offered by the provision of the "open border" between India and Nepal, and travel to find work opportunities in Indian cities, they are also subjected to high levels of ill-treatment and suffering while crossing the border and while living and working in India. For marginal Nepali migrants, the circulatory nature of migration does not appear to be as transformative as might have been expected: while life in the destination may well be urban and modern, their positions remain marginal. Most of them work in poorly paid jobs that do not allow them to save sufficiently to send money back home regularly. They remain socially and economically marginalized in Indian cities. Thus, while the idea of freedom remains extremely important in men's migration decisions to move away from the regimented life in the villages, Nepali migrants' actual experiences are often of suffering and lack of freedom. Engaging with the local term *phaltu* (useless, empty),[14] this book argues that, while large numbers of poorer men seek to assert their masculinity through labor mobility, in the form of both earnings and wider experience beyond village life, this does not automatically translate into an affirmation of identity. Many struggle to save money and end up working in difficult environments that offer few possibilities for social mobility. Following Mary Beth Mills (1999), this book approaches young migrants not only as *workers* but also as *consumers*. In the context of Nepal, Mark Liechty's work has demonstrated the emergence of middle-class consumers in Kathmandu and its effect on the sociocultural and geographical aspects of the city (Liechty 2003). Despite being working-class poor, the migrants traveling to work in India are equally consumers. These migrants have created their own world-view of migration to India that is associated with adventure, freedom, excitement, and consumption, which offers powerful means by which migrants can maintain a sense of meaning and purpose, despite the many difficulties they face.

Most migrants attempted to assert their patriarchal idea of masculinity through rituals of drinking and socializing on weekends, and, for some, visiting sex workers. It is this world-view that works to sustain a steady flow of poorer migrants from the Nepali hills to the Indian plains. The remaining chapters advance this argument by discussing the political economy of rural livelihoods and the social meanings, ideas, aspirations, and experiences of migration among Nepali men who travel to India. I place this migration in the wider context of economic and political inequalities between the two countries and an "open border" that not only operates as a filter of economic values but also creates the position of Nepali migrants as neither natives nor aliens.

The remainder of this book discusses these central arguments as follows:

Chapter 1 focuses on the significant changes in the political economy of livelihoods in rural Nepal—that is, the gradual weakening of traditional forms of attached and caste-based division of labor in the past few decades. It discusses not only the diversification of rural livelihoods from land- and agriculture-based to nonagricultural and non-land-based sources of employment but also the widespread mobility of labor inside and outside the country. These processes have significant impact in configuring young men's subjectivities.

Chapter 2 provides a historical perspective on the *culture of migration* among young men in rural Nepal, with a specific focus on how the hill economy has long relied on the comparatively large economy of the region's immediate neighbor to the south. It offers a history of migration in the hills of Nepal, including Gurkha recruitment as well as the more recent trend of migration to the Gulf States that has attracted global attention.

Chapter 3 draws on ethnography and interviews with young men in rural Nepal and shows how migration has become a rite of passage among the young men, and how their strategic responses to livelihood insecurities are shaped not only by wage differentiation and economic calculation but also by a complex set of gendered sociocultural considerations, particularly relating to ideas of modernity and masculinities. With a focus on local notions of masculinities, this chapter discusses how these shape the decision of men to migrate to India.

Chapter 4 commences with an ethnography that follows the departure of migrants from their villages. This involves crossing the rural-urban border as well as the border between Nepal and India. Building on my experience of traveling with migrants to Mumbai and others parts of India and returning home, this chapter focuses on the actual experience of travel that has rarely been considered in the study of labor migrants. It explores the journey and the border crossing and reveals the feelings of excitement and ambivalence experienced by migrants. It reveals how the very act of border crossing disciplines young men and turns them into docile migrants.

Chapter 5 focuses on the lives of migrants in Mumbai and other parts of India. It shows how migrants end up living in Mumbai's slums or substandard housing in other parts of India, working in jobs that are casualized and underpaid, and having no access to official social protection. It discusses how masculinity in patriarchal family contexts that prize the authority and respect of men is often thrown into crisis by labor migration under the kinds of coercive conditions prevailing in Mumbai and other destinations in India.

This chapter goes beyond the notion of Nepali migrants as marginal, as passive, and as victims and shows how young men working and living in cities like Mumbai, within constrained working and living conditions, not only explored ways of realizing their dreams but also became involved in a variety of consumption activities.

Chapter 6 focuses on migrants' risk behavior in Mumbai. The concern of policy makers was more about women as carriers of HIV for most of the 1990s (especially with the discourse on trafficking), and male labor migration did not feature centrally in the HIV discourse. However, since 1998–1999, within the discourse on mobility and HIV, there has been a major shift toward representing male labor migrants as carriers of the epidemic. Building on ethnography of Nepali migrants and their social lives, this chapter offers a critique of policy discourse that blames migrants as carriers of disease without locating them within the wider context of structural violence and concepts of masculinities.

The *Conclusion* consolidates various arguments made in the previous chapters, discussing how migration to the Indian city of Mumbai offers an escape for poorer men from rural areas who are otherwise left with few economic opportunities to manage their livelihoods and support their families. However, the migration of men to Indian cities is not always met with success, and many work under very difficult conditions and struggle to save money. The social meanings of labor migration associated with adventure, freedom, excitement, and consumption offer a powerful avenue by which male labor migrants can maintain a sense of meaning and purpose despite the many difficulties they face. Therefore, what appears as a hegemonic masculinity in their villages in Nepal is only a subordinate masculinity in the context of Indian cities. Taking the example of young men's participation in the Maoist insurgency (1996–2005), this chapter makes the point that men who do not migrate may be under pressure to perform other ways of asserting their masculine identity. It concludes by exploring possibilities for change in the lives of these migrants.

1

Political Economy
of Rural Livelihoods

The context in which young men from the hills of Nepal struggle to secure their livelihoods and take part in gendered goals
is not of their own creation. Young men's gendered lives and
livelihoods in the middle hills of Nepal must be located in the
history of the extractive state and dynamic political economy of
the region. This chapter focuses on the historical socioeconomic
conditions and state policies in the nineteenth and twentieth
centuries that forced poorer households in the hills to emigrate
in search of work opportunities both inside and outside Nepal.
It also outlines significant changes in the political economy of
livelihoods in rural Nepal in recent decades that form the context
for young men's subjectivities. I hope here to provide background
for understanding migrant workers' class and gendered identity
formations within the historical context of Nepal's transformation.
I discuss the diversification of rural livelihoods from land- and
agriculture-based to nonagricultural and non-land-based sources of
employment and the widespread mobility of labor inside and outside
the country. I describe the idea of the silent revolution epitomized
in the gradual weakening of traditional forms of attached labor, in
which workers are contractually obligated to a specific employer
for a specific time period, and of caste-based division of labor,

alongside the profound ideological impact of *bikas* (development) and modernity in reconfiguring young men's cultural world, lives, and livelihoods. A major theme that runs through this chapter is that rural Nepal is on the cusp of a major transformation from the relatively stable reproduction of social and economic relations based on feudal and caste-based systems to more fluid and open conditions. The old socioeconomic order is changing, if not collapsing, giving way to a new order. As I discuss below, this reading of Nepali society and economy runs in contrast to the pessimistic conclusion reached by Piers Blaikie, John Cameron, and David Seddon (1980, 2002) in their studies on social change in Nepal. They concluded from their longitudinal research that the only social change in the previous twenty years in rural western Nepal was the "degree of continuity" toward deepening poverty and inequalities. Though there had been some changes in the semi-feudal system, they concluded that there was very little change in the rural class structure.

Livelihoods and gendered identities of young men are increasingly shaped by dynamic socioeconomic processes such as the circulation of labor, the incorporation of the rural economy and society into globalized flows, and the commodification of labor and land, to name but a few. In considering these issues, this chapter argues that while male labor migration was an escape from suffering caused by exploitative state policies in the eighteenth and nineteenth centuries, it has come to be understood as an expression of freedom in the recent context of changing political economy. Over the past two hundred years or so, the very meaning and context of migration has undergone a phenomenal change.

Extractive State Policies

There is historical evidence of exploitative social relations of production and of extractive state policies that created conditions for the impoverishment of the peasantry in the middle hills of Nepal (Regmi 1971, 1978, 1988; Shrestha 2001). Exploitation of labor arose from the three related processes of forced and obligatory recruitment of labor, the unjust distribution of land, and the extraction of rent by state functionaries, all of which contributed to the marginal position of peasantry in the hills.

First, during the eighteenth and nineteenth centuries, the Shah and Rana rulers recruited labor for their territorial expansion of the Gurkha Empire and during various episodes of warfare between different states (Regmi 1988). Peasants were recruited not only to fight but also to serve as porters to help transport goods such as weapons and other supplies (Shrestha 2001). They were also recruited to build roads, temples, palaces, and other buildings for the rulers. This forced labor system was unpaid. Through the systems of *rakam* and *jhara,* the state was able to impose a labor tax and extract free labor from the peasants. *Rakam* entailed the provision of administrative and military services to the state, such as transporting mail and supplies, mining, and managing check posts, whereas the *jhara* system provided labor for construction and the repair of roads, bridges, irrigation channels, and other public services. These forced labor systems did not allow the peasants to make any economic gains, as there was no return for these services (Regmi 1978). Military officers were permitted to treat peasants and their children badly when they failed to provide labor as requested (Shrestha 2001). The rulers and others in positions of power, often based on caste and patronage, made excessive use of unpaid labor. The poor peasants and their children were expected to work for free on the farms, in the mines, or in the home. Men from Palpa went to work as laborers in copper mines in nearby areas such as Baglung, Parbat, Gulmi, and Myagdi. More recently, young men, mostly Magars, from poorer households went to live and work for affluent households in the village or neighboring towns or Kathmandu, often without any pay and in exchange for food and accommodation. Not only were peasants unable to focus on their own farming, increase productivity, and improve their well-being; they were also systematically marginalized by the state, despite the fact that they were subjects (Regmi 1988). Peasants were unable to produce enough to feed their families, compromising not only their livelihood security and well-being but also the provider role of men within their families. Such a social structure was a direct assault on men's roles.

Second, there was unequal distribution of land based on loyalty and caste-based patronage, which benefited the high caste and those with social networks within the ruling class, marginalizing the already impoverished. Those close to the ruling class were able to accumulate land through grants made by the rulers (Regmi 1988; 1978). This process led to a landed class who controlled the means of production. Absentee landlordism was prolific in different parts of the country. These landlords would employ local peasants to cultivate their land and would extract more rent than was invested back into the land. The agrarian system under the Shah and Rana rulers revolved around land control and surplus appropriation (Regmi 1988). Within these unequal agrarian and socioeconomic relations, peasants were hard pressed to manage their livelihoods with no or little entitlement over land. In my fieldwork area in Palpa, the land distribution is unequal. In 2005, my surveys showed that the distribution of paddy land (*khet*)[1] among the population was that 44 percent did not have access to it, about 26 percent owned 1–4 *ropani*[2] of land, about 18 percent owned 5–8 *ropani,* and 12 percent owned 9–25 *ropani.* Similarly, the distribution of *bari/pakho* (dry field)[3] was that 2 percent did not own it, about 76 percent owned 1–10 *ropani* of land, about 14 percent owned 11–20 *ropani,* and 7 percent owned 21–50 *ropani.* While only one household identified as landless, most of the households owned too little land to generate a consistent surplus. I analyzed household socioeconomic status in the management of income and expenditure through a survey conducted in 2005. My survey showed that members of about half the households believed that, together with whatever they were able to earn from different economic activities, including remittances, they had more or less enough to manage their household expenses. About 20 percent had been able to save enough to invest in the education of their children, build houses, or buy land, whereas about 25 percent had found it difficult to cope with daily survival and were dependent on loans, and in a few cases were still engaged in attached labor.

Third, peasants were subject to hardship from additional exploitation through the extraction of rent through local administrators, temples, and other state officials and institutions. According to Mahesh C. Regmi (1978), since the nineteenth century in rural Nepal, those known as *mukhiya* and *zamindar* were not just landowners but also representatives of the central government, collecting revenue as well as performing various judicial and administrative functions of the state. The state extracted free labor from the peasants. Regmi mentions that land was appropriated by various elite groups through the systems of *Rajya* (land owned by principalities in far western hill regions), *birtas* (land owned by priests, soldiers, and the royal family), and *jagir* (land owned by military and government personnel). This allowed elites to extract tax as well as rent in the form of money, commodities, and labor without any compensation to those who had previously owned the land (Regmi 1978). This provided the landowning elite with an abundance of resources. These forced systems did not allow the peasants to make economic gains, as there was no return for their services; on the contrary, they "allowed the state to exercise authority over the peasant not only as a tenant but also as a subject" (Regmi 1978: 104). The rulers saw the collection of rent as a way to fund their armies, bureaucracy, and administration (Regmi 1971). These taxes and rent did not supplement the state revenue, nor were they reinvested in agricultural development. Hence, Nepal's continued existence as a poor country during the nineteenth century was because of low productivity—the result of inadequate capital investment in agriculture. Regardless of the productivity of the farmland, the households in the fieldwork area held to the requirements of their land documents and paid tax (*tiro*) to the government.

While the recruitment to the British Army that started after 1816 did offer an employment opportunity for some hill men, especially Magars in Palpa, it meant that they would be engaged in life-threatening and dangerous work while away from their families and farms. This had significant implications for gendered division of labor and identities. The women back home had an increased role in running the household, including managing the agricultural activities. While the men received secure employment, they were absent and mostly unable to look after their parents, wives, or children. When the hill men and their families, especially the mothers, showed little interest in recruitment into the army, British recruiters used force and coercion to compel people to enlist. Although Gurkhas, soldiers from Nepal serving in British and Indian armies, have been represented as the "bravest of the brave" within the imperial narratives, the experiences of Gurkhas and their families are characterized by suffering (Des Chene 1991). Over the years, the recruitment of these hill men into the British Army contributed to the shaping of the economic and social structure in the hills (Hitchcock 1961). Income from recruitment to foreign armies not only provided cash to hire workers to sustain agriculture; it had a major impact on the aspirations and identities of young men and women in the villages.

These exploitative state policies had an enduring impact on peasant livelihoods and survival, prompting peasants to escape suffering in the hills in search of work opportunities elsewhere. As early as the 1850s, hill men faced with economic insecurities began to travel to Sikkim, Bengal, Assam, Darjeeling, Bhutan, and Burma in search of work opportunities across the border. Not only did this lead to out-migration; it also meant that many of those who chose more formal employment (e.g., service in the Indian Army) decided to settle in India or in other parts of Nepal rather than return to the villages.

Changing Face of Rural Nepal

In a longitudinal account of the political economy of west-central Nepal, Blaikie, Cameron, and Seddon (2002) concluded from their empirical research that the only social change in the previous twenty years in rural western Nepal was the "degree of continuity" toward deepening poverty. They argued that there had been very little change in the rural class structure and concluded that there had been no significant changes in the development of commercialized agriculture or in the cost of hired labor, and no improvement in livelihoods. Though there had been some changes in the semi-feudal system, this had not translated into a capitalist agriculture as predicted. The authors, however, acknowledged that migration and urban growth had been underestimated in their previous study (Blaikie, Cameron, and Seddon 1980) and that these appear to have resulted in significant changes in labor relations and livelihoods.

In a study conducted in the mid-1970s in a Gurung village north of Pokhara, Alan Macfarlane documented a temporary migration pattern, with many men from the village leaving for service in the British and Indian armies (Macfarlane 1976). Soldiers returned with their pay and pensions, and the profits from army service were invested in the village. Macfarlane's study showed that over a third of the total income in the village came from army pay, pensions, and civilian work abroad. More importantly, this was the only source of cash income to the villagers. In a more recent account (Macfarlane 2001), reflecting on thirty years of change in a Gurung village north of Pokhara, Macfarlane found that the importance of migrant remittances, as described in his original study, had declined, with remittances reduced to a trickle from the few laborers abroad who saved some money and sent it home. This study demonstrated a significant change to the nature of migration. From the mid-1970s, when army recruitment dried up, village men went first to India and later to East and Southeast Asia, the Middle East, and a few to Europe and America. When these men and the remaining army service men retired, they no longer came back to the village but settled in towns, in particular in nearby Pokhara. Further, Macfarlane argued that a beneficial effect of this out-migration had been to prevent ecological crisis due to population pressure on land and environment as predicted in the original study, but it had meant that the people left behind bore the burden of out-migration through material impoverishment (Macfarlane 2001).

Another study conducted by Jagannath Adhikari (2001) over a decade beginning in 1990 in a village of the Kaski district showed how migrant remittances, which were the main source of cash, had a dual impact on labor opportunities in the village. During the early 1990s, remittances assisted "marginal farmers" and "landless laborers" in their livelihoods "through the creation of land-renting and labor employment opportunities within the villages" (J. Adhikari 2001: 248–249). Remittance-receiving village households invested the cash in agriculture and were able to employ agricultural laborers to work on the farm. However, toward the end of the 1990s, there was a trend toward migrant households investing remittances in land, housing, and businesses in urban areas. There was a gradual decline in investment in rural agriculture and shrinking work opportunities for laboring households. This led to a further escalation of rural to urban migration, especially within poor and disadvantaged communities.

As the three studies referred to above show, rural Nepal today has a complex and rapidly changing reality. While historical factors have shaped class differentiation and the livelihoods of the poor, as I discuss below, rural Nepal has been going through a silent revolution characterized by changes in the political economy and livelihood structures. Lives and livelihoods of people in Palpa are becoming increasingly divorced from farming and land.

One defining feature of the hill political economy is the relative decline of agriculture in the economy, although the rhetoric of Nepal as an agrarian country remains in key scholarly work, policy documents, and mainstream development thinking. Such an imaginary of peasantry in Nepal is based on theoretical, epistemological, and policy models that fail to take into account the empirical reality of changing political economy in Nepal. In the following paragraphs, I outline key features of changes in the political economy of livelihoods.

Diversification of Livelihoods

As a number of studies have documented, rural households have been drawing on multiple sources of livelihood, both farm related and nonfarm related, as a form of insurance (J. Adhikari 2001; Blaikie, Cameron, and Seddon 2002). While agriculture has not been completely abandoned, most households rely on nonagriculture-based wage labor both inside and outside the village (J. Adhikari 2001; Blaikie, Cameron, and Seddon 2002). Economically, my fieldwork area did not differ much from other hilly regions in western Nepal. While subsistence farming was a widespread practice, the vast majority of households were engaged in diverse economic activities. The people I worked with identified themselves as subsistence farmers in the sense that they produced mostly for consumption and not for trade (Miller 2002; Raithelhuber 2003). The agriculture was characterized by rice cultivation in *khet*; cultivation of maize, millet, beans, and vegetables in *bari*; preservation and use of fodder on dry and *pakho*;[4] and animal husbandry. Employment outside the village, at both long and short distances, was an important source of livelihoods for most of the households. More than half of the households received remittances from family members working in different locations outside Nepal. Nonetheless, all households identified farming as their primary occupation. Households identified themselves as farmers whether or not they depended financially on agriculture. People I worked with consistently spoke about declining agricultural productivity and how it was becoming increasingly difficult for them to gain much from agriculture. However, the very identification of themselves as people from the village meant that they also identified themselves as farmers. This identification as farmers was strongly reinforced by various development programs as well as radio and television programs that broadcast messages about peasants being attached to farming and land. However, there was a strong perception among young men that there is no benefit to farming and that it is, essentially, unproductive.

Land fragmentation, decreased availability of arable land due to land degradation, availability of work outside the village, access to markets, and the need for cash income have brought changes to the nature of livelihoods in Palpa. Most households could hardly rely exclusively on agriculture- or caste-based attached labor for their subsistence. Many households depended on two or more sources for subsistence. The most common sources of livelihood among the laborers were farming, which

Jeep service along the newly built motorable road carried people from the village to the town and beyond. (Photo by Jeevan R. Sharma.)

has increasingly become focused on cash crops as well as milk production; wage labor (both inside and outside the village); informal-sector jobs in nearby markets or towns; and migrant remittances.

People in the area I studied once used the trade routes to go down to the plains or other places (Smadja [1922–1932] 1999), but since the building of the 176-kilometer Siddhartha highway in 1969[5] this area has been well connected to the Tarai,[6] Kathmandu, and beyond. The construction of the highway has been a major factor connecting Palpa to the outside world and transforming it (Smadja [1922–1932] 1999). There are frequent buses to different destinations within Nepal, and the Indian border of Sunauli is just 68 kilometers from Tansen. Small roads reach all sixty-five VDCs of Palpa, including my study area.

The construction of roads and other development activities has impacted people's lives in different ways. One visible change has been the growth of settlements close to the newly built roadsides, forming small bazaars like Aryabhangyang, Bartung, Dumre, and Humin, among others (Smadja [1922-1932] 1999). These new settlements have provided opportunities to start small shops, hotels, and bars. There has been growth in the construction of new houses from modern building materials like cement, iron, and gravel that have been imported from outside, mainly from the major towns of Butwal and Bhairahawa in the Tarai.

Small shops started to be seen in the villages, which sell goods coming from other parts of Nepal, particularly the Tarai and India. People eat rice bought from a local shop in the village or from Tansen, imported from the Tarai. Snacks made of millet and maize are no longer preferred by the younger generation, but noodles, bread, and biscuits are consumed. People regularly use soap, shampoo, batteries, and many other goods that require cash. The shops in the villages supply LPG cooking gas, reflecting the increased use of gas in local households. When they go to Tansen, people are seen bringing vegetables such as tomatoes and cauliflowers to the village. Two village shops sell vegetables brought from Tansen, which originally came from the Tarai or India. The need for cash means that the households produce milk and dairy products, chickens, and goats to sell in the market instead of consuming them.

With the intervention of the agricultural programs, introduced by the government in partnership with aid agencies and NGOs, and the building of roads, there has been a significant transformation in agricultural practices (Smadja [1922-1932] 1999). Traditional farming techniques have largely been replaced with modern practices, mostly through the works of junior technical advisors, who give advice on modern farming and animal husbandry (Stone 1989). There are many shops in Tansen and small towns like Aryabhangyang, Bastari, Harthok, and Rampur that sell modern fertilizers, pesticides, and seeds (*bikasi*). People in the villages listen to programs about agriculture broadcast on the radio that often encourage people to adopt new farming techniques. It is common to see new farming techniques pushed through by the District Agriculture Office and the programs of NGOs like Helvetas-Nepal. With the encouragement to use modern fertilizers and pesticides, many people in the village have adopted these practices, though people maintain a contradictory perception of modern farming practices, which parallels Akhil Gupta's observation in the northern Indian village of Alipur[7] in the 1990s (Gupta 1999: 2–5). In this ethnography, Gupta discusses how the farmers in Alipur contrasted the properties of chemical fertilizers with local organic manure. The farmers talked about how the chemical fertilizer had increased productivity but had contributed to the degradation of soil and reduced the taste and strength of the produce. Despite the role of the widespread adoption of modern fertilizers and pesticides in increased agricultural output, people in Palpa believe that their use not only has increased the cost of farming but also has negatively impacted the quality of the produce. Like the farmers of Alipur, the farmers in Palpa have become caught up in the discourse on modern development.

While people continue to grow grains, there has been a significant change toward cash crops like ginger, coffee, and vegetables. Given the demand for fresh vegetables in Tansen, a few farming households have begun to experiment with vegetables (cauliflower, tomatoes, modern hybrid beans, modern cucumbers, etc.) in their fields. People living at higher altitudes of the village grow a particular type of beans (known as *gahate dal*), which are used for household consumption, while the surplus is sold in a local market in Tansen. People previously sold milk and other dairy products through Tansen on their own initiative. This practice was transformed with the introduction of dairy cooperatives in the villages since 1990.

An important aspect of consumption includes communications and media. Whether cooking at home or plowing the field, listening to the radio has been very common among the people in the village. In Palpa alone at the time of my study, there were three FM stations, and, in addition to these, people listened to FM transmissions from neighboring districts. People mostly tuned into local FM radio, and only a few people in the village tuned to Radio Nepal. Similarly, electrification has facilitated the growth of television ownership. While most people continue to watch Doordarshan (Indian National Television), the erection of a television tower on the top of Srinagar hill in 1997 has meant that more people watch Nepal Television (the national television of Nepal) than previously. There has been a growing interest in commercial satellite television programs, which is reflected in the growing subscription to cable television in Tansen and the erection of disc antennas in small bazaars.

Similarly, the use of the telephone has been very common. In 2004–2005, there used to be three landline telephones in the study area, but none of them were working during my visit. They were disconnected by the government, as it suspected that they were being used by Maoist activists. Many people from the village went to Tansen to make phone calls. There was no mobile phone reception in 2004–2005, but the situation changed dramatically in the following ten years, and now almost every household has at least one mobile phone. In recent years, the use of mobile phones for making telephone calls and also for Internet access, mainly for social networking sites such as Facebook, has become commonplace.

With the expansion of roads and markets and increased mobility, there are varied work opportunities for laboring households, including petty trade, milk production, weaving, and commuting or migrating to work in service sectors, or construction work in nearby markets and towns. Very few people are involved solely as agricultural laborers, and only a few of them have continued traditional bonded or caste-based labor relationships. Households at the lower end of the socioeconomic spectrum work as wage laborers in the agricultural sector, and as construction and migrant workers according to availability, social networks, and kin relations. For laboring households increasingly relying on wage labor outside their villages, the associated transport, accommodation, and health care expenses are significant, often eroding returns and remittances back to the village. New sources of demand for labor outside the village have enabled laboring households to raise their wages locally and to break away from caste-based labor relations and other demeaning practices in their villages of origin. Women are restricted to housework and the care of children and the elderly. Because of widespread outmigration by men, women's participation in local agricultural activities, and therefore their workload, has increased, but it is not clear whether women's agency in decision making has increased as a result as well.

According to the 2011 Nepal Living Standard Survey (NLSS), the share of the agricultural sector in household income has decreased from 61 percent to 27.7 percent from 1995–1996 to 2010–2011, whereas the share of the nonagricultural sector in household income has increased from 22 percent to 37.2 percent during the same period (CBS 2011). Similarly, the share of wage earners in the agricultural sector decreased to 35 percent from 53 percent, while the share in the nonagricultural sector increased to 65 percent from 47 percent in the same period (CBS 2011).

The 2011 NLSS found that household dependency on the agricultural sector had marginally decreased from 79.9 percent in 2003–2004 to 76.3 percent in 2010–2011. It found that the share of agriculture in wage employment had decreased from 53 percent in 1995–1996 to 35 percent in 2010–2011, whereas the percentage share of the nonagricultural sector in wage employment increased from 47 percent to 65 percent during the same period. In the same period, there was a decline in agricultural wage employment from 12 percent to 2.8 percent. Between 1995–1996 and 2010–2011, the average nominal daily wages increased by 325 percent in agriculture and by 255 percent in nonagriculture. According to NLSS 2011, the share of farming income in household income decreased from 61 percent to 28 percent from 1995–1996 to 2010–2011, whereas the share of nonfarm income in household income increased from 22 percent to 37 percent during the same period. The NLSS also documents an increase in the percentage of households receiving remittances from 23 percent to 59 percent, with the total amount of remittances increasing rapidly from NRs 13 billion in 1995–1996 to 259 billion in 2010–2011. NLSS 2011 also notes that 80 percent of the remittances received are primarily used for daily consumption, along with 7 percent for repaying loans, 4 percent for household property, and 3 percent for education of children.

Anthropologist John Hitchcock conducted a study in the hills of central Nepal in a Magar village in the late 1950s that concluded that cash income from working for the Indian or British Army in India was the main basis to cope with increased monetization and to improve the economic status of many in the village (Hitchcock 1961). With the increase in the availability of trade items from nearby markets, there was an increase in monetization—cash was in high demand. The salaries of soldiers and, more importantly, their pensions became the primary sources of cash for many households. Hitchcock concluded that households connected with the army were able to improve their economic status, while the others had difficulty coping with the increased cash requirements. Similarly, income from recruitment in foreign armies has remained an important source of cash income in selected households in Palpa. Income from recruitment into the British and Indian armies has declined in the study area because of a decrease in demand as well as increased competition. The households have relied on a number of other sources of cash income, including, but not limited to, migrant labor, commercial agriculture, and petty trade.

The ownership and nonownership of land continues to be an important aspect of rural power relations. In addition to owning land in towns and cities, village landlords have invested in their children's education and have extended networks in state administration and local politics. Yet, the growing diversification of the rural economy is no doubt having its own influence on social relations that are no longer based on only land ownership and social relations governing land but that emanate from access to education, office jobs, foreign employment, and new forms of patronage, including affiliation to political parties and links with outside political or business elites, among others. The households that have invested in schooling and secure government jobs, those that have developed political networks in the towns and cities and initiated various forms of trade and businesses, have emerged as influential. Salaried employment and income from businesses and various political, economic, and administrative networks have been important in shaping these social relations. State and market forces have penetrated even the remotest parts of the country, and the use of cash is now widespread. "Rural Nepal," as it is portrayed in the development discourses in Nepal, is no longer a reality. Rural Nepal is increasingly integrated with the national and global economy and culture.

Widespread Mobility

The diversification of livelihoods is intrinsically linked to intensification of labor mobility inside and outside Nepal. Unlike the mobility driven by impoverishment, the new forms of migration are linked to the quest for multiple sources of livelihood and also to aspirations for consumption, and this signifies a weakening of traditional social relations of production.

As the productivity of agriculture diminishes because of land fragmentation and poor investment in agriculture, alternative sources of livelihood have emerged in Palpa, drawing on different forms of mobility. Buses and jeeps that travel to villages in Palpa, thanks to the massive road construction in the last two decades, bring young men commuting to nearby towns like Tansen or cities like Butwal in the Tarai for work. Construction sites, stone quarries, agro-businesses, not to mention hotels and restaurants, are full of young men from the villages. Migrating to the plains or nearby towns and cities from interior rural areas has been very common among those looking for new opportunities for employment. Work in construction and migrating to work in India, on the other hand, has also been continuing over the years, and improved roads and connections have made it easier for members of rural households to return home to work in their fields on a seasonal basis. More recently, the trend of migration toward the Gulf has offered rural households, particularly those that can afford it, new income opportunities.

Declining agriculture, alongside the gradual relocation of local landowners to cities and towns, has reconfigured livelihood spaces for peasants and resulted in the weakening of traditional social relations and labor arrangements, including the caste-based division of labor, now replaced by commodification of labor and circulation of cash. Although traditional forms of semi-feudal labor have not disappeared completely, and some poorer households are still engaged in semi-feudal and caste-based labor arrangements, most laboring households are exchanging their labor for cash, commuting to work as wage laborers in the construction and informal sectors in nearby markets and cities or across the border in India, while those who can afford it are involved in long-distance migratory labor.

Here it is useful to point at the gender dimensions of the transition of labor from agriculture to nonagriculture and/or caste-based attached labor to wage labor. Most often, it is men who appear to be making this transition, with women still working in caste-based attached labor and/or agricultural labor. Often those who are left behind in the villages, and especially those without skills and good health, remain quite vulnerable. It is the women, the elderly, and the destitute who are more vulnerable as a result of ongoing transitions in labor.

The shortage of labor in rural areas as a result of widespread mobility has increased bargaining power and the price for wage labor. This has no doubt benefited laboring households whose access to cash has enabled many of them to take part in various nonfarm economic activities such as small trade and agro-business or to finance labor migration of members of the household.

The opening up of the countryside, through the construction of roads, transport, travel, mobile phones, availability of modern commodities, media, and schooling, along with the popularity of ideas of modernity and *bikas* (development), has accelerated the aspiration for, as well as the practices of, mobility on a larger scale than ever before. As anthropologist Stacey Pigg has convincingly argued, the idea of *bikas* in Nepal has a particular effect in representing the village as a traditional place to be left in the past and urban areas as modern places to be desired. This idea of *bikas* has heightened aspirations for mobility in rural Nepal (Pigg 1992). Hardly any area of rural Nepal remains unaffected by the exodus of young men, and, increasingly, young women, across the border to India and more recently to various global destinations, including the Gulf States and Malaysia (Seddon, Adhikari, and Gurung 2002). Perception of new opportunities has been a key factor in attracting people from the rural agrarian economy into urban areas. Increased mobility of labor has reshaped labor relations and has had widespread implications for the ways in which labor has been organized, though mobility has not always had a transformational impact on the existing feudal labor relations in poorer households.

Changing Social and Labor Relations

One of the key aspects of the silent revolution taking place in the hills is in the domain of labor and labor relations. Through the specific caste-based labor arrangements, many of the poorer households traditionally relied on their landlords or those with a wealthier economic status for their livelihoods. Decline in agriculture as well as diversification of livelihoods to nonagricultural and non-land-based livelihoods have significantly altered the social and labor relations in the study area. The shift of livelihoods from the domain of traditional social relations into more open forms of social relations has impacted not only the material conditions but also the subjective positions of the laboring class. More recently, the expansion of market forces and the increased involvement of the state in development activities, party politics, and, in the last decade, the Maoists' discourses on feudalism and the discourses on development and rights advocated by NGOs and various local groups have all challenged the feudal system of labor.

This shows that there have been some clear changes in labor relations in rural Nepal, directly challenging the traditional feudal labor relations that have existed for a long time. Those who previously exercised authority not only have been compelled to give away their power; in some cases, they have been forced to meet the needs and demands of the laboring class. Hence, the laboring class has also identified the limitations of the landlords, and has been taking advantage by increasing the wage rate for labor work. Shortage of labor and the increased cost of labor has been a common complaint in the study area. This subsequently has had an effect on the bargaining capacity of the laborers and eventually on their relations with their landlords. Although, in some cases, laborers are dependent on their landlords and have established new forms of labor arrangements, the feudal relations of labor have been greatly weakened.

The availability of cash and the access to markets have created new ways in which labor is utilized and, more importantly, the way in which labor is being valued. The traditional practice of labor exchange and the reciprocity attached to it did not have any monetary value; it was governed by a motivation that was not purely economic. Tradition and caste relations played a key role in shaping labor relations. Practices of labor exchange were highly prevalent for those seeking labor in agriculture. The exact value of labor was not expressed in the labor exchange or attachment system, and it was even considered "morally wrong" to put a value on labor. Such exchange and attached form of labor was beneficial to the landlord or the stronger party, and exploitation was not questioned. However, since the relationship was built on the exchange of gifts and reciprocity, the landlord or the service user was expected to offer generosity, respect, and protection in exchange for the services. In the study area, it was common for the rich households to keep several workers, often from the same family, to manage the work inside and outside the household. Within such a system, the employer had the moral responsibility to look after the welfare of the workers and their families. Over the years, such reciprocal relationships had been normalized into a tradition by both parties, leading to social reproduction of the class structure. While the laboring family was protected, it did not have any opportunity to escape the caste system. These exchanges have been on the decline as more and more poor peasants are now working on a daily-wage basis in agriculture, construction, or other sectors of the economy. The value of money is also attached to loans, as debtors have started repaying their loans in cash instead of working unconditionally for others.

While overall the transition from feudal to nonfeudal working relationships has been beneficial to the laboring households, there are disparities in how the benefits have been distributed. For young people in particular, the new dispensation offers opportunities that did not exist before to escape from the drudgery and rigidities of traditional village life. For them, the detachment that has come with the weakening of the feudal system and its associated structural violence has definitely been positive. Migration, nonagricultural wage labor, and employment in the informal-services sector represent both changing aspirations and opportunities. But there are groups who are left behind by the gradual weakening of the reciprocal relationships inherent in the feudal caste system, which were exploitative at the core but also provided a form of social and economic safety net in times of need. Those who are too old, weak, or ill to adapt or who lack skills face perhaps greater vulnerabilities than before. Similarly, some friction in social relations is to be expected as some members of the upper-caste old guard find it difficult to transition to a situation where the increased assertion of the laboring class clashes with their perception of their past inherited authority.

The historical practice of sending children to work has continued, although this too has gone through changes. A few of the poorer households send their children (usually ages 10–14) with someone they know, mostly their relatives or someone from the village, to work as domestic helpers in the middle-class families in towns and cities.

This practice of sending children away for domestic work has been common among both the Bahun and Magar households. Contact with influential people (*thulo manche*) in the cities in the middle-class houses opened up opportunities to visit the cities and possibly seek employment opportunities for other members

other organizations. Therefore, the laboring classes have gradually turned from being subjects of landlords to citizens of the state and more able to articulate their demands and their rights.

A gradual transformation of the socioeconomic structure is taking place in rural Nepal. While the drivers of change are diverse, and include the opening up of rural areas through a complex mix of migration, political agitation, education, and communication, it is clear that the old system based on caste and the reproduction of feudal labor relationships is being replaced by an emerging system based on the commodification of land, labor, and cash—and the incorporation of rural areas into globalized socioeconomic flows.

Conclusion

The changing political economy and subject positions of the peasantry have had cultural consequences and a gendered impact on young men. Ideas associated with development (*bikas*), schooling, radio, television, mobile phones, and consumerism have significantly impacted how people in rural Nepal think about themselves, their work, their farming, and their aspirations. The commodification of land, labor, and money has had important consequences. Farming is neither profitable nor an attractive option for young men. There is tremendous pressure on young men from poorer households within farms and villages to take on the gendered breadwinner role. Young men are eager to escape the regimented life in the village and aspire to a salaried job in the city and the opportunity to take part in modern life. For them, out-migration is thus a natural response to escape the insecurities in the villages, but they rarely have the necessary social and political networks needed for securing salaried employment. Their marginalized position within the feudal system in the villages continues to shape their social position, disadvantaging them even when pursuing economic opportunities away from the village. Thus, young men from poorer households migrate to cities, where they mostly end up in precarious working conditions.

History and Culture
of Migration in Nepal

Migration in search of work is not a new phenomenon in Nepal. Historical and ethnographic evidence suggests that migration has been a significant feature of household liveli-hoods, shaped by exploitative state policies as well as wider pro-cesses of social transformation both inside and outside Nepal (Des Chene 1991; Hitchcock 1961; Hutt 1998; Shrestha 1990). This chapter provides a historical perspective on the *culture of migration* in rural Nepal, with a specific focus on how the hill economy has long relied on the comparatively large economy of their immediate neighbor to the south, India. Migration has been so pervasive that it has affected not only those who move but also those who stay behind. The decision to migrate is an accepted livelihood strategy for economic survival and well-being. Mi-gration, however, has come to shape the gendered identities of those who move and those who remain. This chapter offers a history of labor migration from the hills of Nepal, including the history of Gurkha recruitment and the more recent trend of labor migration to the Gulf States that has attracted global attention. It discusses different waves of out-migration and how these have shaped cultures of migration in the hills.

Mobility and Immobility

The differences in scholarly understandings of the characteristics of hill populations in the Nepal Himalayas, particularly in relation to migration, are provocative. Despite the fact that the vast majority of social scientists working in the region have noted different forms of migration in their fieldwork, there is a strong tendency in early scholarly work, largely dominated by anthropologists, to view life in the hills of Nepal as a discrete and timeless society unaffected by the outside world. In different ways, this "sedentary bias" (Malkki 1995: 208) has been influential in research on Nepal.

In classical anthropology the traditional approach is to look at "bounded space," examining the local, bounded, community as the object of study. In this sense, the community's relations with the rest of the world are of secondary interest to the ethnographer, if they are considered important at all. Even though "peasantry" itself is considered to have come into being only when connections to a dominant outside group have been established, classical anthropologists tend to focus on the community as a coherent and independent entity, and the relationship with the wider world is often ignored (Kearney 2004a). Despite repeated observations of the migration of young men made by anthropologists (see Mead 1930), most ethnographies represent communities as timeless cultures unaffected by outside forces. In his popular treatise, Ronald Inden argues that the colonial ethnography on India tends to represent India as a land of self-contained and inward-turned villages consisting of cooperative agents (Inden 1990). Such a conception of village society, in India and elsewhere, has recently been seriously questioned in postcolonial studies and critical anthropology.

Drawing on her ethnographic fieldwork among Hutu refugees who lived inside and outside of a refugee camp in Tanzania, Lisa Malkki explores the traditional ways of thinking about identity and territory that are reflected in scholarly work and nationalist discourses. She argues that there is a tendency in the modern world to locate people and identities in particular spaces and with particular boundaries and thus mobility is viewed in negative ways (Malkki 1992). She discusses mobile/nomadic identities or nomadic metaphysics in opposition to sedentary metaphysics (Malkki 1992). Similarly, Tim Cresswell has argued that a place-based "sendenterist metaphysics" has been developed in cultural geography and the humanities in general in which places and roots are given priority over and above mobile states of existence and forms of identity (Cresswell 2003). The idea that people belong to a particular place undermines the ubiquitous nature of mobility and fluid boundaries that are at the heart of social life.

In a stimulating analysis of perceptions of syphilis, Cresswell shows how human mobility has been linked to the concept of morality (Cresswell 2000). Here, Cresswell reveals that the disease is explicitly linked to the concept of mobility, and therefore mobility is viewed as a problem.

Until recently, it was standard practice among anthropologists to consider community studies to be the primary locale through which anthropologists developed an in-depth understanding of the community (Gupta and Ferguson 1997). Kearney calls the earlier approach "parachute anthropology," referring to the way the anthropologist figuratively drops into a community from out of the sky and takes that place as a bounded, self-contained unit of analysis, with little attention to how it is situated in regional, national, or even global contexts, which more or less shape its internal features (Kearney 2004a: 18). This internal focus on a community perfectly suits classical anthropology, which emphasizes long-term fieldwork in small communities, and these anthropologists make very little effort to match the wealth of detail on internal structure with analyses of external linkages. With the isolated community as the ideal unit of study, the impression of immobility is unintentionally promoted in the social science literature.

A reading of early accounts of Nepal produced by Western travelers, missionaries, and British officers shows a colonial tendency to represent Nepal as an exotic, traditional, and unexplored region. The first account of the region was produced by an Ital-

ian missionary named G. Tucci, but it is the writing of Colonel
William Kirkpatrick (Kirkpatrick 1969), a British officer serving
in British India and charged with the first Western diplomatic
mission into Nepal, that has a wider readership (Beine 1998). His
work is the first among only a handful of early sources that have
provided background information on the nature and interest of
anthropologists and others working in Nepal (Allen 1994). Beine
(1998) comments that Kirkpatrick's view is affected by colonial
logic and an ethnocentric view of discrete "indigenous people"
that was held by the leading anthropologists of those times.

Another frequently cited study is B. H. Hodgson's *Essays on
the Languages, Literature, and Religion of Nepál and Tibet* (1874),
a collection of articles written between 1828 and 1838. During
his twenty-year stay in Nepal (1820–1843), Hodgson produced
in-depth accounts of various ethnic groups. Beine (1998) argues
that Hodgson's accounts demonstrate a clear colonial agenda.
Similarly, written reports by British officers who visited Palpa represent an exotic picture of Palpa's landscape and people
(Smadja [1922–1932] 1999: 41). All of these colonial writings tend
to represent Nepal as a closed and exotic society, mostly agrarian,
inhabited by a traditional people requiring development through
a civilizing mission.

Among most of the early anthropologists, an interesting
example demonstrating colonial dominance is the examination of religion, in this case Buddhism and Hinduism, or tribe
and caste. Analyzing the scholarly discourses on religion of the
Thakalis, William Fisher argues that earlier scholars made an
attempt to understand the Thakalis on the basis of the idea that
Hinduism and Buddhism are distinct, and Hinduism and the
caste system are recent phenomena among the Thakalis (Fisher
2001). The underlying element in such a representation is the
immobility of a closed society, which has had only recent contact with people from outside. Yet, various forms of migration
have had a significant effect on the heterogeneity of the Thakalis
and their quest for community solidarity and identity (Fisher
2001). Modern ethnography in the hills of Nepal has focused on
providing a detailed sociocultural account of a particular eth-

nic group, with very little interest in the group's linkages to the outside world.

The idea of Nepal as a peasant society dependent on agriculture (Blaikie, Cameron, and Seddon 1979, 1980, 2002; Macfarlane, 1976, 2001; Shrestha 1989) and natural resources (Conway, Bhattarai, and Shrestha 2000; Eckholm 1976; Ives and Messerli 1989) is particularly visible in several scholarly works that have had significant influence on policy and public debate in the region. These studies are based on the theoretical model that rural populations are dependent on agriculture and natural resources, and this informs the scholars' analytical categories. The assumptions, often implicit, are that the solution to poverty in the region lies in agricultural development, management of natural resources, and distribution of land.

Rural development programs in Nepal have been organized around conceptualizing Nepal as a peasant society dependent on agriculture and natural resources without taking seriously the ubiquitous presence, normalcy, and importance of mobility. Any report on different aspects of Nepal's development, at the local level or the national level, starts with a paragraph on the centrality of agriculture and natural resources in the life and livelihoods of the Nepalis.

A report released by the World Bank in 1989 highlights the importance of agriculture in the livelihoods of Nepalis, looks at its failures, and recommends developing Nepal by systematically modernizing the agricultural sector. It states:

Because 90% of Nepal's population live in rural areas, the key to alleviating poverty lies in improving agricultural performance. The reasons for the poor agricultural growth reflect numerous problems in the agricultural system, many of which have proven thus far to be intractable. These include the inadequate transport infrastructure; a large number of poorly fed livestock with low productivity; an inadequate and declining forage base; declining soil fertility due to environmental degradation, particularly in the Hills; and adverse and erratic weather. Nepal has not followed inappropriate producer pricing and trade policies and therefore these cannot be blamed for agriculture's poor performance. The major constraint to agricultural growth has been ineffective irrigation delivery, particularly in public irrigation schemes where only a small part of the command area actually receives reliable delivery. Other factors that have contributed to low growth and productivity include problems in the delivery of fertilizer, slow progress in developing yield-increasing technologies, and weak research and extension. (World Bank 1989: xiii)

Again and again, various agencies have reported that agriculture is the most important source of livelihood for 80 to 90 percent of Nepalis. While policies have been framed differently under different development regimes by different agencies, there has been a uniform voice coming from policy documents that agriculture is the most important livelihood option available to Nepalis and that it must be the central element in any strategy for economic development in Nepal. While there has been no disagreement among the agencies that agriculture is one of the central elements in the livelihoods of Nepalis, it is surprising to see that even Nepalis who do not own land and/or derive their sustenance from farming have been automatically categorized as farmers just because they live in rural Nepal. Furthermore, powerful development donors, including the World Bank, the UK's Department for International Development (DFID), and USAID, among others, continue to portray rural Nepal as an agricultural region where farming predominates as a livelihood. This perspective appears partial and inconsistent when compared to my observation that lives and livelihoods in my fieldwork area are becoming increasingly divorced from farming and land. At the local level in Palpa, agriculture (*krisi*) dominated programs supported by the District Development Office, which did not mention out-migration or the significance of migrant remittance for household livelihoods. Development donors and institutions active in Palpa, including the Asian Development Bank, Helvetas (a Swiss NGO), and the Food and Agricultural Organisation, had

funded a number of programs focused on agricultural development ranging from irrigation, vegetable farming, milk production, market access, and improved technology, among others.

Michael Hutt's "Going to Muglan: Nepali Literary Representations of Migration to India and Bhutan" (1998) and "A Hero
or a Traitor? The Gurkha Soldier in Nepali Literature" (1989)
show that such an aberrant view of migration is equally evident
in Nepali literature. Hutt's studies of literary writings show that
out-migration from Nepal to India and the recruitment of young
men as Gurkha soldiers is always viewed as a result of dispossession in the hills. The literary writings represent these out-
migrations as stories of loss and suffering. Migration has been
systematically viewed as unusual, and often a threat to the hill
economy, society, and culture. It has been seen as an exception
and often a crisis, leading to other crises.

The picture that emerges from the literature is not monolith-
ic—that is, existing literature does note mobility and migration
of different forms, but these are often treated as less significant
practices. A few works reflect the mobile life among the highlanders (Furer-Haimendorf 1964, 1975). Christoph Furer-Haimendorf noted that during winter, highlanders migrated to the
South to the warmer areas of the district along with their families and livestock. From this new temporary home, they traded
with various parts of Nepal for the whole winter season. In the
summer, they went back to their highland home again and traded in the North with bordering towns of Tibet such as Taklakot.
Several studies have documented men's migration for work to
India as a livelihoods strategy in the hills of Nepal (Hitchcock
1961; Pfaff-Czarnecka 1995; Thieme and Wyss 2005; Thieme
and Müller-Böker 2004). The practice of recruitment to a foreign army among certain hill ethnic groups, like Magars and
Gurungs, has received some scholarly attention as a defining
feature of people's livelihoods and identity (K. Adhikari 1993;
Des Chene 1991). The vast majority of the scholars working in
the hills of Nepal have collected empirical evidence on migration, but most of them have treated it as a peripheral variable
within the ideal of the bounded unit of a village community.

In the social sciences, including anthropology, agrarian studies, and development studies, peasantry is largely seen as rooted in the soil and immobile (Kearney 1996). In this imaginary, peasants have no reason to look for employment outside this mode of existence. The category of peasant hardly fits into twenty- to twenty-first-century realities, when most of the people whom we might call peasants are part-time workers in the informal economy in the cities (Kearney 1996) and who make sense of their migration experiences in sociocultural terms. This delinking of peasant with the soil or agricultural resources has important implications on how one conceptualizes production and reproduction of poverty in rural areas. Within anthropology, the earlier sedentary approach is being challenged in the era of globalization during which population mobility is seen as fundamental to people's lives. Certain scholars have recognized that mobility has had an important impact on peasant lives in which rural and urban cultures and economies are connected (Kearney 2004a).

With the emergence of debates about the value of mobility, more recent developments in anthropology and other social sciences have involved a rethinking of the very foundation, methodology, and subject matter of the discipline. On the methodological front, George Marcus has advocated a "multi-sited imaginary," if not a multi-sited ethnography, which forces ethnographers to move beyond a single locale (Marcus 1995, 1998). The idea of a changing conception of the field is extensively discussed in a volume edited by Akhil Gupta and James Ferguson, who argue that anthropology appears determined "to give up its old idea of territorially fixed communities and stable, localized communities, and to apprehend an interconnected world in which people, objects and ideas are rapidly shifting and refuse to stay in one place" (Gupta and Ferguson 1997: 4). Despite this recognition, they note that the discipline has become more defensive in favor of fieldwork in a localized context. Drawing on her research among the Nepali Gurkhas who fought in the British Army and who traveled to different parts of the world during their careers, Mary Des Chene writes how her own research would have benefited from a multi-sited and traveling anthropology to different destinations where Gurkhas had lived (Des Chene 1995: 73–74).

Overall, fluid boundaries and mobile epistemology are recently emerging concepts in social sciences. In recent years, it has become increasingly impossible for social science researchers to ignore the mobile and complex nature of social life, and there are now new methodologies to capture this complexity. The work on labor migration and remittances by David Seddon, Jagannath Adhikari, and Ganesh Gurung (2001) for DFID proved instrumental in bringing more attention to the debate on male labor out-migration from Nepal in the scholarly and development discourse. Since then there has been a proliferation of research activities, largely funded by development agencies, as well as commentary and public debate on out-migration and its impact. Yet, the focus has largely been on the impact of remittances sent by labor migrants who are on temporary contracts for work in international destinations in the Gulf and Southeast Asian countries. Occasionally there has been public debate about these migrants' ill-treatment and exploitation. The poorer households that continue to send migrants to India have, however, received scant attention from scholars, policy makers, civil society, and media.

Waves of Out-Migration from the Hills

The history of Nepal is the history of migration and mobility. The idea of Nepal is rooted in migration (Whelpton 2005). Migration and mobility have involved transhumance trade in the borderland regions, labor migration within Nepal, modern-day slavery practices such as keeping children and women from rural areas as domestic workers (often called servants) in middle-class houses in cities like Kathmandu, religious pilgrimage, travel to seek education in Banares in India and latterly in other parts of the world, work opportunities in India and other parts of the world, recruitment into the British and Indian armies, and distress migration in the face of extractive state policies and unequal distribution of land. In this book, my focus is on migration in search of work opportunities in cities in neighboring India among marginal households. Poor households have long relied on young men's migration to India as an obvious livelihood strategy in different periods of Nepalese history, resulting in a culture of migration in the middle hills of Nepal. I distinguish different waves of out-migration in the following paragraphs to show how different forms of migration have very different historical roots and routes. In his discussion of the formation of the Nepali diaspora, David Gellner writes, "As far as the modern Nepali diaspora is concerned, three distinct waves and types of migration can be distinguished: first, overland, mainly seeking work and land, and mainly towards the east; second, again overland, but more focused on seeking work in Indian cities; and finally, third, travelling by plane to work in the Persian Gulf (or 'arab' as Nepalis refer to it), in Southeast Asia, and beyond, or for education and work in the developed world" (2013b: 138).

First Wave of Migration

The first wave of migration began in the eighteenth century, when state policies and agrarian changes forced peasants in the hills to move off their land and seek their livelihoods elsewhere, both within Nepal and across the border into India (Regmi 1978). The establishment of Nepal under the leadership of King Prithvi Narayan Shah in 1768 led to massive changes in land and labor relations in Nepal. The poverty caused by the oppressive land, taxation, and labor policies of the state, and the resultant rural indebtedness and loss of land, threatened the very survival of the low-income groups, prompting them to migrate in search of work opportunities (Shrestha 1990: 292–297). Furthermore, Nepal's Muluki Ain of 1854 (the National Code) created the framework of a caste-based society, whereby members of occupational castes and ethnic groups were pushed into the margins by state-led policy (Whelpton 2005). The original Muluki Ain of 1854 contained a five-tier national caste hierarchy in which the people were divided into the following categories according to ascribed ritual purity: wearers of holy cord, non-enslavable alcohol drinkers, enslavable alcohol drinkers, impure but touchable castes, and impure and untouchable castes. The high-caste hill Hindus (Bahun, Thakuri, and Chetri) were placed at the top. Below them were the traditionally non-Hindu groups under the rubric of *matwli* (alcohol drinker). Hindu castes that were said to be impure but touchable along with Muslims and Christians were ranked one above the bottom, and Hindu castes deemed as impure and untouchable were placed at the bottom. The system pushed untouchable and impure castes into the lower strata, in terms of not only sociocultural hierarchy and status but also economic position.

During the late eighteenth, the nineteenth, and the early twentieth centuries, migration was mainly eastward to northeastern India (primarily in Darjeeling), Bhutan, Sikkim, and Burma. The opportunities for work in the bordering states of India in sectors such as tea plantations, coal mining, and construction attracted a larger number of Nepalis from poorer households as laborers. Nepalis traveled across the border, in both the eastern and western part, to work as porters in hill stations like Darjeeling, Nainital, and other towns in Himanchal Pradesh. Working as porters and laborers became a routine job for many Nepalis. In the East, large numbers of people from the Rai and Limbu ethnic groups left for Darjeeling around the 1850s to work on tea plantations (Hutt 1997).

Following the earlier migrants who went to work on plantations and in coal mines, many Nepalis went to work as dairy farmers in the Indian state of Assam starting in the middle of the nineteenth century (Nath 2006). The British encouraged Nepalis to cultivate and graze cattle in Assam and other parts of the region, because they were the first to pay grazing fees and thereby contribute revenue to the British. Accordingly, dairy farming became a major occupation among Nepali migrants in Assam, mainly those from the Bahun (Brahmin) and Chetri castes who had such skills back in Nepal (Nath 2006).

The colonial government in India encouraged Nepalis to migrate to the Northeast to work in forests, on road construction sites, in mines, in fields, and on plantations to meet the growing demand of labor. Given the limited economic opportunity back in

Nepal, Nepali migrants began to travel to the Northeast in search of work. On tea plantations, the migrant workers and their families received housing, rations, medical facilities, and schooling for their children, among other benefits (Besky 2014). This practice continued after Indian independence, when Nepalis continued to travel to India to work in the construction and industrial sectors. Large numbers of Bahun and Magar men from Palpa migrated to work in Burma, West Bengal, and Assam, where they worked on tea plantations, construction sites, and mines, or as porters. In Assam, among international migrants, Nepali migrants form a large demographic second only to Bangladeshis. These migrations have sparked political and social conflict in Assam, with "natives" worried about being dominated by "immigrants" in political, economic, and cultural spheres. More recently, Nepali migrants in northeastern India have found themselves on the receiving end of a nativist backlash (Nath 2006).

Second Wave of Migration

The second wave of migration started with the recruitment of young men to serve in the army of Sikh ruler Ranjit Singh and in the British Army in India (Seddon, Adhikari, and Gurung 2002). This wave of migration has roots in the Treaty of Sugauli, signed between the British and Nepali governments in 1816 following the Anglo-Nepalese wars of 1814–1816. Although the then Nepali ruler agreed to the British demand for recruitment of Nepali men into their army, the Nepali government is believed to have resisted the recruitment of Nepalis by the British until 1885 (Shrestha 2001). This could have been due to the perception that the recruits would bring back revolutionary ideas to Nepal and because such recruitment was seen as an assault on Nepal's sovereignty. The Nepali government changed its policy in 1886, when it allowed free recruitment of Nepalis into the British Army. Nepali men who serve in the British Army are known as Gurkhas, which is a distortion of the word Gorkha, a district in western Nepal. Because the British were initially not allowed to recruit in Nepal, they encouraged the settlement of Nepalis outside of the country by offering work opportunities on tea plantations and in mining and construction work in Assam and the Northeast. However, Nepali rulers turned a blind eye to recruitment inside Nepal by local agents, who were called *gallas* (Hutt 1997). Once the Nepali government allowed recruitment, by 1887 Gorakhpur, the border city in India, became a formal headquarters of Gurkha recruitment for those from west-central Nepal (Hutt 1997). By 1902, there was a recruitment center in Darjeeling for those from the Rai and Limbu ethnic groups. These men migrated in order to work, not to settle permanently. Most Nepali families were against the idea of sending their children for recruitment into the army. Many mothers would send their sons to hide in the forest or with relatives to avoid the recruitment agents because the casualty rate in the British Army was very high, and many Gurkhas had lost eyes and hands in the war (Des Chene 1991).

In my fieldwork area, an elderly Magar man told me that, for as long as he could remember, Magar men had been recruited to foreign armies, both British and Indian, as a means of supplementing the livelihoods of the households. Most in Palpa, he recalled, had been sent to different parts of India, while a few had been sent to Hong Kong, the United Kingdom, Malaysia, and Burma. The names of those places were familiar not only to the *lahures* (returned soldiers) who had been there but also to the people left back in the village. It was usual practice among the retired *lahures* in the village to tell stories of battles and experiences in different places around the world. I listened for hours to some of their stories, which they were very enthusiastic to share. They contained not only the experience of war but also descriptions of the places, peoples, and foods. The experience was reflected in the frequent use of English words such as "recruit," "fight," "attack," "position," and "camp." The village households with *lahures* (both current and retired) displayed photographs from different places in the verandas (*pirhi*) outside their houses, where visitors would be greeted when they arrived.

Out of seventy Magar households I interviewed during my fieldwork in 2004–2005 in Palpa, fourteen households had *lahures* with the Indian Army and only three households had *lahures* with the British Army. There were a total of seventeen men in the army and twelve retired army men in the survey households. Many Magar informants told me that recruitment to the British and Indian armies had declined sharply in recent years because of a reduced need for recruits and increased competition for places. At the same time, there was increasing pressure from Maoist activists opposed to the idea of recruitment to a foreign army. A 24-year-old male Maoist activist that I met in the village said, "This is an unfair practice, where the blood of poor innocent Nepalis is sacrificed for the benefit of the imperial expansionist." Recruitment into a foreign army was viewed by the Maoist activist as a direct form of exploitation by the British and Indian governments. This was reflected in the forty-point demand submitted by the Maoists to the government before they declared the people's war on 17 February 1996. The Maoists' demands included controlling the Nepal-India border. Another demand stated, "Gorkha recruitment centres should be closed and decent jobs should be arranged for recruits." Additionally, the Maoists asked for a review of the unjust treaty of 1950 between Nepal and India. In one instance, for about forty hours on 20 October 2003, the Maoists abducted a British Army officer along with three soldiers and three porters who were there to recruit hill men from a village named Lakhani, north of Pokhara.[1] Despite this, none of the households in the village told me that they were directly threatened to stop sending their family members for recruitment, though, depending on their income level, a few households with *lahures* paid forced donations (called *chanda*) to the Maoists.

Third Wave of Migration

A major distinguishing feature of this wave of migration is that the destinations are the cities, metropolises, and towns going through major transformations. In addition to finding jobs, migrants were also getting drawn into the world of consumption.

Substantial migration has been seen from the hills to the plains and across the border into Indian cities to make up for the low income of the hill regions and to cover the needs of local rural communities throughout the year. This wave of migration started in postcolonial India around the 1960s, and a major feature that distinguished this wave from the previous waves of migration was that Nepali migrants were now traveling to work in Indian cities and towns. The newly independent India, with its growing urbanization and middle class, saw the creation of service-sector jobs in Indian cities, from domestic work and security guard positions to work in hotels and restaurants. This was directly related to the processes of social transformation in India, where urbanization created the need for a particular kind of labor.

Large numbers of Nepali men migrate in search of work in India, and these migrants account for just under half of all of Nepal's migrants. Pushed by difficult economic conditions at home, the hill men have long relied on the comparatively large economy of their immediate neighbor to the south, where they migrate in search of various work opportunities. The flow of Nepalese migrants has been facilitated and sustained by kin and friendship networks among migrants and their households (Thieme 2006).

This particular wave of migration had a major gender dimension because it was mostly young men who traveled, leaving their families behind. Unlike work on the tea plantations or in the fields, where Nepalis migrated as family units, migrating to Indian cities as a family was almost beyond imagination, given the risks involved, the unavailability of accommodation, and the nature of work itself.

Since the beginning of the 1990s NGOs have become increasingly active in combating the trafficking of an increasing number of women and children from Nepal to Indian cities like Mumbai (Joshi 2001; Pigg 2002). NGOs estimate that some 120,000–150,000 girls and women work in brothels in India.

Fourth Wave of Migration

Known as *bidesh tira jane* (going abroad), the fourth wave of migration from Nepal started in the mid-1980s, accelerated in the 1990s, and dramatically increased in the mid-2000s, when people from Palpa continued to migrate to work in India but also began to migrate to new destinations, mainly the Gulf States and Malaysia. Excluding India, the official data for Nepal in 2010 show that Malaysia (32.04 percent), Qatar (28.71 percent), Saudi Arabia (19.81 percent), and the United Arab Emirates (UAE) (12.68 percent) are popular destinations in the Gulf States (Government of Nepal 2010) for Nepalis. In 2010, about 5–7 percent were estimated to have migrated to Australia, European nations, Japan, the Republic of Korea, the United Kingdom, the United States, and other countries with globally strong economies. My household survey in Palpa in 2005 shows that the Gulf States (Qatar, UAE, Saudi Arabia) and the Southeast Asian countries (Hong Kong and Malaysia) are popular destinations: Just over 30 percent (56 individuals) of the current absent population migrated to these locations, and about 15 percent (10 individuals) of returnees came from these destinations.

In 1985, the government introduced the Labour Act to regulate migration for work to about a dozen countries. The act banned recruitment of Nepalis without government permission. More people from Palpa began to go to different foreign countries, particularly after 1995. The opening of new markets for Nepalese laborers in these destinations and the decentralization of passport issuance in Nepal contributed to this escalation of migration, which has become an extremely important part of the Nepalese economy and culture. The booming export of manpower overseas in the 1990s led the government to decentralize passport issuance, and after 1997 people could get a passport from the District Administration Office (DAO) in Tansen. A clerk who worked at the passport section in the DAO told me that every day more than twenty to thirty people sought passports. Young men in Palpa were seen queuing in the DAO for passports, which then cost NRs 5,000. Prior to 1997, passports were issued by the Ministry of Foreign Affairs in Kathmandu, and people who needed a passport were required to visit Kathmandu with the necessary documents for a minimum of six to eight days, which involved a huge cost.

At the time of my fieldwork in 2004–2005, several men from the village had been planning and preparing documents to go to these countries for work. As a result of the relatively high salaries and job security during the contract period, more men have now become attracted to this form of migration, though it required a substantive investment compared to the village standard. To migrate to the Gulf and Southeast Asian countries as unskilled workers, people needed to invest about NRs 100,000–150,000 to pay for the cost of preparation of various documents, recruitment agent's fees, and airfare. This was no doubt a lot of money, given the village standard. For the poorer households, this amount was probably more than their total wealth. Even for the well-off households, this amount was quite a lot, as they often did not have cash. While some people sold property, others took loans from relatives, moneylenders, or banks. From the perspective of both the sending households and the migrant, the money was considered an investment that could lead to the betterment of their lives. While the households arranged money and made the migration of one or two individual men possible, the migrants left with increased responsibility toward their household members.

As most of the migration to the Gulf and Southeast Asia took place through recruitment agencies (known as manpower agencies) based in Kathmandu, many potential migrants traveled to Kathmandu with an experienced and/or knowledgeable kinsman to approach the "reliable" and "trustworthy" (*bharpardo, biswasilo, nathagne*) recruitment agencies. In other cases, men in the villages were initially approached by the agents of recruitment agencies with an attractive offer. The agents could be the kin of the potential migrant or could approach the potential migrant through kin or directly. Three such agents I met during my 2004–2005 fieldwork in Palpa told me that they would get paid NRs 5,000–15,000 for each person successfully recruited for the manpower agencies. There were several individuals working as agents in and around Tansen.

One very popular manpower agent was a former member of parliament, who lived in Tansen and was well known for arranging migration to different foreign destinations, including Europe. There were rumors that this agent was earning a lot of money by sending people abroad. Earlier a very popular politician, he now gave very little time to politics but was busy with his new enterprises. One of his neighbors in Tansen commented, "His house has always been busy with visitors; earlier with his party cadre, now with his clients." He was always traveling between Tansen and Kathmandu with a small bag, which contained documents and passports. It is believed that he has sent more than five hundred people to work abroad since he started this work in 2001. I met two young boys who had been visiting him for the past two months and whose migration to Europe was being arranged at a cost of NRs 700,000 each. Another agent was a relative of a clerk at a manpower agency in Kathmandu. He had been arranging migration abroad for a few people from my study area. Yet another agent was a returnee from Qatar, who lived in the village and took a group of men to his contact at a manpower agency in Kathmandu. I learned that recruitment agencies kept a few staff whose sole work was to find potential clients from different parts of Nepal.

Contrary to the popular perception of such agents as exploiters, from the perspective of the potential migrants I spoke to, the agent played a crucial role in making migration successful. They were aware that the agents took money from the recruitment agency but it was mostly viewed as fair remuneration for their work.

Culture of Migration

In villages and towns throughout the middle hills of Nepal, migration for work features as a regular theme of conversation among the people, with a particular focus on aspirations, planning, organization, benefits, and costs. Many stories, poems, novels, films, and songs illustrating the pervasive culture of migration have been written in Nepali during the last few decades (Hutt 1998). A powerful example of the culture of migration and associated suffering is found in the popular Nepali novel *Basai*,[2] by Lila Bahadur Chetri, which portrays the life of Dhane Basnet and his family, who were forced to leave their settlement in a hill village in eastern Nepal as a result of poverty, debt, and economic exploitation. The seventy-page novel tells the story of the family's dispossession and forced migration from Nepal. It highlights the everyday reality of poverty and caste- and gender-based oppression that has continued to force people from the hills to the Tarai or across the border to India for decades. It is probably the most widely read Nepali novel because it has been required reading as part of the university curriculum in Nepal. More recently, in 2017, a song (with a video) named "Saili" that highlights the emotional costs associated with out-migration became viral, with more than 12 million views on YouTube within six months of its release. The song tells the story of Nepali men migrating abroad for work, leaving behind their children and family, and dreaming of having fun in life after 40. Over the years, subsistence hill agriculture combined with male labor migration has remained the key feature of culture and livelihoods in the middle hills. Migration and associated remittances have sustained hill agriculture for decades; the practice of out-migration has been embedded in the gendered lives and aspirations of young men. "An important aspect of the relationship between India and Central Nepal is the close connection arising from the stringencies of hill agriculture on the one hand and the cash value of Indian employment on the other" (Hitchcock 1961: 15). Writing on modernity in the context of urban Kathmandu, Liechty (2003) shows the significance of having close friends and family living in a foreign country. For those who stay back, having family and friends living and working in a foreign country offers not only a source of pride but also important insights into other cultural worlds.

Any fruitful analysis of the sociocultural meaning of migra- tion to India requires a discussion on how it is referred to, dis- cussed, and imagined in the sending context. One way to begin to make sense of this is by looking at different local terms and expressions people use to speak about men who go to work in India in relation to those who stay back or those who migrate elsewhere. These include *lahure* (one who is recruited into a for- eign army), *jagire* (one with secured employment), *phaltu* (one who is useless and has no engagement), and *chaure* (one who is useless, wrinkled, and unable to grow). These are important in the sense that they represent different forms of masculinities in the local context.

Commonly known as *lahur jane*, migration of male family members to join foreign armies (Des Chene 1991; K. Adhikari 1993) is very much linked to the identity of the Magars. Among the Magars, the success of a man's life is measured in terms of his ability to join a foreign army. It has become the answer to the question—what do Magars do? The presence of the Indian Army Pension Camp and British Army Welfare Society within a two- to three-hour walk of the villages of Chilangdi and Khorbari, respectively, signifies the ubiquitous importance of *lahur jane* in the life of the Magars in Palpa. I observed many retired Indian Army *lahures* from surrounding villages and districts come to the pension camp to collect their pensions. Holding their pension documents (*pensing patta*) in their hands, many of them were seen walking around the teashops, seasonal hotels, and restaurants outside the pension camp. The collection of these pensions supported the local economy around the camp.

Although the term *lahure* has historically been associated with those who went to work in a foreign army, it is sometimes used to refer to those who go to work as migrant workers in the Gulf, Southeast Asia, or India or as a generic term to refer to men who went to work outside of Nepal and contribute to the households left behind. This form of migration is meant to contribute to the smooth functioning of the household and to opening opportunities for its socioeconomic mobility. The term implies travel to a foreign country, excitement, hardship, and an eventual return back home. *Lahures* do not leave the village just to earn money; they also return with the experience of a different culture, whether from India, the United Kingdom, Malaysia, Singapore, or the Gulf countries. Not all of them return home, however; some choose instead to settle elsewhere in Nepal, and their earnings often enable them to purchase land and property there. The Magar men showed overwhelming interest in *lahur jane* because of both the material and the symbolic value it offers. It plays an important part of life among the Magars.

By local standards, a *lahure* can earn a substantial amount of money that far exceeds the economic position of anyone else in the village. Moreover, the pension allows for security after retirement. It opens up opportunities for a better quality of life, not just for the *lahure* himself but for the entire household. By the village standard, the presence of a household member in the British Army means that the household will be counted as one of the richest and most influential in the village. The Indian Army does not offer as much when compared to the British Army, but the households with a member in the Indian Army are able to meet most of their cash needs. While aspirations to be recruited to the British Army far exceed desires to join the Indian Army, entrance to the former is, unsurprisingly, more competitive than to the latter.

The symbolic value of *lahure* is a very important because the position earns respect in the village. *Lahures* are considered to be more experienced and knowledgeable, and villagers, mostly kin, go to them for advice or even a loan when they need cash. The status the position brings to the entire household is highly cherished by the *lahure* households. Those unable to secure recruitment as *lahure* are disappointed and look for other opportunities to migrate. After all of her three sons were unsuccessful in getting recruited as *lahure,* a Magar mother said to me:

> Our "fate" [*bhagya*] is quite bad. None of them [her sons] could get selected. They are all "useless" [*phaltu*]. After several attempts we managed a loan and sent the "second son" [*mailo*] to Qatar and the "first son" [*jetho*] to Bombay. The "youngest" [*kancho*] is still wandering around the village; wondering now what to do? He might begin "to plough the fields" [*halo jotne*]. I don't know why, even after having three sons, our status is like this. We had great expectations when we had three sons; what did we do to turn out to be like this?

The retired *lahures* prefer to wear their clothes from their army days—primarily a woolen cap or a sweater—and walk around the village. This signifies that the person is either a *lahure* himself or some close relative of a *lahure*. Most of the returned and retired *lahures* are known as *lahure dai, lahure kancha, captain,* and *subedar,* among other titles, rather than by their names. A teacher who is the son of a retired captain of the Indian Army is not known as "teacher" or by his own name but as "captain's son" (*captain ko choro*). In fact, most of the people in the village do not even know these people's actual (formal) names. The value is not just social and economic but political too. The *lahure* households are able to lend money, donate to welfare services like schools/health posts/drinking water schemes, consume the best food, and hire labor. Such an economic position helps them earn status and turn their economic status into political power. Moreover, if one decides to return to the village after retirement, it offers opportunities for an influential political position in the village.

Boys have been brought up with the expectation of being a *lahure* when they grow up, while girls have been brought up with the expectation of getting married to a *lahure,* who, it has been said, can offer security and happiness. Boys are often told that one of the major goals in life is to get recruited to a foreign army, which ensures the livelihoods of the household. Children are told the stories of *lahures,* of their experiences and time abroad. There was one instance during my fieldwork in Palpa when a returned *lahure* was sharing his experiences from different countries in the village, close to a tea shop, and a group of village men from different social groups as well as youth and children were listening to him. Such a scene, where young schoolchildren listened to such tales, was common in village teashops. Children were constantly exposed to *lahures,* who often got much more attention than anyone else in the village, coming and going from their own households and community.

The elders told me that in earlier days not everybody wanted to become a *lahure,* as it was considered dangerous. Several people from the village died, while others returned disabled. An elder remembered the time when several *gallas*[3] used to come to the villages to convince the younger men to join the foreign army, but this is no longer the trend. These brokers brought with them sweets to convince (*phakaune*) young able-bodied men to join the army. There was a time when the young men were advised to be conscious of unknown persons (*parai* or *nachineko manche*) and *galla,* who might take them forcefully for recruitment. This had certainly changed in recent years, with increased competition, and brokers no longer visited the village to select the young men. With the number of spaces in the army reduced, there was a significant increase in movement for work to India, the Gulf, and Malaysia. Though fewer jobs were available in foreign armies and there were fewer *lahures* in the village, people maintained a strong memory of *lahures* and *lahur jane* in their everyday lives. They would often talk about a father, a grandfather, an uncle, or some other relative who was a *lahure.* It was considered to be a matter of pride for the entire family.

The term *lahure* had become integrated into the everyday conversation in the village so much so that it was used as a sign of respect for some men who had never been outside the village. A common use was in relation to the display of wealth, comfort, goods, or knowledge. It was quite possible that a man who wore new clothes and walked about in the village would be teased as a *lahure.* During my fieldwork in Palpa, a Bahun uncle called his nephew, who was sleeping on the veranda during the day, *lahure,* and required the nephew to accompany him to the field. In this context the uncle used the term *lahure* to wake up his lazy nephew when he was expected to accompany other family members to work. Here it is important to consider the ethnic dimension of the use of the term. In the Bahun conception, the term *lahure* also signified people who lacked intelligence and spirituality but enjoyed material comfort, which was again part of their understanding of Magars. For Magars, recruitment into a foreign army, for its symbolic and material value, was at the center of what it means to be a man. However, the high-caste

Bahuns and those with *jagire* ridiculed *lahures* for their service in foreign armies to earn money. Therefore, a *lahure* was recognized as a successful man only within his own group.

People used the term *jagir khana jane* (literally, "to eat *jagir*"— i.e., land) or *nokari garna jane* (literally, "to work as servants") to refer to the migration to work in professional or semi-professional secured jobs, whether inside or outside Nepal. The terms *jagir* and *nokari* cover jobs that are more or less permanent, or in some cases temporary but ensured a degree of job security with regular payment. Mostly the term *jagir* refers to civilian jobs within Nepal, but some *lahures* are also known as *jagires*. The term *jagir* was a form of land assignment in return for state service, which was a common means of payment to soldiers in the Nepali army in the nineteenth century (Regmi 1976: 71–86). Though these days those who are employed by the state or private agencies do not get paid in the form of land, most of them use the salary to purchase land, which signifies their particular relation to the state as servants.

Jagires are considered to be responsible men who are able to ensure income through a regular salary and thus are able to take care of their duties as men effectively. Among Bahuns it is the core of what it means to be a good man: working for the government (*sarkari jagir*) as a paid employee stands as a desired characteristic of an ideal man.

In certain situations, the terms *lahure* and *jagire* are used as the reverse of *chaure* or *phaltu*. *Phaltu* is a very common word used to categorize people who are unemployed, who wander around, or who work in relatively undesirable, low-wage manual labor with no job security. This is contrasted with a few people commonly known as *jagire* or *lahure,* who receive higher pay, have higher intelligence, and hold white-collar jobs with some level of job security. The term *phaltu,* which means "useless," is used to refer to unproductive men who cannot earn and demonstrate their worth as responsible men. Other uses of the term *phaltu* are in relation to anything useless or that lacks worth, whether it is a person or a conversation or things. It is also used to refer to the men who wander around in the village instead of working or to the unemployed men in the cities. The term *phaltu* is used in this context to categorize the men who fail to fulfill their responsibilities.

At the same time, the term *chaure* is used in contrast to the term *lahure* to categorize men. In this context *chaure* means those who work in a relatively undesired and useless setting in India such as domestic work and are looked upon as "old," "weak," and "wrinkled." *Lahures* are referred to as men who display lots of cash, bravery, and experience of a foreign place, and *jagire* are men who are educated and have salaried employment, while *chaures* are men who cannot display money, are weak and incompetent.

All this shows that the experience of migration to India for work has had complex meanings in the local conception. The different meanings show that people use a variety of terms to categorize men, depending on the nature of work and the experience they underwent. Although going to India to work as manual laborers is more common but comparatively less desired and people often call it *phaltu kam*[4] or *sano tino kam*,[5] it is more desirable for men to go to India in search of work than stay in the village. There they manage their farm and/or work on others' land and this is commonly referred to as *halo jotne* (literally, "plowing the field") or *bhari bhokne* (literally, "carrying weight") or simply *phaltu*. In this sense, going to work in India provides an escape from the derogatory status of *halo jotne* or *bhari bhokne* and is a means to look for opportunities to be referred as *jagire* or *lahure*. These different categories reveal that there is no such thing as a homogeneous masculinity, but rather a range of different masculinities that are related to experiences of movement for work (Connell 1995).

Here, it may be useful to link this to the historical evidence on agrarian relations during the nineteenth century, where peasants were compelled to share a proportion of their income with those who did not have a role in production (Regmi 1978). This showed that the importance of going to India was not just as an escape from the exploitative social structure but also that the social structure had an impact on the construction of local categories of manhood. Compared to staying back in the village, going to work in India opened up possibilities of being modern and developed, exploring a distant place, and demonstrating the conception of manhood.

Rural young men are no longer interested in farming and do not see their future in rural areas. Development discourse, which views the village as a traditional place to be left in the past and urban areas as modern places to be desired (Pigg 1992), has impacted the meanings of migration in the local context. Thus, aside from the impact of the physical movement, migration to India or any other place has been a movement in the ideological space of development and modernity too. The significance of movement to India lies in the possibility of what it offers to the individual man who moves and his household and in how it relates to the experience of other men in the community. In the context of discourses of development this has had an effect of creating rural and urban areas as social categories of differentiation (Pigg 1992). A similar observation has been made by Mary Beth Mills in her study on young rural women involved in the migration process in Thailand. She argues that economic compulsion was often not the major driving force behind women's decision to migrate to Bangkok, but rather it was the desire to participate in a "modern" (*thansamay*) life (Mills 1999).

Conclusion

As we saw in this chapter, while significant differences exist, a particular scholarly construction is dominant in the production of a different sort of sociopolitical conception of hill society in Nepal. A quick review of studies shows that the conception of the rural population in Nepal as sedentary and immobile remains problematic and paradoxical given ethnographic and historical evidence that shows that different forms of migration have been an important part of life among the hill population in rural Nepal for many generations. This chapter has sought to challenge the explicit and implicit assumption that rural livelihoods in Nepal are dominated by agriculture and farming and that the solution to rural poverty lies in improving farming and the distribution of land.

Looking at different forms of migration makes it clear that conditions for out-migration from the hills of Nepal have been shaped by not only extractive state policies but also processes of social transformation taking place in the destinations of migration, whether they be encouragement by the British to migrate to northeastern India, recruitment into the British Army, the urban transformation in the Gulf countries or in Indian cities, or the developed economies of the North that rely on skilled manpower and flexible student labor. As we have seen, the structure of migration that encourages migration of individual male migrants has a particular gendered implication.

3

Leaving the Hills

Young men from the villages are no longer interested in farming, and they do not see their future in rural areas. In addition to the economic uncertainties and pressures, discourses of development, schooling, and modernity have contributed to the downgrading of farming as an occupation. Over the years, out-migration has become a rite of passage among the young men in rural Nepal. This chapter builds the argument that young men's strategic responses to livelihood insecurities in the hills of Nepal are shaped not just by wage differentiation and economic calculation but also by a complex set of gendered sociocultural considerations, particularly relating to ideas of modernity and masculinities. With a focus on local notions of masculinities, this chapter discusses how these shape the decision by men to migrate to India.

Decision Making

The question I posed in my fieldwork—Why do men go to work in India?—seemed irrelevant to those who were either working in India or lived in the households that sent young men to India. To most of the people I interacted with and studied, the question was foolish, and the answer self-explanatory. The practice of men going to work in India was simply considered the obvious choice as a part of managing the livelihoods of their households. While households that could afford it had men travel to the Gulf or other countries that were considered to be more attractive destinations, even though getting there was costly, the poorer households saw India as an obvious destination. Thus, the first thing to be said about this form of migration to India is that there is nothing exceptional about this practice. A more interesting question to consider concerns the conditions under which people made their decisions about migration. Although the neo-Marxist perspective shows the structural context in which these decisions are made, it provides very little insight into the actual process of decision making from the people's perspective. This structural perspective says little about the ways in which people experience their migration and what they themselves hope to gain from it.

The neo-Marxist framework overemphasizes the political-economic contexts that influence migration decisions, while simultaneously disregarding people as active agents in managing their livelihoods. A rational economic approach to migration tends to focus on economic decision making and consequently does not analyze the cultural, political, and social contexts in which these decisions are made. My fieldwork on migration to India shows that economic necessities are significant in determining choices people make about movement, but the motivations for such choices are far more complex and cannot be confined within the logic of economic rationality. This implies that the reason men go to work in India must be viewed in relation to a specific context in which the decision to move was taken, incorporating both social and cultural dimensions. Examining how households and the men who moved from them made decisions about workers going to a particular place in India gives insight into how these individuals are not just reacting to larger forces but are active in making decisions. Although each of the men interviewed had his own story and reason for going to India, the stories reflected several common experiences and themes. In the paragraphs that follow I discuss how men referred to the decision making and the organization of movement to India in relation to political economy, identity, family, and relationships. Examining the dynamics of this migration, I argue that migration is a gendered sociocultural process that can be understood within the framework of masculinity.

Practice of *Bhagne*

One of the common themes that ran through most of the stories of migration to India was *bhagne* (running away). *Bhagne* refers to adolescent boys leaving home as young as 10–12 years old without consulting their parents and going to different destinations in the Tarai and different cities in India.[1] Elderly members of the village said this was a common practice in village life, though I was repeatedly told that it had declined in recent years. Most of the adults and old men I interacted with in the village laughed when they recalled their own experiences of *bhagne.* The Nepali men working in Mumbai told me that they left home with their friends or others without informing their parents when they were young and later found some work and extended their stay. Their accounts indicated that it was a very common practice during the earlier days. During my fieldwork in Palpa, four local boys ran away, leaving their homes without informing or consulting their parents—this was a reduced number from times past. Until the late 1980s, *bhagne* was common, but in the previous few years it had become the exception among the adolescent boys. In recent years the emphasis on education and schooling had made a significant impact in reducing *bhagne.*

Children and adolescents were instead being encouraged to go to school, as it was widely believed that schooling opened up new prospects for social and economic mobility. Parents wanted their children to complete the School Leaving Certificate (SLC), which they believed would increase life chances for their children. Interaction with the parents and others in the village revealed that it was not considered right for the young boys to run away; it signified deviant behavior (*bigranu*). The parents of these young boys considered it a matter of shame (*lajmardo kura*) for the family and believed that their children must have run away under the influence of others (*aruko laha lahai ma lagera gayeko*). They instead wanted their children to go to school and prepare themselves for better prospects. While schooling was more common and this led to a reduction in *bhagne* from the village, there was evidence that the pressure of schooling and the discipline itself led to *bhagne* among several young boys. From the perspective of those involved, strict discipline, poor performance, and corporal punishment in the schools were the major reasons behind the boys' running away.

In terms of their attitude toward childhood and children, the Bahuns were more concerned about the discipline and control of their children than Magars. Among the Bahuns, the socialization of children involved strict control, with several disciplinary codes and punishment for deviant behavior. Children were perceived as minors who were not able to make their own decisions. For the adolescent Bahuns, *bhagne* provided a good escape from the strict control of their parents and the school. Among the Magars, most of them displayed a more liberal attitude toward childhood and children when compared to Bahuns. While the Magar parents told me that they would like their children to get educated and complete schooling, they did not display a moral panic, like Bahuns, when children went away without consulting them. One Magar mother whose 13-year-old son had left home a few months before told me that the decision had been made by her son, who was not doing well in school and whose only option, therefore, was to leave home and explore work opportunities. She heard that her son was working in Delhi and believed that he would be back in a few months, with or without money. She was not concerned about discussing her child's future prospects, and this was indicative of the idea that among the Magars *bhagne* was not always viewed as deviant.

An important aspect of *bhagne* behavior was that it was gendered—that is, it was always performed by adolescent boys.[2] Adolescent boys left home in small groups from the village, usually motivated and/or accompanied by some experienced men who worked in India or the Tarai, who came to their village for holidays. In most of the cases, the adolescent boys either borrowed money from their friends or stole money from their parents for their travel expenses. In a few cases, an experienced migrant financed travel expenses, took the boys along, and eventually found work for them. Those who were unaccompanied by experienced people usually took the address of some of their relatives or neighbors in their destination city and lived with them once they reached there. After spending a few weeks in one or two cities, some of them returned home, while others continued to work and came home only after earning some money. The boys usually sent letters or messages with someone with an apology for their behavior. At home, the parents were usually worried about the absence of their children unless they knew their whereabouts. Many of the Bahun parents went to look for their children or sent messages to the relatives working in the Tarai or India, while others believed that their children would return in a few months' time. From the perspective of the parents, it was important to find out whether their children went willingly with people they knew or whether they had gotten lost (*haraunu*). The biggest worry for the parents was establishing whether their children were safe. While none of the children or adolescents were lost from the village, rumors that strangers came to villages to kidnap children to sell them for organs such as kidneys were not uncommon. The people in the village were aware of the practices and discourses about trafficking from Nepal to India.

In Mumbai, I met a Magar boy who was 14 years old and was working as a domestic servant in the flat of a middle-class household in suburban Mumbai. He worked mostly in the home, cleaning the house, shopping, and washing dishes and clothes, among other things. He got about an hour's free time in the evening that he spent in the teashop where other Nepalis gathered. He had run away from a village in Palpa with two of his school friends about ten months previously. They had traveled with a distant relative who had been working in Mumbai for the previous two to three years. They were studying in the local school in the village until one day they decided to leave and travel to Mumbai. At the time the boy left the village, he was studying in class 4 (in primary school) and was an average student in his class. According to him, it was common for school children in his village to run away to India to work. He had two brothers, both married, who were working as manual laborers in Delhi, and two sisters, recently married. His parents (who were about 60) were small farmers who managed their farm and worked as agricultural labor in the village. He told me his father had worked in Delhi and Mumbai for more than twenty years while the children grew up. When the boy and his friends ran away, none of them informed their parents about leaving home to go to Mumbai. However, their parents came to know about them, as many other friends in the village knew about it. He secretly sold a hen from his home to cover the travel expenses. His distant relative who accompanied him found him a job that paid him about IRs 1,000 per month plus food and accommodation. He had already sent IRs 5,000 to his parents through a man from his village. For his parents, who didn't have a stable source of cash income, the money sent by their son was significant enough to meet their expenses for a few months. He planned to go home after a few months and to decide at that time if he wanted to continue working in Mumbai or continue his studies.

Similarly, a Bahun boy of 15 had left home in Palpa with a friend when he was 12. At that time his family was facing economic hardship, and there were frequent quarrels at home, so he decided to leave the family. He used the English word *tension* and Nepali phrase *dikka lagdo* (sad and annoyed) to explain the situation in his family. At that time he was studying in class 6, and his father wanted him to finish his SLC and then look for a secure employment or *jagir*. He knew that several men from his village were working in different cities in India and were earning money to contribute to the family. He too thought that, by going to Delhi, he would be able to work and earn some money. He left for Delhi with a friend who arranged money for the travel. Both of them left the village in the early morning and took the bus from the highway to the border town of Bhairahawa and then to Delhi. The friend who accompanied him was four to five years older than he was and had been to India earlier with his uncle.

After reaching Delhi, they went to a neighbor from their village who was working there and stayed with him. Within a week, the neighbor helped them to find a job in a shop and later in a hotel. After a month his friend left for home, but he continued to work there. Even after working for a year, he was not able to save money, as he was paid only IRs 600 per month. He then he went to work in Mumbai, and one of his brothers joined him. He worked as an assistant in an architecture firm, which paid him IRs 4,300 per month. His family members were happy with him. He was able to send about IRs 20,000–30,000 home annually and was satisfied with his work.

Young boys from the village often went to Indian cities (or sometimes to cities like Butwal in the plains) to wander around, see different places, go to the cinema, and engage in work, and within a few months later they would either return home or continue to work there. Though the *bhagne* did not necessarily lead to secure employment, it nonetheless provided freedom and opened up economic opportunities for these boys if they chose to stay and work. The experiences of *bhagne* meant that the boys left as minors but transformed themselves into adults by the time they returned home. Before going away, these young adolescents had heard about life in the cities through the radio, returning migrants, and their school textbooks, and they believed that the *bhagne* would open up avenues to see new places and explore opportunities for work. Many of them were able to learn to work and save some money through these experiences.

In Palpa, almost any conversation on *bhagne* was full of giggles and laughter that signified its association with fun, excitement, and a desire to see a distant place. Most of the men with careers of migration to India started with *bhagne* and continued from there. This has implications for understanding the practice of *bhagne* as a rite of passage to adulthood. At the same time, as discussed earlier, ethnic dimensions are important to understanding the meaning and significance of *bhagne* among the village men. Unlike Magars, who displayed a more liberal attitude toward childhood and children, the high-caste Bahuns, who socialized children with strict control and severe disciplinary codes, clearly

For young men, work in India provided an escape from plowing the fields. (Photo by Jeevan R. Sharma.)

Schooling had a major impact on young men's decisions to leave the village. (Photo by Jeevan R. Sharma.)

understood *bhagne* as deviant behavior. And, under the influence of global discourses on child rights and increased emphasis on schooling and completion of the SLC, *bhagne* became increasingly viewed as a problem and not a normal practice.

Although *bhagne* did not always lead to employment, it nonetheless provided a wider experience of travel and offered exposure to new things for the young men. They enjoyed the freedom and learned about the wider world away from their home village and away from the strict control of their parents. Young boys spent a few months wandering as runaways, without necessarily being economically productive, and this was socially accepted.

Survival Strategy

Despite the long tradition of *bhagne*, most of the men I spoke to emphasized that they left for India because of the situation back home (*ghar ko awastha*). They referred to migration to India as an escape from the difficult economic conditions and as an opportunity to improve their socioeconomic situations and fulfill their obligations as "good men." Men were unable to secure the material needs of the household, and thus it was a natural response for them to look for opportunities to earn cash. This was best reflected in the case of a young unmarried Bahun of 19, who was working as a helper in a restaurant in Mumbai, leaving behind his parents and two young sisters. When I reached his house in Palpa, his father was lying on a mat made of straw (*gundri*) on a veranda (*pirhi*) outside the house. Suffering from diabetes and tuberculosis, he could barely function. His mother was busy working on a piece of dry land (*bari*) beside their small hut, while two of his sisters (ages 6 and 7) were playing in the courtyard with other children from the neighborhood. The condition of the house and the appearance of the family members showed that the household was relatively poor. They owned insufficient land to provide them with grain for the entire year. Depending on the situation, they had to buy grain for four to six months. The father had been working as a security guard (*caukidar*) in Delhi for seventeen years, which had provided crucial income for the household, but he had fallen ill two years before and had not been able to return to work. This meant that the responsibility for earning money had fallen to the son, and the only option available was to follow in the footsteps of his father and other relatives who had been going to India for work. Eventually, he went to Mumbai, supported by his uncle who lived next door. He was excited when his mother told him about the possibility of going to Mumbai with his uncle, and he immediately accepted it. Though he had heard a lot about Mumbai and many of his friends had been to India, he had never had a chance to go to Mumbai. His uncle took complete responsibility for paying the fare, accompanying him, and finding work.

When I met him in a tea stall next to his workplace in Mumbai, he told me that he had been able to send money home on a regular basis. He was planning to go home in the next three months but expected to come back to work after a month. When asked why he had decided to come to Mumbai, he said, "The situation at my home (*gharko awastha*) was not good, so I came with my uncle to find work." As the only able-bodied man in the family, he felt that he was responsible (*jimmawar*) for earning money and regularly sending it back home to ensure the smooth functioning of their household (*ghar chalaune, ghar herne*). Though he did not believe that it was possible for him to earn a lot of money, he believed that it was possible to earn reasonable money and improve his family's situation back home (*kehi awastha sudharne, kehi ramro hola bhanera*). To him, earning money to support his family was vital to his identity as a son (Osella and Osella 2000). He was particularly concerned about the health of his father and the education and marriage of his two little sisters, and the family's future. While his situation seemed to have been triggered by his father's illness, the practice of going to India was not uncommon in his family history and immediate social network. His situation is similar to that described by Osella and Osella in the context of southern India:

> For boys in the poorest labouring families, adolescence hardly exists: they move from an impoverished and de-

prived childhood in which their parents are unable to protect them from the knowledge of adult realities into a young
manhood, which immediately demands that they take their
share of responsibility by dealing with those realities. Taking
on responsibilities at home, bringing cash and paddy, building a new thatched house—all this enables a boy to enter the
men's world. (Osella and Osella 2006: 40)

He was considered a good son among the poor laboring households in the village. Nevertheless, because the work was temporary,
poorly paid, and insecure, his effort to go to India and provide
for his family was ridiculed in the village context, where finding
secure employment as *jagire* or *lahure* dominates the hegemonic
styles of masculinity.

While the practice of going to India for work offered socioeconomic mobility for only a few, it nonetheless played an important role in sustaining the cash needs of most of the households.
A few people became quite successful, like a Bahun man of 30,
who initially came to India as a domestic worker at the rate of
IRs 300 per month but was now managing an expensive guesthouse and earning more than IRs 30,000 per month. This kind of
example meant that people saw Mumbai as a land of possibilities
and opportunities. After this man completed his schooling, he
had a choice either to study in Kathmandu with the support of
his maternal uncle or to follow in his father's footsteps and go to
India to contribute to the household expenses and the education
of his younger siblings. He went to India with a neighbor and
started working as a domestic worker. He later went to Mumbai to work as an assistant in a guesthouse, which was arranged
by his maternal uncle. After more than five years, he was managing the guesthouse on a contract basis and was able to earn
a good amount of money. Following his economic success, his
entire family moved to the Tarai, where they bought some agricultural land and built a house. By village standards, this was a
significant achievement. He was extremely busy in managing the
guesthouse, always wore formal suits, and the security guard at
the entrance of his building always referred to him as "big man"

(*bada admi*). The ability to earn money and improve the socio-economic status of the family was crucial to his identity as a successful man.

While the socioeconomic situation of the household played an important role in the Bahun man's decision to migrate to India, his responsibility as a man in the family appeared to be crucial in this process. Such migration was not only a reaction to economic desperation. It is equally worth noting that not only impoverished young men from the village migrate to India. Even members of village households with teachers and local political leaders as well as members of well-to-do households have gone to India to find work. In recent years opportunities have arisen, for those who could afford it, to migrate to other foreign countries, mostly in the Gulf or Southeast Asian countries, for work. Thus, although it was the most obvious option available for those from the poorer households in the hills of Nepal, they were not the only ones who migrated to India for work.

Escaping Relationships

Migration to India was not always characterized by a need to work and provide for the family. The experience of several men showed that migration was an escape from difficult relationships at home. One Bahun man of 38 from a relatively well-off household in Palpa, who was working as an assistant in a doctor's clinic in suburban Mumbai, told me that he escaped because he could not cope with the pressure to be a successful son. Frustrated with his inability to run a business and make substantial profit, he escaped to India without telling his family. A few years earlier he had seen the potential for business in steel roofing and had opened a shop in a nearby town, which was fully supported by his father. Despite strong protest from his brothers, who were more or less established in different sectors in Nepal (a civil servant, a local political leader, and a teacher), he decided to go ahead with his plan of starting the business. His lack of know-how in running a business meant that he was unable to collect money from the creditors and went bankrupt within two years. This was a humiliating experience for him, and he found it difficult to face his family and other relatives. He left home for India at the age of 24 with NRs 5,000 in his pocket. At that time he did not have any idea about where to go or what to do. He told me, "I felt like running away." With no previous experience or contact, he went to the Indian town of Gorakhpur and took a train to Mumbai. Though he had never been to Mumbai, he decided to go to there on the spur of the moment when he saw a train leaving the station. He had heard of Mumbai in his village from relatives and neighbors, and his father had been there. On the train journey he met two men from the neighboring district who were going back to work in Mumbai. A friendship developed on the train, and he lived with them for fifteen days before finding the job with the doctor as his assistant. Though initially he did not plan to work for very long, later he felt strongly that he needed to earn some money before he could return home. Back at home, everybody was worried about his absence. There were rumors that he had died, while other rumors circulated that he had lost his leg. His father came to know of his whereabouts from someone in the village and visited him after two years. Though his father wanted him to return home, he insisted that he would not return unless he had earned a substantial amount of money to pay his father. After six years, he returned home and got married. After fifteen years of work in Mumbai, he had earned a good amount of money. Though he lived in a shared room in a slum, he had used his savings to buy two rooms[3] worth IRs 300,000 in the same slum. He believed that the situation in Mumbai was far more favorable for his children and wife than the situation at home. He was looking for better housing outside the slum so that his wife and children could join him. His case suggests that though money was certainly an important part of his decision to migrate to India, the move was closely linked to protecting his masculinity. He went to India primarily to escape the humiliation of being labeled an unsuccessful man by his family and the community.

The following two cases show how movement to India can be

a strategy to deal with relationship problems at the family level. For a Magar man of 25 from Palpa, it was his romantic relationship with a girl from a lower caste three years before that had led him to determine to go to Mumbai. His decision to marry a girl from a different caste was not accepted by his family. Though he had hoped that his family would eventually accept her (*bhitraune*), it had not happened, even after more than a year of their marriage. Furthermore, he was repeatedly pressured to leave his wife if he wanted his share of *ansha* (the family property). While he had been to Delhi before for a short time with his friends when he was 14, this time he decided to leave for Mumbai with the support of his friends and in-laws already working in Mumbai, who provided him with the necessary financial and social support to find work. As a man, his decision to go to Mumbai was prompted by the need to find a means of income to support his new family, and to escape from the everyday problems he faced in the village. At the time he had a one-and-a-half-year-old child. He noted that it was not an easy choice for him to sever ties with his parents but that his wife and child had to come first.

Similarly, both the culture of migration and infertility seemed crucial elements in the decision of a 52-year-old Bahun man from Palpa who had been going to India since he was 15. When he was young, he went to Delhi with his friends for fun. When the money he had stolen from his father ran out, he worked in a hotel (restaurant) for three months to enable him to earn his bus fare to return home. Since then he had been to different parts of India, including Delhi, Bangalore, and Calcutta and had several years of experience in Mumbai. He had a total of more than twenty-eight years of working life in India. He married at the age of 19. Despite trying for four years and undergoing various treatments, he and his wife did not have children. Listening to the advice of a local healer, he married again at age 23 without the consent of his family. He had severed his relations with his family members and relatives when he remarried in the hope that he would have children, but this did not occur. He went to Mumbai after his second wife ran away, blaming him for infertility. He had been left with virtually no social support in the village, and he found it difficult to live in the village under the new circumstances.

People in Palpa mentioned several men and women who left the village when relationships between families and neighbors soured or when people were alleged to have been engaged in illegal and illicit activities, such as murder or theft. In other cases, young men and girls ran away to India when they married a partner of their choice without their parents' consent, particularly when it involved cross-caste marriage.

These cases show that migration to India occurs not only in relation to work and providing for the family. Migration allowed these men an escape from difficult situations in their families and relationships.

Violent Conflict

Nepal's Maoist insurgency (1996–2005) had a major impact on rural Nepal. What initially started as a rural insurgency in the midwestern hills of Nepal eventually spread to other parts of Nepal, impacting the security, life, and livelihoods of a large number of people. Those in rural areas like Palpa found themselves caught between Maoist intimidation and forced donation on one hand and police or Nepali army reprisals on the other. During my 2004–2005 fieldwork, there were frequent ambushes and confrontations between state forces and the Maoist insurgents in and around my fieldwork area. Strikes and roadblocks constrained the mobility of people in the study area. Daily commutes between the town and the village and between villages were scrutinized by the warring parties. In Palpa, Maoist activists had targeted government employees for extortion (often called "donation"), and those employed by the police and army were forced to give up their jobs or risk their lives by becoming informants for the Maoist activists. Security forces frequently questioned and interrogated people in the village, including health workers and teachers, significantly reducing people's mobility. Men in Palpa referred to the escalating conflict in Nepal as prompting them to migrate to India in search of security and livelihoods. To indicate those who saw their migration as a means of escape from political conflict in the country, the men frequently used the phrase "caught in the middle" to refer to being stuck between the then Royal Nepal Army and the Maoists. There were a few cases in which the political instability, particularly the Maoist movement, had affected them directly, and that was the reason for making decisions about migration. A married man age 29 from Palpa had quit his position with the Royal Nepal Army because of pressure from the Maoist activists in his village. His job was a main source of income for his family. Although when I had met him in India, he had denied to me that he had quit his job out of intimidation, the timing of having quit during the state of emergency led people in the village to refer to Maoist intimidation as the primary impetus. He told me that the (political) situation in Nepal was not very good, and that he had a responsibility to look after his mother, his wife, and two children back in the village. People in his village believed that his resignation had not been accepted by the army, and that therefore he had fled (*bhagnu*) to India. He had secretly returned home only once.

A Magar man of 22, who was a domestic worker in Mumbai, had left home to avoid trouble from security forces back in Palpa after his brother had joined the Maoist militia. Though he was sympathetic to the Maoist insurgency and supported his brother's involvement, he did not join the armed militia because his parents needed to be looked after. He found it difficult to stay in the village as the Royal Nepal Army men often came and abused his relatives and friends, who were sympathetic to the Maoist insurgency. Later, his mother arranged for him to go to Mumbai with his maternal uncle, who was already working there. A Bahun man of 25, who worked as an assistant to a medical doctor in Mumbai, shared a similar story. Trained as a health assistant, he had left Nepal the year before, after he found it extremely difficult to continue to run his private clinic close to his native village. He had to cope with the pressure to treat the Maoist activists when they were injured in the conflict. At the same time there was surveillance and a threat from the Royal Nepal Army. Apart from the risks, his business was going quite well, and he was able to earn good money. The threat from the escalating conflict had meant that he was pressured by his in-laws to close the clinic and go to Mumbai, with the support of his brother-in-law, who was already working there. Eventually, as told by his in-laws, he left behind his wife and children when he went to Mumbai. Though he missed his wife and children, he did not have plans to bring them to Mumbai, as he saw his migration as short term. He wanted to return to Nepal and open a clinic somewhere else, if not in his previous place, but his in-laws had been pressuring him to find "regular and stable work" and stay in Mumbai until the risk was reduced. Though he was trying to find work in urban areas in Nepal, he believed that he did not have the right "connections" (*aafno manche*) or enough money to do so. Without social networks and connections, often based on kinship networks, it is very difficult for a young village man to find a job or start a business in cities.

While there was widespread talk that the political instability and the Maoist conflict had led to an increase in the number of people going to Mumbai in recent years, except for a handful of people who were directly forced to out-migrate as a result of conflict, I did not find evidence that the conflict had suddenly or significantly escalated out-migration. Furthermore, interaction with Nepali migrants in India showed a complicated relationship between the escalation of conflict and migration to India. It was extremely difficult to conclude that the violent conflict had led young men to flee from the village. The fact that several men went to India at the time of escalating violent conflict made it easy to speculate that their migration was triggered by conflict, but the existence of the ongoing practice of migration to India in their households and social networks made it difficult to single out the conflict as the reason for their migration to India. Any inference on this aspect of Nepali society, without a careful study, should be treated with caution.

This range of stories about the decision making around migration shows that migration to work in Indian cities is a part of men's life in the hills of Nepal. One particular characteristic of those who went to work in India was that most of them were unmarried when they started to go to India. Such migration offered an escape from difficult situations at home and was viewed as a way of dealing with such situations. In particular I have shown that such difficulties were very much related to the masculine identities and the responsibilities of men in the hills of Nepal, and the decision to migrate was prompted by their desire to protect or prove their status as men. For the village men, life in the village would not always offer opportunities for demonstrating masculine pride, and in many situations might even constrain it. It was in this context that these men viewed their migration as a possibility to attain their masculine identity by being able to secure some money, experience a distant place, and return to reintegrate themselves within the village life.

Conclusion

Young men's decisions to leave the hill villages were informed in part by their desire to escape farming and the regimented life in the villages. The development discourse has had considerable impact on the decisions of young men to migrate. Such discourses have inspired young men to leave farming to go to school and have also led to their perception of rural life as better left behind in favor of urban life. Men's decisions to migrate to India show that while economic considerations seem quite important in determining the choices they make about migration, the choices are, in fact, far more complex, as they are embedded in gendered sociocultural norms, meanings, and expectations. Men's migration to work in Indian cities does not automatically earn respect for them when compared to other opportunities for out-migration, such as attaining secure employment inside or outside Nepal, being recruited into the army, or going to work in the Gulf or in Southeast Asian countries. Nevertheless, it was the only available option for many young men who desperately wanted to avoid being stuck in their village. It offered the young men an opportunity to escape the regimented order in the village, travel, earn some money, and (if they were able to eventually find secure employment) potentially transform their economic and social standing. Given the existing networks, India was an obvious destination for young men from poorer backgrounds who could afford to travel across the border in search of freedom and experience.

4

Border Crossing

This chapter discusses border crossing from the vantage point of Nepali migrants. Not only do the border and its regime play a central role in keeping a separation between, on one hand, production from labor in the destination and, on the other hand, the reproduction of the labor force in the source communities (Burawoy 1976); the very act of crossing the border plays a key role in disciplining young Nepali men and turning them into docile migrants. In other words, the act of border crossing, whether it is going toward India to work or returning home to Nepal, has an effect on the gendered and class subjectivities of the migrants. Nepali migrants' desire to cross the border into India is informed by ideas of freedom from the constraint of life in the rural hills, but the very act of border crossing, paradoxically, takes freedom away from these migrants by subjecting them to interrogation, extortion, frisking, ill-treatment, and humiliation.

Border

Borders are traditionally defined as international boundaries between nation-states (Alvarez 1995: 449). The idea of state sovereignty is intrinsically linked to the state's control over its territory and is a precondition for state coherence. Borders are thus political constructs and reflect the imaginary of politicians, intellectuals, lawyers, and state agencies (Baud and Van Schendel 1997: 211). National boundaries are shown clearly in the maps of states and international agencies, and they have become the subject of intense debate and discussion in the movement of population, goods, and natural water resources. "Border" in this sense means both the literal boundary that demarcates two states and works to create and sustain a difference and a range of technologies of governance that define it and make it real (Kearney 2004b: 132). People, animals, goods, rivers, and forests that cross the border are subject to various forms of regulation by the states.

Methodological nationalism, which takes the nation-state as a unit of analysis, has contributed significantly to the relatively unknown field of borders and borderlands in social sciences. More recently, a number of anthropological studies have emerged that look at the border from the vantage point of those who live in the borderland and those who cross it. Within border studies, scholars have looked at the border both in its literal sense (i.e., concerned with formal geopolitical boundaries) and in a metaphorical sense (i.e., culturally) (Kearney 2004b). This chapter is primarily concerned with the former, from the vantage point of migrants, without ignoring the latter.

Michael Kearney suggests that boundaries and their corresponding border regimes have two missions. The first mission is a "classificatory" one that serves to define and categorize the identities of persons who are divided by borders and those who cross them. These identity categories include nationality, language, ethnicity, and the markers of social class. The second mission of borders is to filter the economic "value" that flows across them; in doing so, borders usually serve to uphold class structures and inequalities (Kearney 2004b: 133). In short, a border's mission is one of deciphering and filtering.

No matter what the missions of the border may be, its significance to national sovereignty, or how it upholds various regulations, people have always ignored these borders and regulations when it has suited them (Baud and Van Schendel 1997: 211). Generally speaking, there has always been an enormous gap between the rhetoric of border maintenance and daily life in borderlands (Baud and Van Schendel 1997: 220). The political need to maintain the border operates using a very different logic from that of the everyday lives of people who rely on crossing the border. "Premodern" borders in northern South Asia are fuzzy and contested, and local populations often carry on daily life across them regardless of any border regime (Gellner 2013a).

Nepal-India Border

One of the first things to point out about the Nepal-India border is its paradoxical nature—that is, it is a border where a regional and emerging power meets a poor country. In terms of territorial size, population, and development, there is little comparison between India and Nepal. As a land-locked country surrounded by India, Nepal is economically dependent on India, and its only access to international trade is through India. Along with cultural, ethnic, linguistic, economic, and political continuities and spillovers run inequalities and differences between the two countries. These similarities are reflected in cross-border kinship networks, marriage practices, language, culture, and shared history. The differences become more pronounced as a result of different economic and political systems, which provide distinct entitlements and benefits, that govern the populations on either side of the boundary. Nepal borders with India on three sides—west, east, and south—and with China to the north. Nepal and India share an "open border" of more than 1,751 kilometers without any clear demarcation. The history of this open border between India and Nepal probably goes back to the nineteenth century, after the demarcation of the India-Nepal boundary in 1816 in the Treaty of Sugauli following the Anglo-Nepal war of 1814–1815. The Nepal-India Peace and Friendship Treaty of 1950 and the letters of exchange that followed the treaty speak explicitly about the open nature of the Nepal-India border. Article 7 of the treaty states, "The governments of India and Nepal agree to grant, on a reciprocal basis, to the nationals of one country in the territories of the other the same privileges in the matter of residence, ownership of property, participation in trade and commerce, movement and other privileges of a similar nature."[1] It is to be noted that the treaty does not explicitly mention the phrase "open border," although there is a clear provision of equal and reciprocal privileges to the nationals of both states. The border, however, is not without controversy and boundary disputes—smuggling, trafficking, and the infiltration of criminals and "terrorists" all occur. The India-Nepal border is guarded by SSB (Sashastra Seema Bal), an Indian security force that was founded in 1963 to win the hearts and minds of people in the Northeast and the Himalayas following the India-China war of 1962.

Three aspects characterize the "open" nature of the Nepal-India border. *First,* although there are several conflicts and disputes between the two countries on the issue of police atrocities, ill-treatment of migrants who cross the border, encroachment, smuggling, mobility of criminals, floods, diversions and dams, and there is widespread perception that India has intensified the security apparatus at the India-Nepal border, the border is not securitized like other borders such as India-Bangladesh or India-Pakistan in South Asia. *Second,* formalized by the treaty of 1950, the authorities allow the citizens of both countries to cross the border without having to produce official documentation and offers equal treatment to citizens of both countries, at least in policy, while the movement of goods is allowed along twenty-two designated transit points with custom regulations on both sides. *Third,* the Nepal-India border can be categorized as an "interdependent borderland," using the typology constructed by Oscar Martínez (1994), where both sides of the border are linked by regular economic, familial, and human resource flows crossing the border itself (Hausner and Sharma 2013). People move freely across the border for everyday affairs, including shopping, selling of goods, going to schools, visiting health facilities, and meeting relatives. This is shaped by close cultural and economic continuities and spillovers, as people continue to share language, marriage, and familial relations.

Despite these spillovers and continuities, several issues have contributed to strain the relationship between the two countries. This has caused some factions, in both Nepal and India, to call for greater regulation and tightening of the border. Nationalistic sentiments on the Nepalese side decry the economic consequences of out-migration of able-bodied men to India, the harassment of Nepali migrant workers in India (or of Indian migrants in Nepal), and the trafficking of Nepali women and children into India. Other subjects that have contributed to debates on border control and its management include smuggling and illicit trade across the border, movements of those involved in crime and "terrorism," the lack of citizenship cards in Nepal's Tarai, boundary disputes, flooding, and the perception of inequality in water resource sharing. For example, the sanctions imposed by India in 1989 and more recently in 2015–2016, the Maoist insurgency in Nepal and its links with Indian Maoists, ethnic conflict in Nepal's Tarai, the hijacking of an Indian Airlines flight from Kathmandu airport, and various terrorism-related incidents in India have all escalated the border control debate. Given the significant differences in population size between the two countries, Nepal saw a heated debate in 1980s and 1990s on the implications of an open border for demographic imbalance and citizenship.

Both the colonial regime in India and earlier Nepali rulers had an interest in keeping the border relatively free. The open border facilitated the flow of cheap labor in both directions, but more specifically from Nepal to India in the form of recruitment of men from the hills into the British Army. As a part of the tripartite agreement between Nepal, India, and the United Kingdom signed in November 1947, Nepal allowed the recruitment of Gurkhas into the Indian Army, primarily because it faced the burden of rehabilitating 200,000 soldiers discharged from the British Indian Army at the end of World War II. The Ranas, who then ruled Nepal, also feared that the well-trained but unemployed Gurkhas might pose a threat to their rule. For India, the recruitment of the Gurkhas was a foreign policy tool to garner goodwill among the people of Nepal (Das 2008: 881).

Similarly, the open border facilitated the flow of raw materials from Nepal into India, and, conversely, Nepal has been a market for Indian manufactured goods and commodities.

The Nepal-India border has come under increasing scrutiny from policy makers, academics, and civil society, with some calling for strict management of the border while others support maintaining the unique arrangement of the open border. There is widespread perception in the media that the border is being increasingly securitized, with the Indian side escalating the presence of security personnel and establishing checkpoints. Migrants who travel across the border are regularly subjected to ill-treatment.

Journey

James Clifford provides an interesting metaphor of "routes" (which is the title of his book) to argue that "routes" and not "roots" are central to understanding human society. Arguing that "every man . . . was a traveller," he contends that traveling rather than dwelling is an important area for study (Clifford 1997). Clifford's insights are very useful in studies of migration, which have mostly been based on either the sending or receiving context, particularly when considering what goes on during travel. Therefore, understanding the experience of migrant hill men who go to work in India requires us to study not just the places they leave and arrive in, but also their journeys. I address this gap in the literature by describing the travel experience of these men. This account is based on my own experience traveling with a group of three men who were on their way from Palpa to Mumbai. Characterized by ambiguity and insecurity, their travel experience demonstrated that the border is a liminal site where migrants stand on the threshold of renegotiating their identities.

Crossing the Sunauli Border

Almost every day on my way to the village in Palpa from the town of Tansen, I observed men leaving for India in groups of three or

five, and often there were a few young men accompanied by a
returnee on his way back to India. They made their way to Tansen
to catch a bus to Butwal, a town in the Tarai about forty kilometers
away. Playing loud popular Bollywood music, the buses to Butwal
depart every twenty to thirty minutes from the noisy bus park in
Tansen carrying about twenty to forty passengers. It takes about
two to three hours to travel to Butwal, which had frequent buses
to the border at Sunauli, which was about thirty kilometers away
and would take another hour by bus.

The journey to India is long and offers, in addition to excitement, significant risks of being cheated or robbed. Depending
on the precise destination, it takes about two to four days to
reach India—the group I joined took two days to reach Mumbai from the Nepal border. Traveling through the Tarai and cities like Butwal, many migrants hear from others about bitter
experiences of suffering illness and being robbed and cheated.
These stories include frightening encounters with dangerous
people from the different culture of the plains and the experience of being asked to pay the fare more than once on local
transport. People spoke of consuming food that knocked them
unconscious and of being robbed in the hotels. Men take precautions by traveling in groups and keeping money hidden in
their inside pockets; they avoid eating anything given to them
by strangers and staying overnight in hotels. Places like Gorakhpur and Sunauli—the border towns—are considered to be the
worst offenders. These towns are particularly treacherous when
migrants are attempting to return home with their savings and
gifts for their families.

I traveled with a group of three men from Palpa going to work
in Mumbai, after meeting them in Bhairahawa, a commercial town
on the Nepali side of the border.[2] Two (Hari and Anil)[3] were traveling for the first time, while the third man (Kumar) was returning to his work in Mumbai after spending three weeks at home. I
knew both Hari and Anil, who were young men, but I had not met
Kumar before, who was older and related to both young men.

With his fifteen years of work experience in Mumbai, Kumar
was our leader. He told us that it was important to look confident

at the border crossing; otherwise, it was possible to be harassed by police or other officials, including "strange-looking people" (referring to thugs the police turn a blind eye toward) trying to cheat migrants. He told us that we needed to be extremely careful while traveling, as people could not be trusted in this part of the journey. Because of the heat and our fear, the group felt a mounting anxiety as we left Bhairahawa. After getting off the bus, we took two rickshaws at the Sunauli border to reach the bus station on the other side, where we could get a bus to the train station in Gorakhpur. Our fear and anxiety must have been evident, because as our rickshaws were heading toward the border crossing, two policemen standing at the side of the road beckoned us. They stopped our rickshaw, looked through our bags suspiciously, and began to ask questions in authoritative voices. Where had we come from? Where did we want to go and why? Though questioning is a regular occurrence at the border, it was nonetheless frightening and humiliating. The day was very hot, and the road was full of dust, with several vehicles crossing both ways. The border appeared a strange place, with many large, loaded trucks waiting to cross along with rickshaws and many other travelers. We could see as we crossed officials with customs, immigration, police, and an anti-trafficking NGO named Maiti Nepal.

Apart from having commercial advertisements, the border was a site of trafficking, reflected by the billboards at the border area and in the activities of NGOs like Maiti Nepal (Hausner 2005), which had a small office at the Sunauli border with two members of staff constantly checking the movement of women and children over the border. At the time of the border crossing, I saw a Nepali family (a man and woman with their 16- to 18-year-old son and daughter) being questioned by Maiti Nepal's staff. Another couple crossing the border was also stopped and questioned. The frustrated husband was trying to convince the staff that his wife was accompanying him to Mumbai, where he worked, but the officials did not believe him. He had never had to prove to anyone in the village that he and his wife were married. Initially, the wife kept quiet, but later she angrily accused the staff of creating an unnecessary problem. The couple did not have a Village Development Committee letter of recommendation, which the Maiti Nepal staff requested. It was the fact that the wife was arguing their case that eventually allowed them to move on. Other people in the queues remarked that this was a typical scene at the border. Later I met the couple in the railway station in Gorakhpur, and they told me that they were unnecessarily hassled by "those people," as the wife referred to the Maiti Nepal staff. During our conversation, the wife asked me, "Now you tell me, now [if] we need documents to prove that we are husband and wife, why don't they go to our village and ask for it?" It was considered extremely difficult for women to cross the border, and almost everybody I spoke to had experienced this. The helpless husband stood beside his wife and smiled at me as his wife continued to complain.

As we entered the Indian side of the border, our rickshaw was stopped by the Indian police and then by Indian immigration. They asked us: Where had we come from? Where were we going? What were we carrying? While we did not face significant trouble from the officials at the border crossing, the experience of facing different types of officials made us feel very vulnerable. The threat of ill-treatment and extortion at the hands of these different officials was obvious to us. One of them jokingly asked if we were Maoist insurgents or had any links with the Maoists. The border-crossing experience continued with encounters with a series of officials and men.

Before we reached the bus stop, our rickshaw was stopped by two intimidating men who wanted us to buy bus tickets from them to travel on their bus. Scared as we were, we said that we would like to go by jeep (which is much faster and more comfortable for the same price), but they forced us to buy tickets from them and to travel on their bus. When I objected, they physically forced us to take the tickets and to travel in the crowded bus, standing for the three-hour trip to Gorakhpur. While I had traveled to India by road as a student before—always with my middle-class friends, dressed well, and interacting with the officials in English—I had never been treated this way. When I resisted (in Hindi), we were told, "Go. . . . [G]o back to Nepal. . . .

[Y]ou don't get anything in your home, so you come. . . . [G]o. . . . [G]o run" (*Chalo. . . . [C]halo bhago Nepal jāo. . . . [K]uch khaneko nahi milta, phir chale aate ho. . . . [C]halo. . . . [C]halo. . . . [B]hago*). I was pulled aside by Kumar, who asked me not to argue. He told me that this was a very common experience at the border and advised me to stay quiet. The experience was threatening, as we found ourselves helpless. Although I was a Nepali citizen myself, I stood out as being of a different class from the men I was traveling with. It is possible that my presence made a difference to the way the men I was traveling with were treated, and they were treated less harshly than they otherwise would have been.

On the bus, many Nepali men were watching over one another, which gave me a sense of relief. A song from a Bollywood film was playing loudly in the background. A man working in the Indian Army (*lahure*) was standing next to me on the bus. Referring to the use of force, he told the conductor that he should let the passengers choose the bus they wanted and that they should be given a seat. The conductor responded by becoming aggressive and speaking abusively. It was a highly tense and frightening situation as the conductor and his associate tried to drag this *lahure* off the bus. Realizing he had no choice, after resisting being ejected, the humiliated *lahure* and everyone else simply kept quiet. This was a particularly poignant result, because although a *lahure* is considered to be a brave man, in this instance his vulnerability was obvious and he had no choice but to remain silent.

We finally reached Gorakhpur, a crowded city, where many Nepalis congregate at the railway station. Just outside the railway station were several Nepali restaurants and lodgings aimed at Nepalis. On the railway platforms many Nepali men waited for trains going to various places. Some of them had reservations, while others were planning to travel via the waiting list and/or the crowded third class. We stood in the queue for about two hours and finally managed to get our tickets via the waiting list. In the meantime, we were approached by several ticket brokers who promised to get us confirmed tickets. We declined these offers, as such brokers were known for cheating and issuing fake tickets. Several other Nepalis waiting in the railway station preferred to group together and stay prepared to foil any attempt to cheat them. We were aware that the brokers were attempting to cheat us because we looked like typical migrants. The train finally approached the platform, and we joined the crowd boarding the train. Though we did not have reservations, we went into the reservation coach in the hope of securing seats with a bribe. After paying IRs 250 extra for each person, we managed to get seats to Mumbai, a journey of thirty-six hours. The other option for travel was to sit on the floor in the same coach or move to the crowded third-class coach, which had hardly any space even for standing passengers. The train was a new experience for the two young men in our group, which prompted a long conversation about the railway in India, travelers, and different places. On the coach we met other Nepalis—a group of four men from Syangja and two groups of families from Palpa—returning to work in Mumbai and Pune after spending their holidays at home.

The tension was palpable when the ticket taker (known as TT) and police came around, making everyone in our group feel self-conscious and vulnerable. The man from Syangja told us about harassment that he and his cousin experienced from the TT when they were traveling together. The TT had approached them and asked for their tickets but did not return the tickets to them. After three to four minutes the TT returned and asked for the tickets again. When they told him that he had taken their tickets just a few minutes before, he threatened them. Finally they had to pay IRs 400 each to continue traveling. This kind of experience was not limited to Nepalis, however: it was common for many travelers.

But the journey was also fun. The excitement of seeing new places, eating different types of food, and traveling in the train was apparent in the group. The journey included singing songs, playing cards, and conversation that compared life in Mumbai with life back in the hills. During the journey, Nepalis generally trust other Nepalis in matters like looking after the luggage. From the perspective of people from the hills, to be perceived as trustworthy, you need to look like a *pahadi* (with the racial features of a hill person) and speak Nepali, and it helps even more if you come from a neighboring district. During the conversation, a few people developed friendships after discovering that they knew the same person or had something else (Nepali politics or a favorite movie) in common. Here it is useful to draw a comparison with Nepalis' issues and identity in India (Hutt 1997; Subba and Sinha 2003).

Crossing the Border in Mahendranagar

More recently, in 2010, I crossed the border in Mahendranagar by *tanga* (horse-drawn carriage) with three young men who were leaving for Delhi. The *tanga* took an hour and half to cross a twelve-kilometer border zone from Mahendranagar, on the Nepal side, to Banbasa, an Indian market town where we could get buses for our onward journey. Our *tanga* crossed the Nepali checkpoint just before the no-man's land. It was guarded by armed Nepali police who did not stop us. After the checkpoint on the Nepal side, we continued on a dirt road. After about five minutes, the *tanga* helper asked us to get off, and we had to stand in a queue to be questioned and inspected by a member of India's border force (known as Sashastra Seema Bal). The armed police looked inside my bag and asked if I was a student. I told him that I was going to Nainital for my holidays, and he let me go without further questions. Each and every traveler was questioned, and their bags inspected. As we remounted the *tanga* and continued, we found that the border gate was closed. It was 6:15 P.M., and we were told that the border gate closed at 6:00 P.M. We were told that this was a regular occurrence and the gate would open after paying a bribe to the official who controlled it. The helper of our *tanga* collected five Indian rupees from each passenger, passed it to the official, and the gate opened after about twenty minutes.

I also did fieldwork with Nepali migrants in Uttrakhand and Himanchal in India on this trip, and I returned to Nepal through the Banbasa-Gaddichauki border. Once, when I got off the local bus in the Indian border town of Banbasa, several rickshaw pullers approached me and other travelers who were continuing the journey toward the Nepal border. I saw a couple of young boys and a middle-aged man together who were from Jumla: two of them were carrying rucksacks and another was carrying a plastic sack, and they were also being approached by another rickshaw puller. I joined them to cross the border, and we fixed the price of IRs 30 for each rickshaw after bargaining for a few minutes. However, when we reached halfway, both the rickshaw pullers stopped their rickshaws and asked for us IRs 50 for each rickshaw. Frustrated with such a demand, we tried to convince them, saying that we were returning home and that we also had to work hard to earn money, but finally we had to give in to their demands for the higher price to drop us at the bridge. After getting off the rickshaws, we carried our bags and crossed the long and narrow bridge on foot. There were many travelers crossing the bridge carrying heavy luggage on their backs. Two of the men from Jumla seemed quite confident, while the youngest one was a little nervous. The boys were dressed in jeans and T-shirts, one of them had colored hair, while the middle-aged man had a shirt and trousers. They were coming from Hariyana, where all of them worked as security guards (*caukidar*), earning about IRs 3,000 per month plus some extra income from cleaning the cars of the residents where they worked. While the middle-aged man had not been to school, the other two had completed high school and were waiting for the final results of the School Leaving Certificate exam. As we approached the end of the bridge, one of the boys began to tell the others that they should look confident and answer whatever questions they were asked by the police. The youngest boy and the middle-aged man seemed more nervous now. They told me that they were not carrying much money with them, as they knew that border police would search them and that there was a possibility that the border officials would try to extort money from them. The confident-looking boy told us about one of his uncles who had been given fake currency while exchanging money at the border.

As we came to the customs checkpoint immediately after the bridge, a policeman called us toward him using an authoritative gesture and asked where we were coming from. There were four officials present. One was sitting in a hut, another was sitting on a chair outside the hut, and two policemen were standing with batons in their hands. We were made to stand in a line and go to them when they called us. When my turn came, the official asked me if I had Indian rupees in 500 or 1,000 denominations, to which I replied no. He pointed to a banner that read that it was prohibited to carry Indian rupees of denominations of 500 and 1,000. Then he repeatedly asked me if I had read this and whether I had understood the notice, and also whether I was carrying such paper notes. As soon as I replied that I had understood the notice and I did not have any 500-rupee notes, he asked me to empty my pockets and started to frisk me. He searched all of my pockets and asked me to remove my shoes. Another official simultaneously opened my bag, emptied the contents on the table, and looked inside all the clothes I had packed. I kept repeating that I did not have any 500-rupee notes. They agreed to release me from their "inspection" once I told them that I worked for a university and had previously studied in India. After inspecting my ID card, they finally let me go. I was quite relieved, as I had heard rumors of custom officials who threatened and stole money from Nepali migrants. Then they called my fellow travelers one after the other, who went through a similar ritual of physical search and were spoken to in an even harsher way than to me, reflecting the idea that class plays a significant role in the border regime. Even though there were female travelers, I saw no female officers, thus reflecting the masculine nature of the border. I waited for my fellow travelers and observed how they were searched. They had clothes, utensils, a pressure cooker, and a mobile phone, among other things. The policeman asked if he could take the mobile phone or if he could purchase the pressure cooker. The officials asked one of them where they were coming from and asked him to show them the tickets from their journey. The policemen were desperately trying to find something in their pockets or luggage that they could confiscate, and one commented, "You [are] useless; how can I believe you have come back home with empty pockets"? The word "useless" was used to ridicule the men for their failure to earn money despite working in India. The policemen saw the returnee migrants as a source of extra money. The men who retuned without money were a disappointment to them.

They checked everything, including inside the men's under-wear, which of course was humiliating. One official asked, "Why don't you have money, having worked in India?" He said, "Show me all your money," to which they replied, "No we don't have any money." The official threatened them and said that if he found money, he would take it all; the travelers simply nodded and smiled. It was like a game. Because the official was frustrated with the physical search, he asked one of the men to remove his shirt, and also looked inside his underwear. This was the bare life, both literally and metaphorically, of marginal migrants at the border. They were reduced to a state of being without any entitlements and rights. In the end the policeman took IRs 50 from the pockets of each of the three men and let them go. We were sweating in the heat and dust. My fellow travelers seemed relieved that the main search point was over, although there were further border search points for the Indian border force, Nepal Police, and Armed Police of Nepal. One of them was very happy that the IRs 12,000 he had hidden in his luggage had not been found by the officials at customs. We boarded a *tanga* that moved after fifteen minutes or so. While we were waiting, a distraught middle-aged man came along saying that the police had taken the IRs 15,000 he was carrying for a relative. The bills were packed inside a small cloth, and he did not know that his relative had sent it in 500-rupee denominations. Others in the *tanga* suggest-ed that he go and offer to give the policemen some bribe of IRs 1,000 or 2,000 in return for the rest. I never learned the fate of this man, but the other passengers in the *tanga* commented that this was a common affair. Once I reached the Nepal side, I met a middle-aged man who had had IRs 3,000 taken by the same cus-tom officials, all in units of 100 rupees. Border crossing involved encounters with various authorities who made travelers feel like vulnerable, powerless victims of extortion. The entire border-crossing journey of about two kilometers took a little more than two hours, starting with transporters, thugs, immigration officials, and civilian police on both sides, and then all the armed police and antitrafficking officials.

The border-crossing experience always involves this game between the border guards and the migrants; sometimes the guards win, while at other times the migrants win. Yet, the migrants remain vulnerable in a space controlled by police and border guards. Except for questioning by the antitrafficking NGO Maiti Nepal, border crossing from Nepal to India is relatively less stressful for women, girls, and children; those who travel with them; or the transporters and thugs who want to make money by dragging potential customers their way. The reason why Nepali migrants go through excessive searches when they return from India to Nepal is because they are thought to be carrying significant amounts of money and other valuables.

Conclusion

All this shows that, apart from the excitement of seeing new places, people, and culture on their journey to Mumbai, it is also a humiliating and exploitative experience for many migrants. During the journey, the young men's sense of being men was threatened in an isolated place with very little protection. As discussed above, these men went through threatening experiences, with constant questioning and attempts to cheat them. Seen in the context of the Nepal-India border, "open border" is a paradoxical concept. On one hand, it signifies an "openness" that has enabled the mobility of the migrant workers I traveled with, whereas on the other hand it signifies an excessive border regime evidenced by frisking, extortion, and other forms of questioning and surveillance. The border between Nepal and India functions as a filter, in line with Kearney's (2004b) argument. The border regime not only treats poor Nepali migrants in a humiliating manner; it also sustains the social and economic conditions for producing docile and vulnerable migrants. In this sense, the border serves to create docile migrant workers who lose their savings to the state-sanctioned agents. The border-crossing experience can sometimes seem like an exciting game, but the actual experience of humiliation is a precondition for the creation of docile migrants and contributes to the poverty of their households. Travel and border crossing, and in particular navigating the danger and risks of this process, play an important part in renegotiating men's gendered and classed identities.

Marginal Migrant Workers
in Indian Cities

Nepali migrants in India are highly mobile, are dispersed, and often work in "invisible" positions within private homes, presenting significant methodological challenges for the researcher. They are difficult to find, as they do not necessarily reside in a defined location or work in a fixed place. It is not possible to map them geographically in a particular locality. Nepali migrants end up working in jobs that are casualized, underpaid, and without access to any official social protection, and they end up living in substandard housing in Indian cities. These exploitative working conditions, where men's agency is often negated, are in sharp contrast to the patriarchal family contexts in the hills of Nepal, where men command authority and respect by virtue of being men. This crisis of masculinity is caused by not only the act of leaving the family behind but also, more vividly, the difficult and exploitative working conditions that prevail in Mumbai and other destinations in India. Nepali migrants occupy an ambiguous political position in India, as they are treated neither as foreigners nor as citizens. This chapter goes beyond the notion of Nepali migrants as marginal, passive, and victimized and shows how, within constrained conditions, young men working and living in cities like Mumbai not only try their luck at and explore possibilities for realizing their dreams but also begin to negotiate their gendered agency through consumption activities.

Life in Mumbai

Mumbai is far from Palpa, approximately two thousand kilometers away. Even though there is an open border between Nepal and India, Mumbai is located in a different country. It takes about three days for men from the village in Palpa to get to Mumbai. For those in the village, Mumbai signifies progress, exposure to modern life, availability of paid work, and opportunities to transform their lives by earning money. In contrast to the hill village in Nepal, Mumbai is a densely populated global city and an imagined land of opportunity for work and consumption.

While cities like Mumbai have always attracted migrants to work in factories, Indian cities began to attract a considerable number of migrants after independence. It is the growth of the middle class in Indian cities like Mumbai that has created increased work opportunities for Nepalis from across the border. The growth in high-rise flats and housing colonies has led to a rise in demand for security guards and domestic workers. Similarly, Nepalis are in demand in the service hospitality sectors such as hotels, food stalls, and restaurants. Owing to their Gurkha identity, Nepalis, in particular, are preferred for work as security guards. In Mumbai, the growth of the Bollywood film industry has also attracted Nepali migrants, who are thought of as honest and reliable workers. This image of Nepali migrants is built on the identity of Nepali Gurkhas, who were represented as the "bravest of the brave" in British military writings (Caplan 1991).

Like most migrant workers, Nepali men travel to Indian cities on their own, leaving their families behind. They are not only citizens of a different country but also residents of rural areas, and most of them are identifiable by their appearance. They are poor and disadvantaged in language and educational credentials. I found that most cannot speak English or Marathi, the local language used in Mumbai, while only a few have conversational proficiency in Hindi. In Mumbai, they must learn to live and work among the unknown and unfamiliar surroundings often in casual and flexible work settings. Only a few of them have knowledge of the difficult working and living conditions before they arrive, and often they find that they are living in a room shared with four to six others in the middle of a slum community in suburban Mumbai, and working for long hours, often in difficult and exploitative conditions.

For most, the disparity between their workspace and their personal dwellings is stark. While the working space of Nepali migrants is largely in prominent economic hubs in Mumbai, where they work as security guards in banks, companies, hotels, or homes of economically and/or politically influential people, they go home to live in marginal slums and substandard housing. I here focus primarily on the gendered life experiences of Nepalis working as security guards, domestic workers, and help in hotels and restaurants. These men experience a complex tension between fulfilling their desires and their obligations as men in the face of difficult circumstances that often put their identities as men into crisis.

Work

Working life is an area where gender differences are defined, maintained, and reconstituted. It is an important space where men accumulate material and symbolic capital to assert their identities. In this section I examine what life was like in Mumbai for those who escaped the middle hills of Nepal in search of working opportunities and possibilities.

Depending on the situation, some jobs are already arranged for these men by their relatives before they arrive to work in India, while other migrants find jobs within a few weeks of their arrival. In all situations the role of the accompanying person or the social networks is crucial in finding employment (Thieme 2006). The support of social networks is so important that without them it is virtually impossible to find a job or place to live in Mumbai or other cities. In the vast majority of cases, Nepali men from Palpa do not travel to Mumbai without knowing someone beforehand who can support them.

Upon arrival, the newcomers receive free accommodations and food from these supporters until a job and appropriate accommodations can be arranged for them. Until that time, the newly arrived men often wander around the locality, meet other friends/relatives, help with housekeeping (cooking, cleaning, and washing dishes), play cards with others living in the same accommodation, and (when there is nothing else to do) sleep. This same hospitality is expected of them, in turn, once they have established themselves and the next groups of migrants arrive. If they are lucky to find someone else who is free, they may accompany each other to see different places. During my fieldwork, the conversation of the newcomers focused on the busy roads, crowds, people of different types, the sea, high-rise buildings, different types of food and liquor, and the availability of brothels—everything that was so different from Palpa.

Several newly arrived young men from Palpa visited the locations where Bollywood films were being shot to find jobs as spot boys or assistants, primarily through other Nepalis already working in that sector. Going to the film shoots provided them with entertainment as well as opportunities for jobs. Others found jobs as security guards or as helpers in restaurants with the help of their social networks.

Security Guards

Those who work as security guards are known as *caukidar* or *gorkha* or *bahadur* and are employed in private bungalows, housing colonies, government offices, factories, hospitals, or businesses. This is perhaps the most common job among the Nepali men working in Mumbai.

As indicated earlier, it is the social networks that play a key role in helping the men find this type of work. However, commercialization of the security business under multinational companies such as Group Four has meant that the influence of these social networks, which previously formed the basis of a continuous supply of Nepali men, is slowly being replaced by formal processes of recruitment. For generations, security guards were directly employed by the owners, with the help of previous employees or some other social networks, and a few experienced security guards worked as middlemen to arrange security guards for potential employers. The expansion of the security business has meant that residents and offices have shifted the recruitment of security guards to security agencies like Group Four. The standardization of recruitment, and agencies demanding educational qualifications in these agencies, has meant that most of the Nepalis who dropped out of school early do not qualify for the jobs. Recruitment through security agencies requires the completion of schooling and some understanding of English, along with good physical health and a pleasant appearance. While a few Nepalis working through these security agencies were earning better money and said that it provided better job security, it was the inability to get into the sector in the first place that was considered a major hurdle by many Nepalis. At the same time, men said that working with such companies was demanding, as they have very strict rules and require knowledge of how to complete paperwork. A few men I spoke to believed that, unlike having direct employment, working with a security agency was very difficult in terms of setting up work hours and making other work arrangements. There was a mixed reaction to this development from the informants. While some thought the companies still preferred Nepalis because of the long tradition and association, based on the image of Nepali bravery and loyalty, others believed that Nepalis were no longer wanted, as these companies could hire others at a cheaper rate. This process meant that more Nepalis were looking for alternative employment opportunities in hotels and restaurants, other manual labor or domestic help, diversifying the employment base of migrant Nepali men. In one instance, a Bahun man had kept Bahadur as his surname, as it was thought that those with the Bahadur[1] surname had a better chance of being selected for guard jobs. Such perception was influenced by the colonial discourse on a "martial race" that was reflected in the recruitment of men from certain ethnic hill groups to the British Army.

The working hours of security guards were not fixed, and it was usual to see these men working overtime, often up to fifteen to seventeen hours a day, to earn more money to enable them to save and send money back to their families in Nepal. A few of them working as guards through a security agency worked a fixed ten- to twelve-hour shift, plus some overtime work, on a regular basis. Depending on the situation, their duty involved staying awake the whole night or working during the day on a shift basis. Most of them worked both day and night shifts, as well as working in two places at different times. Long hours of work also meant that it was stressful and it was not possible to do or focus on any other work.

The monthly salary of security guards ranged from anywhere between IRs 2,500 and IRs 5,000 (roughly USD 40–60), but they were able to earn more money by working overtime and by doing other work (e.g., taking children to school, cleaning cars, and shopping) for the residents as well as getting occasional tips from the employers. Though most of the guards worked long hours, it was not always possible for them to dramatically change their living conditions. Despite this, the men I spoke to seemed happy with their jobs, though they hoped to find work with better pay and job conditions later. Although a few of them initially believed that the job was difficult and boring, they found it easier as they became accustomed to it. At the beginning, the language barrier and having to learn a new language proved difficult for many, but as they continued to work they picked up the languages. Some of them even learned Marathi and English. Despite the long working hours, the job of security guard was particularly important for the flexibility it provided to work overtime, earn more money, and assert their manhood.

Security guards are usually given a uniform, a long stick, and a whistle, and many sport mustaches. Dressed as such, the guards move around their buildings, check cars and people who are entering the building, and make an effort to demonstrate their employer's confidence in them. I observed that when the owners of the buildings passed through the gate, the guards would display their deference and discipline with a salute. A security job was considered less demanding—it was called the "stick-holding job" (*danda samatne kam*)—than work in restaurants and domestic work, which required long hours, often in difficult conditions. In the words of one 48-year-old Bahun security guard, the job was very easy, as he did not have to do anything other than be there. In some ways, the job of a guard seemed to compensate for the frustration of Magar men who were not recruited into a foreign army, particularly because of the job's security-providing aspect. But the work also involved loneliness, as the guards spent most of their time standing at the gate, and often there was hardly anyone to talk to, except the domestic workers staying in or visiting the building or other security guards from the neighboring buildings. It was virtually impossible for them to develop friendships through their work. Another difficulty was being attacked by thieves or finding themselves in situations where they were unable to apprehend them. This usually resulted in the loss of their job or, at a minimum, a deduction from their salary over several months. However, when the job was going well, it provided security and recognition for their capability, which sometimes led to an increase in salary. Thus, performance at work in Mumbai provided an important avenue for asserting their identities as men.

Except when guards were hired through security agencies, such positions did not offer paid leave, and the guards did not want to take unpaid leave. This meant that it was very difficult to go home. Here the importance of social networks is apparent again. In order to be able to visit their homes, they had to find someone to work temporarily in their absence or they had to give up their jobs completely. In a practice commonly known as *satta basne* (covering for another person), many of the guards were able to help one another by working for another person while he took leave. Nepali migrants in Mumbai sought to actively mobilize their social networks to their advantage. In a case where a security guard could not find a replacement, he had to leave the job to someone else, usually a newcomer, through a mutual agreement. Sometimes, once a worker had gone home, various commitments and problems at home prevented him from returning to the job on time. This usually resulted in the loss of the job. Other times, on returning, many found that, despite the arrangement, their jobs had been given to others, and they had to find new work. Home visits were important to reinforce the identities of these individuals as men with family responsibilities. Nevertheless, they had to cope with the pressure of keeping their jobs and continuing to earn while also feeling the obligation to return home regularly.

Restaurant and Hotel Workers

Another popular and growing sector in which Nepali men worked was that of the restaurants, hotels, and food stalls spread across Mumbai. It was common to find Nepalis working in Chinese restaurants and food stalls as cooking assistants, waiters, and cleaners. Working in this sector did not always require qualifications or experience other than trust established through their social networks. While some Nepalis in Mumbai look down on restaurant work, a growing number of Nepali men, in the face of fierce competition in Mumbai, found work in this sector. Those working in hotels and restaurants were paid a relatively low salary—about IRs 2,000–2,500 per month, including food and accommodation. Working in this sector meant that the men had to work for the entire day and sleep only after the business was closed for the day, at about midnight. The work involved strict monitoring and direction from the owner or supervisor. Depending on the specific roles assigned, working in hotels required them to remain in front of ovens in the heat, often drenched in sweat, washing dishes and cleaning floors/tables for hours, leaving their hands ashen and rough. The work was considered physically demanding with very little free time to phone their family and friends and little opportunity for sexual intimacy. It was their productivity and not their well-being that was the priority for the employers. Inability to follow instruction and endure work pressure from the owner often resulted in abusive language and humiliation in front of other workers, reinforcing their sense of powerlessness. Very few of these men had ever washed dishes, managed the kitchen, or served food to the guests in their homes. They had been raised to expect the women do the housework. The kitchen domain that had been completely alien to these men back home was now their workplace. The nature of work in Mumbai was crucial in the reconfiguration of their gendered identities as men.

Domestic Workers

A growing opportunity for an increasing number of Nepali boys (between ages 14 and 20) was as domestic workers in middle-class houses in suburban Mumbai. Often invisible, except when they left the home for two to three hours a day, these young men spent most of their time inside the flats of their middle-class employers. Their main work was cleaning and cooking. The owners usually did not like outsiders communicating with their workers, nor did they like their workers spending much time outside their houses. The domestic workers were not expected to interact with visitors and spent most of their time in the kitchen or in the washing area. In one instance, when sent by the owner to buy vegetables, a Magar boy of 14 took time out to go to the newsstand to speak to other Nepalis working in the same locality. This was the only opportunity he had to meet other people from Nepal outside of the direct supervision of his employer. These young men spent most of their time alone, with very little opportunity for interaction; they were preparing and cooking food, cleaning dishes, and cleaning the house and clothes. The employers often inquired about the caste of the worker at the time of the appointment, and it was widely said that Bahuns had a better chance of finding work as domestic workers. Therefore, it appears that caste identity remained important among Nepali migrants in Mumbai.

Four employers I spoke to hired and trusted Nepali men because they found them loyal, but this was not always the case. There were a few who believed that the Nepalis in recent years were not as loyal and hardworking as before and cited examples of Nepalis involved in stealing and other criminal activities.

Increasingly the image of Nepali men was suffering greatly, as they were becoming known as criminals, drunkards, and gamblers, which impacted their chances of finding work. While people who have come to work in Mumbai from other parts of India as well as locals have been equally involved in crime, the involvement of Nepalis in criminal activities has been widely publicized. While criminalization of migrants is not new, Nepalis in India have more recently become the subject of this anti-immigrant sentiment. What is particularly striking in this case is the shift in their image from a positive one of loyal Nepalis (as *kancha/bahadur*) to one of dangerous thieves and goons (*chor, gunda*), which means that domestic workers are heavily scrutinized, monitored, and disciplined.

Living Conditions

After I arrived in Mumbai by train with my traveling group from Palpa, we followed Kumar to his room; he politely told us, "Do not feel bad; we live in a *jhopadpatti* [slum]. What can be done? It is like this; all of us live like this." Hari and Anil, the two boys, had heard the word *jhopadpatti* but never thought about what it would be like living in a *jhupadi*.[2] As we walked through the lanes of the slum, Anil reacted, covering his nose with his hand and exclaiming, "Oho! It smells really bad. . . . [W]hat is it?" This was the smell of open sewage. Kumar replied, "It is like this. You will get used to it slowly. It does not smell to me at all." We all laughed and followed Kumar along the narrow lane, trying to avoid falling in the gutter. Apart from its use for drainage and a walking path, the narrow lane was a space where people bathed, washed and dried clothes, processed vegetables, and let their children play. A housing block that we passed just before we entered the slum settlements was the workplace for some of the Nepali migrants who worked as security guards or domestic help.

The majority of Nepali men working in Mumbai live in slum housing, primarily because of their lower level of income, the high cost of local housing, and the need to save money. A few (mostly those who work as security guards, domestic helpers, and helpers in hotels) are provided with accommodation by their employers. Except for a few families who rented their own single room, most of the Nepali men rented a room (also called *kholi*) in a slum that was shared by four to six people. The number of people sharing a room fluctuated with the arrival of individuals from the village in search of work and the number of people visiting home during holidays.

Most workers lived very close to their workplace, ensuring that they did not have to spend money on travel. The housing consisted of congested rooms with poor maintenance that often lacked basic amenities like water and sanitation. Many rooms did not have a water supply, thus residents had to collect water from public water tanks. Often they had obtained electricity for their rooms illegally by paying bribes. Most of the housing lacked a toilet facility, and they had to go to a nearby busy public toilet or use the shrubs close to the settlement. A few others, who had been living there for a long time and had the intention of staying longer, built a toilet inside their room and maintained their room regularly.

The cost of a room varied, but most of the people paid about IRs 600–1,000 per month for a room. The landlords were mostly Indians who themselves lived in slums but also included a few Nepalis. It most cases it was a precondition to pay a deposit of IRs 5,000–15,000. The newcomers often needed the support of their social networks to enable them to pay the deposit or act as a guarantee.

The room where I stayed in Laxminagar, in western suburban Mumbai, was rented by three men from Palpa. There were five of us sharing the room. They were all Bahuns, and they knew one another very well. Compared to the rooms that other Nepalis lived in, the room I had was far better, with a rent of IRs 1,500, excluding the electricity bill. It was a relatively large room with two beds, a kitchen in one corner, and a space for taking a bath and cleaning dishes in another corner. There was an old cable television, which served as a source of entertainment, making it possible to watch more than thirty television channels. The room had a fan to cope with the Mumbai heat, which was aggravated by the steel roof.

A few men who worked as security guards were given free accommodation in a pump house or in a small room, usually under the stairs, provided by the owner of the building. A pump house was a generic term used to refer to a small room located within the premises of the building that was used as a store for the water pump or a general store room. Such accommodation was usually free, and they did not have to pay for electricity or water, but they had to cook their own food. Similarly those who worked in hotels and restaurants were usually provided with a common room or the floor in the dining space arranged by the employer, where six to eight people lived together. The employer provided them with food. Because these workers received free accommodation and food, they were paid less money. Domestic workers in residences often slept in the kitchen or in a corridor of the houses they worked in. They went to sleep after everyone else in the house went to sleep and woke up early in the morning before anyone else woke up. Here it is worth noting that Nepali migrants are difficult to reach for social research or delivery of basic services as not all of them live in slums but in dispersed and invisible places. Except for those who were provided with a meal by the employer, workers cooked their own food in their room. Those who stayed together cooked together and shared the cost.

Most Nepali migrants in India lack documentation and the registration required for basic services such as health care, schooling, or subsidized food. Language and cultural differences regularly expose many to harassment and political exclusion. Their marginal position in Mumbai entails poor access to health care provisions, thereby enhancing their vulnerability to ill health. Health problems were common among the men in Mumbai. Men referred to regular incidents of coughs and colds, backaches, skin diseases, fatigue, depression, work-related injuries (often to hands and legs), road accidents, tuberculosis, and malaria among their friends. It was common to find men sleeping in their rooms, tired and unwell. Despite living in cities that offer a wide range of public services, including health care, for the Nepali migrants, proximity to free health care services does not imply its automatic utilization. Most are treated in the private sector, which is costly and results in a loss of income and savings, exacerbating their level of poverty. The high cost of treatment in private clinics meant that men often resorted to taking paracetamol and pain killers (and sometimes self-prescribed antibiotics) from a local pharmacy. The men visited a doctor (in private clinics) when symptoms worsened. As I discuss in the next chapter, the public health discourses that saw Nepali migrants as only carriers of HIV and STIs disregarded their overall well-being and other social determinants of health. Several migrants I spoke to mentioned that they were exposed to violence, abuse, and ill-treatment both in the workplace and in their everyday lives in Mumbai and that this treatment went unreported, unnoticed, and unrecognized. How to protect themselves and stay safe remains a key concern for most migrants. The vast majority of abuse and ill-treatment is ignored and accepted as a part of living in Mumbai. In cases of severe abuse and ill-treatment, Nepali migrants often settle the cases informally, without seeking formal justice. Outside of their membership in Nepali migrant associations and informal Nepali gatherings, Nepali migrants had very little connection with NGOs, labor unions, civil society organizations, or human rights organizations active in Mumbai.

Despite migrants' ubiquitous contribution to the growth and development of cities like Mumbai, they have no access to basic services or protection provisions. The relationship between structural inequalities and poor access to justice thus plays a crucial role in perpetuating the structural inequalities that lie at the heart of their marginalization and poverty.

Consumption

From the perspective of these men, who knew only the constrained life of Palpa, the migration to India was exciting and an opportunity to explore a distant culture and location. Mumbai was a city of large buildings, public transport, brothels, "beer bars," freedom, and the film industry. The experience of men in Mumbai showed that their work offered them an opportunity to earn some money to meet the basic needs of their households and fulfill their obligations as good sons and good men. Working in cities like Mumbai offered these men an opportunity to become involved in the consumption of what was considered "modern goods and experiences." Thus, one important characteristic of life in Mumbai was the transformation that these men went through in their consumption habits, both in Mumbai and back home.

A particular aspect of life in Mumbai for these migrants was to go sightseeing to different parts of the city where there were high-rise buildings, tourist attractions like the Gateway of India, the sea beach, and occasionally films or television serials being shot in studios or outside. Commonly known as *ghumna jane* (wandering around), this involved exploring new places for entertainment. Migrants living in suburban Mumbai sometimes went on weekends to watch Bollywood films being shot in studios with the help of their friends working there. A few men I interviewed worked in the film industry or at least came in the hope that they would find some work there. A few young men spoke of their desire to work in film and watch the films being shot. It was possible that some of these desires were heightened by talk of modernity and development, particularly by the proliferation of glamorous images of modern places and masculinity. Such images were reinforced by the success stories of a few individuals, like Dilip.

Dilip, a 48-year-old man from Palpa, was a role model for many of the younger men who considered migration to India as a chance to improve their socioeconomic situation. Though Dilip went to India to escape from a police warrant on the charge of attempted murder, after several years of work in the film industry, he had become a hero in the eyes of many people in the entire area. Although his was a criminal case, it was informally settled later, after signing a mutual agreement with the complainant. The police then were no longer actively looking for him. He worked as a personal assistant to a producer and earned about IRs 40,000–50,000 a month. Dilip even managed to act in a television serial that was shown on Doordarshan, the Indian national television channel. He had assisted several people by arranging for them to get jobs in the film industry in Mumbai. Whenever he came home, he was surrounded by three or four people, and he bought drinks for everyone and spoke of the opportunities in Mumbai. He wore a big gold chain, several gold rings, and traveled home in an air-conditioned train, something that is largely outside the reach of Nepali migrant workers in Mumbai. Each time he returned to Mumbai, a few young men joined him, in the hope of finding work in the film industry. People often cited the examples of men for whom Dilip had arranged jobs as helpers and who were now working as an assistant production manager and a makeup man. In the film studio, I met a Magar man of 25 who, through Dilip, worked as a helper on the set. His job was to respond to orders during shooting, mainly loading up, unloading, and shifting heavy gear. His work was quite hard for the payment of IRs 150 per day, but he hoped to be chosen by the producer for a better-paid job some day. On the last occasion Dilip had returned to Mumbai after a visit home, he brought back a married man of 30 who was looking for either a good work opportunity or to start a small business in partnership with Dilip's son. After returning from a three-year contract in Malaysia the previous year, this man sought to invest the money he had saved (NRs 400,000) in a business but found little possibility of starting a successful venture because of the escalating violence in Nepal. Staying in Nepal had meant that his savings were quickly getting spent on day-to-day expenses. After speaking to Dilip, he was hoping to start a small shop or a restaurant in Mumbai where he could invest his savings and earn some money. As he was married, he did not want to do contract work again, which meant no leave to go home, but instead he was considering the possibility of going to Mumbai. The success stories from Mumbai and support provided by people like Dilip meant that young men in the village saw possibilities of migration to Mumbai. While men seemed aware that migration to India did not automatically result in success and happiness, it at least opened up possibilities.

Life in Mumbai provided these men with an opportunity to explore freedom away from the strict norms observed in the village. On a Sunday, a group of friends (five Bahuns, three Magars, and one Chetri) would meet in the room of my host in Mumbai to enjoy one another's company (*ramailo garne*). The gathering was characterized by the consumption of alcohol (beer) and meat (chicken) for hours in the room. Because of strict social norms and, more recently, a campaign against alcohol led by the Maoists and women's groups, it would have been difficult to find a similar scene back in the village, particularly for the Bahuns. The cost of the party that I attended in a small room in a slum in Mumbai was somewhere between IRs 3,000 and IRs 4,000 in total. I suspect that it would not have been possible for these men to spend even hundreds of rupees on a party back in their home village. Such an act would not have been socially approved of back in the village. The gathering went on for more than six hours, and they drank beer, ate meat, played music, danced, and talked to one another about their work, life, loves, and problems. Occasionally these gatherings took place in the "beer bar" close to where they lived, which cost more money than what they would spend in the room. Though expensive, the "beer bar" was referred to as a place where they could not only drink and talk but also have women serve them drinks and watch women perform erotic dances. Bimal, a married Bahun man in his late 30s who was self-employed as a real estate agent, was known for visiting different beer bars in the city and spending thousands of rupees. The party scene was revealing in the sense that it showed the possibility of being involved in consumption practices without any restrictions. Such gatherings provided these men with intimacy and an opportunity to meet one another.

On a Sunday afternoon I met four Nepali migrants, mostly in their early and mid-20s, in a local tea stall in Goregaun. The stall was a place where the migrants from Laxminagar (the name of the slum area) mostly met one another over a "cutting tea."[3] The conversation started casually about work, home, friends, mobile phones, the cinema, and so on, and then slowly moved onto love, marriage, sex, alcohol, beer bars, sex workers, and brothels. The men spoke for hours about having fun (*ramailo garne*) by going to beer bars and having sexual adventures.

One of the things that struck me about Nepali men working in Mumbai was their use of mobile phones. Most of the young men I met had a mobile phone, except for those who worked as domestic helpers. Whenever I began to talk to them, a mobile phone would ring with the ring tone of the latest Bollywood song. While having a mobile phone enabled them to be in touch with one another, it was also very easy for their family members back in Nepal to make phone calls to them. Whenever I sought a favor from my informants to speak to other migrants, they always took out a mobile phone and made a phone call. The widespread use of mobile phones shows the desire of these men to consume modern goods. These phones were available in the shops with the starting price of IRs 2,500 or less, and it took about IRs 100 to get the phone connected to the network.

Television and the movies were popular forms of entertainment. Television was so common that, depending on their incomes, men could have cable television supplying thirty channels or more in their rooms. The men with whom I stayed often watched movies, entertainment serials, news, or cricket. They also owned a video player that was used to watch movies borrowed from a video rental shop nearby. Television was put on from the time one entered the room till the time one left. The men considered it usual to go to the movies whenever they were free. Some young men told me that they never missed a newly released movie. They had up-to-date knowledge about the movies, movie stars, and the latest gossip from Bollywood. It was possible for them to watch Nepali movies played in selected movie theaters in Mumbai. Occasionally people mentioned going to watch erotic movies, or B-grade films, as they are called in India, in some of the theaters.

Whenever possible, these men met one another at a convenient place. Apart from the tea stall in Laxminagar, there was a newspaper stand next to the tea stall sponsored by Shiv Sena, a popular Hindu right-wing regional political party with a strong base in Mumbai. Apart from different Hindi and Marathi newspapers, the stand also included two Nepali newspapers (*Nepal News* and *Nepal Sandesh*), which were sponsored (paid for) by a Nepali security guard working in a housing colony in front of the newspaper stand. These newspapers contained news from Nepal, including notices and advertisements of different things targeted at Nepalis, and so the men often got into conversation about the political situation in Nepal and events taking place in Mumbai. These newspapers also carried information about Nepali movies, community events, meetings, announcements from associations, and advertisements for jobs, among other things. Such gatherings also provided these men with the chance to become involved in political debate and mobilization.

Those who read the news from Nepal and engaged in the discussion on Nepali politics afterward indicated their participation in the political processes from a distance. Many of these men were members of different types of migrant organizations and took part in their various activities. Some of these migrant organizations were sister organizations of the mainstream political parties in Nepal; others were activist or welfare-oriented organizations. Although several Nepali migrant associations were active in India, the activities and programs of migrant associations were primarily aimed at political and cultural engagements with the homeland. The participation in migrant organizations thus became an important means of asserting their commitment to belonging in Nepal and contributing to political processes there.

Conclusion

Nepali migrants remain at the margins in Indian cities like Mumbai. Not only are they excluded as poor, as migrants from rural Nepal; they are excluded politically and culturally as well. They occupy a liminal position—that is, they are treated as neither foreigners nor natives. Working and living conditions are difficult and precarious for Nepali migrants, who perceive themselves as inferior and live in segregated areas with limited social networks. Such conditions in Mumbai appear to undermine Nepali migrants' sense of self-worth. The nature of work as well as lack of physical and income security means that there is no prospect of bringing their families. The marginal working and living conditions make them vulnerable to health problems, including STIs and HIV.

Within this constrained way of life, Nepali men working in Mumbai tried their luck, explore possibilities for realizing their dreams, and cultivated new dreams and possibilities. Nepali migrants turned lack of job security to their favor by returning home when work was no longer available or finding a replacement worker when they needed to return home for family obligations. Working in Mumbai offered these men an opportunity to become involved in the consumption of what are considered modern goods, images, and experiences, and to explore freedom away from the strict norms observed in the village. These consumption practices were related to the way of life in the cities like Mumbai but, when compared with their village life in Nepal, they also functioned as key symbols of progress and modernity, which were influenced by the discourses of development. Development discourses, in particular their emphasis on modernization, consumption, and urban life, had a major impact on reconfiguring gendered ideas of being a man. One way to characterize life in Mumbai is the transformation that the village men went through in their consumption practices. Observing migrants' consumption in India allows us to understand the steady flow of poor Nepali migrants who, despite exploitative working conditions, continue to travel to Mumbai.

6

Migrant Risk Behavior
in Mumbai

For most of the 1990s, within the discourses on trafficking, many policy makers were concerned about women as carriers of HIV/AIDS, while male labor migration did not feature centrally in HIV/AIDS discourse (Pigg 2001). Since 1998–1999, however, there has been a major shift in policy discourse toward seeing male labor migrants as carriers of the HIV virus. Many of the reports and articles on "poor and uneducated" Nepali male migrant workers traveling to work in India project these migrants as a "risk population" for the epidemic. "Nepal's open border with India (where HIV infection rates are rapidly rising) and the high level of physical mobility within Nepal and abroad, associated with widespread labour migration and encouraged by the recent development of road transport, means that there is a real danger of a rapid spread of HIV within Nepal" (Seddon 1998: 35).

Building on my ethnography of Nepali migrants in Mumbai, this chapter offers a critique of policy discourses that blame male migrants as carriers of virus and disease without locating them within the wider context of structural violence and gendered meanings associated with migration. It discusses how Nepali migrants are subjected to structural violence that increases their STI and

HIV vulnerabilities. This chapter argues that social forces—the poor working and living conditions—contribute to migrants' taking risks. Structural violence plays a crucial role in the genesis of not only STIs and HIV but also a lack of agency and the stigmatization of migrants. Furthermore, this chapter contends that the role of development discourse and practice in perpetuating structural violence needs to be made more explicit in order to understand the position and action of these Nepali migrants.

Creating Nepali Male Labor Migrants as the Object of Intervention

During the 1990s and early 2000s, there was a regular demand for research and knowledge on the linkages between HIV and male labor migration in far-western Nepal. An inventory showed that in 2001 alone, six different research assessments on migration and HIV were carried out in far-western Nepal (UNAIDS/NCASC 2004: 4). A study by the UNDP's (United Nations Development Program) Participatory Planning and Management of HIV/AIDS project stated that the vast majority—82 percent of migrants—were of sexually active age (14–45), and that a majority of far-western Nepali migrants were married but not accompanied by their wives. The study argued that such a situation put the migrants at an increased risk of sexual contact and thus HIV/STIs (Poudel 1999). In early 2001 another assessment was commissioned by JICA (Japan International Cooperation Agency) in the far-western districts (Poudel 2001). This assessment showed that all the men who tested positive for HIV reported that they migrated to Mumbai—this was 10 percent of the total sample of ninety-nine. The study identified that more than 50 percent of the sample were infected with STIs.

During 2003–2004, a series of articles on male labor migration from far-western Nepal and HIV/AIDS appeared in public health journals (Poudel et al. 2003, 2004a, 2004b). The use of language in the titles of the articles explicitly represented the Nepali male labor migrant to Mumbai as a disease carrier—for instance, "Mumbai Disease in Far Western Nepal: HIV Infection and Syphilis among Male Migrant Returnees and Non-migrants" (Poudel et al. 2003) and "Migration in Far Western Nepal: A Time Bomb for a Future HIV/AIDS Epidemic" (Poudel et al. 2004b), which claimed an alarming need for intervention from policy-making circles. Using the metaphor "time bomb," the article predicted major risks associated with migration and presented a compelling need for intervention.

Nepal's strategy for HIV/AIDS from 2002 to 2006 focused on male labor migration as an important issue for consideration in HIV/AIDS prevention, care, and support programs. The strategy aimed to "address the more behaviour related factors of HIV/AIDS/STI vulnerability, but at the same time advocated a holistic approach to address the broader determinants of HIV/AIDS/STI vulnerability among mobile populations" (NCASC 2002: 19). Estimating the number of Nepali men working in India at around 1 million, the document states, "Migration to India will undoubtedly continue to increase in coming years. Many of these men are contracting HIV/AIDS in India and bringing it back to their wives in Nepal" (NCASC 2002: 3). It identified the mobile population as one of the vulnerable groups and proposed "research" to increase the understanding of the contextual factors and consequential risk behavior, which had contributed to the vulnerability of mobile populations and their families to STIs and HIV/AIDS. It also highlighted "behaviour change intervention" to reduce the vulnerability of mobile populations and their families to STIs and HIV/AIDS and the "creation of an enabling environment" to increase responsiveness to the needs of migrants in their respective host locations.

A report jointly produced by UNAIDS and the Ministry of Health (MoH) viewed male labor migrants as a "bridging population" that carries HIV/AIDS from sex workers to the general population in rural areas. A document released by USAID in Nepal in May 2005 considered high rates of male migration to be one of the primary factors involved in the rapid spread of HIV (USAID 2005). It noted, "Most of these migrants are young men with a low level of awareness about risky behavior and disease transmissions" (USAID 2005: 2).

By 2005, a public health response for targeting male labor migrants from western Nepal had already been configured. This response involved HIV intervention in both origin and destination migration locations. Below, I offer some brief insights into one such intervention in the migrant destination of Mumbai.

HIV Project with Nepali Migrants in Mumbai

Sathi Nepal was a project funded by Family Health International (FHI) in Mumbai. It came into effect when FHI and USAID signed a memorandum of understanding with the Tata Institute of Social Sciences (TISS) in the year 2004. Implemented by TISS, the project aimed to reduce the incidence of HIV transmission among Nepali migrants and their sexual partners through lowering the vulnerability to and risk for HIV transmission and to promote access to care and support services among male Nepali migrants in the Mumbai and Thane districts of Maharashtra.

At the start of the project, FHI Nepal and FHI India undertook an assessment to better understand the situation of Nepali migrants in Mumbai. It involved in-depth interviews with 120 migrants from Nepal. The findings of the assessment indicated that Nepali migrants were getting infected with HIV and possibly transmitting the virus back in their villages in Nepal and recommended the need for intervention with targeted population groups. Interestingly, the study found that a number of men were using condoms. However, consistent condom use with commercial sex workers did not seem to be a regular practice. Further, Nepali migrants in Mumbai did not use condoms with their girlfriends and wives.

The Sathi Nepal project had four major program components—behavior change communication activities, psychosocial support, social mobilization, and advocacy. For behavior change communication, Sathi Nepal carried out various activities, including peer education, outreach education, providing IEC (information, education, and communication) materials, airing satellite radio programs, and organizing different cultural and entertainment programs. They broadcast a weekly radio program in both Nepal and India through satellite radio and distributed radios in the community. Under the psychosocial support component, there were activities like referrals for VCT (Voluntary Counseling and Testing) and care and support. Apart from a project coordinator, a visiting doctor, and two counselors in each of the field offices, there were thirteen trained outreach workers as paid staff of the project, and more than twenty peer educators in different slum communities. The counselor and doctor provided counseling and medical check-ups related to sexual health issues and STIs and, if they suspected someone might be HIV positive, they referred them to a government hospital. To attract Nepali migrants, the project field offices had games such as "Carom-board" and "Ludo" that the migrants could play. However, it was very rare that Nepali migrant workers had spare time from their busy working lives to go and play games in these field offices. The field offices had stocks of various pamphlets and booklets as well as audio- and videocassettes[1] aimed at educating the migrants.

With all the programs and resources, it was evident that the Sathi Nepal project saw Nepali migrants as individuals with high-risk sexual behavior and offered individualized intervention to change their behavior through communication activities that isolated the migrants from the social and cultural context in which they lived. Beyond the subjects of STI and HIV intervention, there was no consideration of the marginal positions of migrants in India or the gendered or sociocultural meanings of this form of migration that increased the vulnerability of Nepali migrants in the first place. Consideration of culture by the project was on an instrumental basis to implement its activities. The project took festivals like Dasai[2] as an opportunity to educate Nepali migrants about HIV and STIs, thereby appearing to reduce its cultural significance.

The field office, managed by a female counselor, was open from 10:00 A.M. to 5:30 P.M. five days a week and functioned as a Drop-in Centre (DIC) for the migrants. The DIC was a single room, not very large in size (10' x 15'), with about ten chairs, two tables, and many IEC materials, including audiovisual tools. There was a cloth curtain (green as used in medical settings), which was used as a partition. There was an assumption that the migrants would come to visit the DIC should they be in need of information on matters related to HIV/STIs. Although I did not see any men in the DIC during my visits, a counselor told me that it was a place where Nepali men would come looking for information related to sexual health and for entertainment. She was of the view that Nepali migrants lacked awareness on risk behavior and that they needed to be provided with education. A medical doctor, who visited the DIC three days a week from 3:00 to 5:00 P.M., told me that his job was to provide health check-ups related to the migrants' sexual health issues. He said that although HIV/STIs were very common among Nepali migrants, they did not seek treatment at the right time. He told me that Nepali migrants did not understand the seriousness of the epidemic and that it could endanger not only their lives but also the lives of others, including their families back in Nepal. The doctor was of the view that the migrants were "careless" and did not look after their health. The focus of the doctor's narrative was very much on the individual migrants and their behavior, with no consideration of the structural context of their migration, its gendered meanings, or their working and living condition in Mumbai.

In an attempt to understand how the staff at Sathi Nepal reach out to Nepali migrants, I spent several days with outreach workers. One day we went to meet two Nepali migrants in their accommodations, and the outreach worker talked with them casually. He spoke in Nepali to the men, who were taking a rest in their room, and asked them if everything was all right.[3] The tired migrants were lying down on the floor and said that everything was fine. We did not stay there long, as the migrants seemed very tired and were trying to catch up on some sleep. They were not interested in our visit. Once we went outside, the outreach worker told me that it is always difficult to find time to meet the Nepali migrants. He told me that the two men in the room visited sex workers regularly and that he has been trying to reach out to them. When I asked him how he knew this, he looked at me and said, "You know about it by looking at their behavior. . . . People feel shy to talk about it, but they don't know that their ignorance is killing them and many others, not just here but also in Nepal. You see, they don't realize the seriousness of the problem."

Toward the end of day, we sat in a tea stall where he took out his diary and made notes. Over a glass of tea, he was writing the names of the people whom he had met that day, as they would be needed for his report. He told me that every month he has a target of the number of people to be reached out to and educated on HIV/STIs. It was not that easy, he said, to meet this target, and reaching out to migrant workers could be quite challenging. The outreach worker was under constant pressure to produce results in his monthly reports and ensure he was increasing the number of migrants he had involved in the program.

Another big component of the project was a satellite radio program named *Desh Pardesh*, produced in cooperation with a team at an organization called Equal Access, based in Kathmandu. Equal Access worked in close collaboration with the field staff of Sathi Nepal for the production of their radio program. The radio program aimed to reduce HIV transmission among Nepali migrants and their sexual partners and used entertainment and education to increase awareness and knowledge of STIs among both migrants in India and the "home" communities back in Nepal. I listened to the episodes broadcast on the radio. With the aim of educating the migrants, nondrama components ("facts," for instance, on the number of Nepali migrants in India, living and working conditions, HIV/AIDS, and condom use) were combined with the ongoing story of a young Nepali man named Narendra, who experienced the difficulties and excitement "encountered" by many Nepali migrants in India. Beginning in March 2005, Nepali communities in both Mumbai and western Nepal were receiving the broadcasts via satellite radio, and many more heard them on FM rebroadcast and the state broadcaster, Radio Nepal.

Migrants' Responses to the Discourse

Given the presence of authoritative discourses that pathologized migrant risk behavior, how did migrants that I lived with view all this? While I did not get into discussion with the migrants about what they understood by "HIV" or "STIs," all of them told me that AIDS was a disease to be avoided by refraining from having sex without a condom and by avoiding bad places[4] (i.e., brothels). They knew what condoms were and where to get them. They told me that a few Nepali migrants had died of AIDS. As one man put it, "Nowadays you hear about it everywhere. If you turn on the radio, it is there. If you read newspapers, it is there. If you go to a health post, it is there. It is not just here, but you will find it back in the village too." Unlike the public health professionals, the Nepali migrants did not bring the topic of HIV/STIs into my conversation with them. Instead, they often spoke to me about their hardship and how they were not able to save much money in Mumbai. When I asked specifically, a few migrants mentioned the presence of STIs (they referred to the names *bhiringi*, or "syphilis," and *luto*, or "scabies") among their friends in Mumbai. It was a common practice among the migrants I met in Mumbai to go to what they called "beer bars," and some spent some of their savings to pay for sex. Many migrants told me that it was a common practice to have girlfriends and to engage in extramarital affairs or to visit sex workers on a regular basis.

Several expressed a dislike of condoms because, they said, condoms did not give them pleasure.[5] In their view, a condom was to be used when having sex with an unknown sex worker but not with their girlfriends or wives. The migrants were aware of HIV/STIs and the importance of using condoms, but this did not stop some of them from engaging in unsafe sexual practices.

There was certainly an opportunity for these men to be involved in relationships, particularly when they were away from home, and involvement in relationships provided a rare opportunity for intimacy. It was a matter of pride for these men, who lived with other men in a small room in the slums or in their workplace, to have girlfriends and sexual adventures. Unlike in their home villages, in Mumbai it was possible to see men and women holding hands, walking in the streets, and even kissing in public. Within the constraints of men living together, the idea of romantic love was very much associated with having girlfriends or visiting beer bars.

Conclusion

Overall, the common public health perception is that Nepali migrants are carriers of HIV and STIs, with no consideration of the broader structural context that makes them vulnerable in the first place. Such a gaze completely ignores the overall health and well-being of low-income Nepali migrants, who regularly suffer from various illnesses for which they visit private clinics. The focus of individualized behavior change communication programs on HIV and STIs pathologized Nepali male migrants and their sexuality as aberrant and in need of education and awareness. The medicalized framework used by projects such as Sathi Nepal labels migrants as the carriers of virus and disease without locating them within the wider context of structural violence and the sociocultural and gendered meanings associated with migration. The docility created by poor work conditions and ill-treatment has contributed to migrants not being able to consider the impact of their sexual behavior. The marginal positions of individual migrants who traveled on their own, leaving their families behind, have left them, by nature, vulnerable to the apparent threats posed by HIV and STIs in Mumbai.

Conclusion

In this book I have traced the linkages between the history and changing political economy of the middle hills of Nepal and the desire, the agency, and the gendered and class-related subjectivities of young male migrants from poorer households in rural Nepal. I have argued that various structural factors—such as significant economic inequality within Nepal—create the conditions for the outflow of able-bodied men to Indian cities. Further, the humiliating experience of crossing the border plays a key role in producing a particular type of docile migrant worker. These phenomena, I suggest, shape the marginal "classed" position of Nepali migrants in India. In particular, this book has examined the sociocultural forces behind rural men's decisions to migrate, the cultural politics of exclusion that pushes Nepali migrant men to the bottom of society in Indian cities, the apparent contradictions embedded in migrant men's struggles for survival, and the way they mobilize consumption strategies and sociocultural meanings associated with migration to defend their decency and dignity. In an attempt to consolidate the various arguments made in the previous chapters, this chapter discusses the sociocultural meanings and experiences of young Nepali men's migration as a classed and gendered project. Further, it explores the question:

What does it mean to be a man in rural Nepal or a similar context in the Global South?

Migration and Masculinities

This book contributes to scholarship on masculinity and young men's migration by describing the close connections between the political economy, migration, and local understandings of what it means to be a man. I have argued that migration from the hills of Nepal to the Indian city of Mumbai offers an escape for poorer young men from rural areas who are otherwise left with limited economic opportunities to support their livelihoods. Over the years, migration has come to be understood as a rite of passage for young men from poorer households. Further, the concept of masculinity appropriately articulates the decision making, the work experience, and how men's gendered identities are reconstituted through the process of their migration. Over the years, this form of migration has been integrated into local meanings of masculinities in the hills, not just impacting those who migrate but also those left behind.

I have argued that rural men's migration is not only an important attempt to pursue economic advancement but also part of their quest for respect and ideas associated with masculinities. The adventure and consumption associated with migration as well as money earned through working in Indian cities is significant in elevating rural men's reputations. For these reasons, migration offers an easily available route for securing transition into adulthood for young men from poorer households in the village. However, this transition isn't automatically guaranteed.

Migration both enables and challenges gendered and class-related subjectivities of young men. Men are expected to migrate and secure successful transition into adulthood, and there is an uncertain gendered and generational transition for those who do not migrate. However, men may have their masculinity threatened as they leave behind their family and village to work in low-wage jobs in Indian cities. At the heart of this form of migration lies a paradoxical process; men must migrate to provide for their families and experience a distant world, but to do so, they have to be away and thus unable to perform their duties as men. Similarly, the men must go through hardship during both travel and border crossing and also while living and working in India.

As expected, migration to Indian cities does not translate automatically into success and freedom. On the contrary, most migrants work under very difficult conditions and suffer. One important implication of migration for masculinity is that there is a contradiction between the men's desire and obligation to migrate and the actual experience of difficult and exploitative working and living conditions in Indian cities and a journey that places a strain on their identity as men. While migration offers an escape from the difficult circumstances in the villages of Nepal, it can create further uncertainties, as it often does not result in the improvement of economic or sociocultural status. Masculinities have to be performed, and the consumption opportunities available in Indian cities become a powerful resource through which migrant men seek to assert their masculinity. But, consumption not only puts excessive economic demands on them; it also increases their vulnerability and the gendered ideas associated with migration, and sexual freedom puts them at risk of HIV infection in Mumbai.

Nepali men actively seek to mobilize consumption opportunities available in Indian cities to assert their gendered identity. The social meanings of migration to India, which is associated with adventure, freedom, excitement, and consumption, offer a powerful avenue by which male labor migrants can maintain a sense of meaning and purpose despite the many difficulties they face, difficulties that create their marginal, classed positions. It is the idea of freedom associated with migration that contributes to Nepali migrants' exploitation.

While migration is increasingly viewed as a form of freedom from the regimented social and economic life in the villages and freedom from the hardship of farming and agrarian life, it does not always result in freedom. Given that Nepali society still primarily defines a man's value in terms of his job (or, more specifically, permanent, full-time employment and stable income), the precarious and low-income nature of migrant work in Indian cities challenges men's sense of manly pride. Nepali men actively mobilize gender strategies of consumption to offset the negative effects of menial jobs and to protect their masculine pride.

Though the practice of going to work in India was largely referred to as "useless" and exploitative when compared to other forms of migration (migration to the Gulf countries or to work for foreign armies) that were associated with better salaries, secure employment, and travel to other international destinations, migration to India provided an opportunity for young men from poorer backgrounds to experiment with the pleasures and possibilities of new forms of commodity consumption, entertainment, and urban autonomy that were not available or accessible to them in the village. It also offered an escape from difficult socioeconomic, cultural, and familial situations and offered an opportunity for young men to experience a distant place, earn and remit money home to fulfil their obligations as men, and try their luck in attaining upward socioeconomic mobility for their households.

Options for Those Staying Back

What about young men from poorer households who do not migrate? How do men from poor households navigate their gendered subjectivities? Limited options are available to them. For young men in the poorer households in the hills, adolescence hardly exists. They are expected to take on adult responsibilities as they transition into adolescence.

These young men could continue to work locally on a farm or as a laborer, neither of which is profitable, nor do they provide gendered status. Regular work and pay are never guaranteed to enable them to provide for their families and meet their cash needs in the increasingly commodified economy in the village. Neither the work available on farms nor laboring opportunities provide prestige within the discourse of "development" that privileges urban life and salaried employment. There is very little opportunity for upward economic and sociocultural mobility, and young men risk being stuck in the village and thought of as *phaltu* (useless). These constraints are shaped not only by historical exploitative systems but also by the rapid socioeconomic and political changes taking place in Nepal.

Schooling has emerged as a significant route for transition into young adulthood. It is widely accepted that completion of schooling could result in a salaried job for young men. Comparatively, schooling is valued more among the Bahuns than the Magars. From the perspective of Bahuns, completion of the School Leaving Certificate (SLC) is an important aspect of their priestly identity as well as getting salaried employment (*jagir*) within Nepal. Magars have begun to put more emphasis on schooling as they believe it leads to better opportunities within Nepal. Yet, completion of the SLC or higher degrees away from home comes with significant cost, which not all the poorer households can afford.

Thus, a potential option for staying back and not being considered *phaltu* requires a young man to go to school and pass the SLC. Within the discourses on development and child rights, children are not expected to be "running away" to India or to be economically active as workers. There is considerable effort to get children to go to school and complete the SLC as it is believed that schooling opens up prospects for economic and social mobility. "It will not be an exaggeration to say that one's 'life-chances' are intimately tied to his/her performance in SLC. The SLC examinations open the door to the 'world of higher education' and the 'world of employment.'" (Mathema and Bista 2006: 5). Referred to as the "iron gate," the SLC controls access to higher education and salaried jobs. It has become a passport to adult life. Passing the SLC is important, but given the high failure rate, taking it is a major risk for many young men. A virtually impossible task for children from poorer households in the villages, passing the SLC has been elusive for a large number of young people who are economically poor or culturally and racially different from the mainstream. Stephen Mikesell (2006: 55) observes, "The rural schools in Nepal basically serve the role of disqualifying rural young people from roles in society and turning them into failures. In the School Leaving Certificate examinations of 1996, my last year of residence in Nepal, not one child from rural schools passed in the first division, which means that rural kids are eliminated from more prestigious college tracks, particularly from being engineers and doctors, the aspiration of middle-class parents for their children." Over the years, student performance on the SLC has stagnated, if not deteriorated. In my study area, the number of students who managed to pass the SLC examinations on the first attempt was very low. After attempting a couple of times, many gave up their dream of completing the SLC. Young men were aware of the stigma attached to failure. Occasional news circulated in the village of those who had taken their lives after failing.

The meaning of education has changed over the years, allowing new patterns and new actors to emerge. Previously, only a few Bahun men from the study area went to Tansen, Banaras, and Kathmandu for their education, and upon completion of their education, they would return to the village to work locally as priests, teachers, and government employees. It was important to go away for education so that they could return to the village and hold some important positions. In recent years, an increasing number of people, and not just Bahuns, have continued to leave the village for education in Tansen and Kathmandu. But unlike earlier students, they do not come back to the village after their studies. Rather they remain in the cities, mainly in Kathmandu, looking for salaried jobs. Young men leave the village not to return. However, the desired transition from completion of education to finding salaried employment is not a straightforward one.

At the time of my fieldwork, finding salaried employment was extremely difficult, as it required hard work, competency in the English language, and social networks in addition to good educational credentials. After completing their schooling, several young men from the village extended their stay in towns and cities searching for jobs. The process is commonly known as *jagir khojne,* and for many it resulted in repeated frustration as employment opportunities became scarce. In cases where they could not manage to find employment within Nepal, those who could manage money to pay for airfare and recruitment agencies eventually went to work in the Gulf or Southeast Asian countries.

I met several young men from the village studying in Kathmandu and Tansen who wanted to see their educational qualifications lead to salaried employment. None of them were interested in going back to the village without securing such a job. The value of educational qualification was seen to be its potential to provide salaried employment opportunities, thus allowing them not to return to the farms. As most of their educations were funded by families in the village, these young men found it very difficult to ask for money from their families as soon as their studies came to an end, and there was a sense of urgency to find jobs so that they could manage to stay in the city without being dependent on their household. They did not want to be seen as *phaltu,* but rather preferred to work in any form of employment that they could find. Many of them worked in underpaid jobs, mostly as hawkers and teachers and tutors in private boarding schools and tuition centers,[1] which did not provide even enough to manage their day-to-day expenses. They continued to work in the hope that they would be able to find a better job some day. Many of them depended on their friends and kinship networks to maintain their life in the cities. A few of them found it difficult to be seen as unemployed and preferred to enroll in one course after another in English language or computing skills.

Having obtained educational qualifications, those looking for salaried jobs needed to respond to jobs advertised in the newspapers by sending out a series of applications and looking for *source force.*[2] It was common to see them browsing through newspapers to look for a suitable vacancy. Men spent thousands of rupees printing out applications, preparing their CVs (called *bio-data*), and sending out application letters by post. After applying for jobs, most of them were never called for an interview, which they attributed to their lack of a recommendation. A job was always possible with a recommendation from an influential person (usually a politician, senior bureaucrat, or other influential person). These applicants had to judge whether a recommendation from a particular person was strong enough to get the job. Before applying for jobs, they would try to find the right channel to get their message across. Men I spoke to believed that it was difficult to find a job without paying a bribe. While some developed connections using their kinship network in the city, others developed connections using friendship or a political affiliation developed in the university.

Even those with an SLC grade found that they remained disadvantaged in the villages because of their lack of knowledge of English and lack of social and cultural networks; even with qualifications, they failed to find jobs and ended up migrating again. These "degrees without freedom" (Jeffrey, Jeffery, and Jeffery 2007), the phenomenon of young men with degree certificates but without secured employment, were prevalent in Nepal.

As I discuss below, the men who do not migrate, succeed in completing the SLC, or secure a job after completing the SLC come under pressure to assert their masculine identity in other ways. This is where the Maoist movement during Nepal's Maoist insurgency (1996–2005) becomes a significant factor.

Nepal's Maoist insurgency attracted a large number of young men from the poorer households of the middle hills. In the context of economic and sociocultural marginalization of young men in rural Nepal, the Maoist agenda for social transformation and an ideology that challenged the hegemony of ideas of modern urban masculinities played an important role in attracting a large number of young men to join the armed insurgency. Young men, mainly those from *dalit* (ex-Untouchable caste) and excluded ethnic groups, were attracted to the Maoist insurgency because its rhetoric addressed the structural equality of all, and the party awarded positions based on merit rather than on age, class, gender, caste, or ethnicity. The radical sociocultural ideology and the everyday practices of the Maoists attracted both young men and women. This had a powerful effect on local young men, who saw themselves as valuable agents within the space of the Maoist party.

For young men, joining the Maoist insurgency was very much an attempt to redefine dominant ideas of being a man in the hills of Nepal. It was a move to escape from being labeled a *phaltu*. For the youth from poorer households, joining the armed struggle did not reward them with a salary or regular payment, and it was not like a "job," but it was certainly attractive, as it allowed them to escape and reject the regimented order based on gender, class, and caste identities. Participation in the Maoist insurgency provided young men and women with an opportunity to escape the hierarchy based on age, the domination, and the traditions that were prevalent in the villages. The fact that the Maoist party advocated for intercaste love marriages appealed to many young men and women who had very little say in the choice of their life partner. Importantly, the ability to earn money or secure employment was not the key attribute of masculinity within the Maoist worldview.

What was life like for young men who left their homes and villages to join the armed struggle? Young men underwent a significant transformation in their worldview and lives once they "became Maoists." From the perspective of those involved, life as a Maoist was transformative, exciting, and difficult. Being a Maoist required young men to take risks, to fight and face physical injury, but also included travel to distant places and opportunities to expand their networks beyond their immediate villages.

By joining the Maoists, young men forged new relationships to the existing power structures in the villages. Living together with other fellow comrades, young men saw the armed struggle as a way of transforming the social relations that had discriminated against them. However, young men did face a hierarchy and regulations within the Maoist party itself. The party regulated courtships, love, and marriage. Young men and women had to receive the permission of their commanders to engage in courtships and marriage.

Life within the Maoist party put some of the dominant ideas about what it means to be a man into question. For the first time in their lives, many men found themselves cooking meals, washing dishes, and looking after their newly born babies in the cantonments and communal living spaces. Men who joined the Maoist party departed significantly from other men in Nepal in the sense that Maoist men were unable to financially support their family members. In this way, responsibility for family was replaced by responsibility toward fellow comrades, society, and the nation. Men went through an intense process of transformation, from being a householder to becoming a man concerned primarily with the nation.

These men actively constructed an alternative modernity based on the Maoist ideology; they rejected the dominant paradigm of consumerism and city life that seemed almost inaccessible to them. These men gave up ideas of achieving hegemonic masculinity when they joined the party.

Overall, the ideology and political education of the Maoist insurgency provided young men from rural remote villages with an opportunity to redefine their position vis-à-vis other men involved in consumption and modernity.[3] Within the social condition of insurgency, it was possible for young men to construct an ideal type of man who was not confined to the "limited" space of "family" and personal well-being but was of the "community" and "nation" at large.

Nonetheless, young men's lives in the insurgency were not necessarily liberating. Within the party organization, their lives were significantly different from their village lives, but the party also often restricted their freedom and sexuality and threatened their identities as men. These men appeared to have redefined their identity in relation to other men, but it was unlikely that these effects would be sustained in a time of noninsurgency.

Possibilities for Change

In the context of marginalization, disempowerment, exploitation, and suffering experienced by Nepali migrants in India, what are the possibilities for change? Could we conceive of Nepali migrants as flexible citizens taking advantage of the open border between Nepal and India? What political opportunities are there for Nepali migrants? Nepali migrants working in India largely remain invisible in the public debate within Nepal, and they remain outside the government of Nepal's priorities, which have focused heavily on international labor migration destinations such as the Gulf countries and Malaysia. Because Nepali migrant workers in India hold a marginal political and cultural position, their concerns rarely receive in-depth and broad coverage in the Nepali media or within public debate more broadly. Similarly, Nepali migrant workers in India are not really a concern of international organizations such as the International Labour Organization, the International Organization for Migration, or other UN agencies. Partly because of their liminal status, Nepali migrants working in India are invisible as migrant workers with rights and protection. The NGOs and development agencies working in Nepal have largely seen migration to India as a problem from the perspective of the trafficking of women and children and the public health risks caused by HIV and STIs. There are very few NGOs, for instance, aimed at protecting the rights and welfare of Nepali migrants in Indian cities. One might think that Nepali migrant associations would be one space through which a potential change could be imagined.

A number of migrant associations in India have been established with the aim of organizing Nepali migrants and providing them with a level of protection. The most prominent ones are the sister organizations of Nepal's major political parties, which have mainly offered safe haven for exiled political leaders from Nepal. Such associations could have been a source for collective mobilization, but they rarely organize activities or programs on the rights and protection of migrants. Except for involvement in resolving minor disputes, the migrant associations have not worked on behalf of Nepali migrants to negotiate better working conditions with their employers in India. These associations have neither the networks nor the leverage with other trade unions or worker organizations in India to achieve any change, nor do they have significant political connections with Indian political parties. In practice, in fact, the activities and programs of migrant associations are primarily about political and cultural engagements with Nepal, and not India, or about social networks. They organize sports competitions and picnics and celebrate Nepali festivals such as Dasai, Teej, Deusi-Bhailo, and Holi. Occasionally they raise funds to help someone, such as a person who has been robbed or who has lost his job, or who needs support with a family emergency.

A small number of Nepali migrants have made attempts to integrate into India by acquiring official documents such as passports, voting cards, and other documentation such as ration cards. Most, however, see their migration as temporary and display a strong attachment to Nepal, although in reality many of them spend most of their lives circulating between India and their homes in Nepal until they decide to retire in Nepal. This attachment to their villages is demonstrated in the different aspects of their everyday lives as migrants: sending remittances on a regular basis; using Nepali language in everyday conversation; the pattern of living together with fellow Nepalis from the same areas/regions; observing various Nepali social, communal, and religious events; continuing engagement with political processes in Nepal (as demonstrated by political mobilization in Nepal and returning home to vote). Because these low-income Nepali migrants remain connected to Nepal, and in an important sense keep separate from India, they have very little political space for collective mobilization to make any demands for their rights in India. Without these rights, their sense of identity and masculinity is being constructed by social forces that are not within their control.

Notes

Introduction

1. This term is associated with Nepali men recruited into a foreign army. The term *lahure* came from the name of the city of Lahore in Pakistan. It was originally used to refer to the hill men who went to Lahore to work in the army of the Sikh leader Ranjit Singh in the early nineteenth century. The term *lahure* has become the everyday designation for anyone going to work abroad, whether for army service or not, but the characteristic *lahure* is still perceived to be the army man. For a deeper ethnography on *lahure,* see K. Adhikari 1993 and Des Chene 1991.

2. The open border between Nepal and India makes it difficult to determine the exact number of Nepali migrant workers in India. Estimates vary between 0.5 million and 5 million. According to the 2001 Census of Nepal, there were a total of 589,050 Nepalis in India, and the Indian Census of 2001 gives a similar figure: 596,696. On the basis of my interaction with Nepali migrant associations in India and a consideration of various estimates made by scholars, I estimate that there are roughly 1 million Nepali migrants working in India. For a useful discussion on the difficulties of ascertaining the number of Nepali migrants in India, see Hutt 1997.

3. The Aadhaar card is essentially an identification card that allows the government of India to record and verify information on every resident Indian citizen, including biometric and demographic data. According to the government, the introduction of this card is to ensure that welfare services are being delivered to those who really need them and to save billions of rupees by reducing welfare fraud.

4. Here I must acknowledge the fieldwork I conducted with my colleague Antonio Donini (Tufts University) in various parts of western Nepal between 2008 and 2013.

5. In 1996, the Communist Party of Nepal-Maoist (CPN-M) started a rural insurgency in the mid-western hills of Nepal that eventually spread to virtually all of the seventy-five districts. By mid-2006, over two-thirds of the approximately four thousand secretaries of the Village Development Committees (VDCs)—the lowest tier of government in rural areas—had been relocated to district headquarters or to Nepali army strongholds. The Maoists effectively denied stable government access and presence throughout rural Nepal. In many areas, they obstructed government-funded development projects and closely scrutinized the work of NGOs. Over the ten-year period, the local population in parts of rural Nepal was caught between Maoist intimidation and forced donation on one hand and police or Nepali army reprisals on the other. The insurgency and counterinsurgency claimed some thirteen thousand lives, in large part civilian.

6. The lower part of the hillsides and the valley floors, which are considered fertile and malarial.

7. Village or village houses that are located in the higher altitude of the hills.

8. For details, see K. Adhikari 1993; Ahearn 2004; Harper 2014; Hitchcock 1966; Miller 2002; Pageni 1991; Ramirez 2000; Smadja [1922–1932] 1999; Stone 1989; and Wilmore 2002.

9. It started with King Prithvi Narayan Shah (A.D. 1723 to 1775) and was followed by his successors, resulting in what would become "greater Nepal."

10. A system of "non-party democracy" instituted by King Mahendra gave absolute power to the monarchy. This political system, which was in place in Nepal between 1961 and 1990, was eventually toppled by the popular people's movement in 1990.

11. Village-level administrative divisions that today are called Village Development Committees (VDCs).

12. Search operation or patrol done by security forces.

13. For more information on missionary hospitals and health-related issues, see Harper 2014.

14. For an ethnography of waiting and boredom in the context of northern India, see Jeffrey 2010.

Chapter 1

1. Irrigated field used for paddy cultivation.

2. Unit for land measurement: 1 *ropani* is 70 feet by 70 feet, approximately 455 square meters.

3. Dry field used for growing maize, millet, and so on.

4. Rocky land not suitable for farming; it is used for growing fodder and as grazing land.

5. The construction of the highway began in the year 1965.

6. The Tarai is the lowland region in southern Nepal. It runs along Nepal's border with India. Historically, the region was sparsely populated due to dense malarial forest. Following the eradication of malaria through DDT spray, the region has attracted considerable in-migration of population due to its fertile agricultural land and is now home to about half of Nepal's population.

7. A pseudonym given by Gupta.

Chapter 2

1. For in-depth coverage of this incident, see Audrey Gillan's one-page article titled "Running for Riches in the Great Gurkha Race," which appeared in *Guardian Weekly* (16–22 December 2005).

2. The novel is used as a textbook in the curriculum for the university intermediate degree (intermediate in arts/intermediate in commerce/intermediate in science), so most of the people who have completed their schooling have read this novel. The intermediate degree is normally taken after students complete their School Leaving Certificate (SLC) and before the bachelor's degree.

3. Recruiters who went to different villages in the hills to recruit men to serve in a foreign army.

4. Useless work or work that does not earn much respect or money.

5. Small work or work that has low status or value.

Chapter 3

1. A similar practice is reported in the Indian hills (see Berreman 1972).

2. There were a few cases of young girls and boys involved in a romantic relationship who ran away together against the wishes of their parents.

3. Migrants used the word *room* to refer to an individual hut in the slums in Mumbai.

Chapter 4

Sources: Portions of Chapter 4 originally appeared as Jeevan Raj Sharma, "Marginal but Modern: Nepali Labor Migrants in India," *Young: Nordic Journal of Youth Research* 21, no. 4 (2013): 347–362, and Jeevan Raj Sharma, "Practices of Male Labour Migration from the Hills of Nepal to India in Development Discourses: Which Pathology?" *Gender, Development and Technology* 12, no. 3 (2008): 303–323.

1. See www.nepaldemocracy.org/documents, accessed 5 April 2017.

2. I had initially planned to travel with a few men from Palpa to India, but at the time a blockade imposed by the Maoists prevented me from being able to go to the village.

3. People's real names have been changed to preserve their anonymity.

Chapter 5

Source: Portions of Chapter 5 originally appeared as Jeevan Raj Sharma and Sondra Hausner, "On the Way to India: Nepali Rituals of Border Crossing," in *Borderland Lives in Northern South Asia,* ed. David N. Gellner, 94–116 (Durham, NC: Duke University Press, 2013).

1. The literal meaning of the Nepali term *bahadur* is "brave."
2. A type of small hut in the hills that looked like a cowshed or firewood shed and signified poverty.
3. A half-cup of tea, served in the street corner tea stall in Mumbai.

Chapter 6

Sources: Portions of Chapter 6 originally appeared as Jeevan Raj Sharma, "Marginal but Modern: Nepali Labor Migrants in India," *Young: Nordic Journal of Youth Research* 21, no. 4 (2013): 347–362, and Jeevan Raj Sharma, "Practices of Male Labour Migration from the Hills of Nepal to India in Development Discourses: Which Pathology?" *Gender, Development and Technology* 12, no. 3 (2008): 303–323.

1. The names of the two films that I saw were *Asha* and *Sneha. Asha* (Hope) is a forty-nine-minute-long video-drama with the message that people with HIV should always remain positive and should never give up hope. *Sneha* (Love/affection) offers the message that people should not discriminate against those with HIV and should give them love, respect, and affection.
2. Dasai is considered to be one of the biggest festivals in Nepal. It is held on the tenth day of the light fortnight (the period of the waxing moon) of the month of Ashvin (September–October) in honor of the goddess Durga.
3. *Sabai thik cha, haina ta?*
4. *Naramro thau.*
5. *Maaja audaina.*

Conclusion

1. Tuition centers are private institutions run by entrepreneurs and individuals for profit-making purposes. They offer supplementary education, covering subjects that are taught in the school. They often employ educated unemployed youth as tutors.
2. *Source force* refers to a kin network for recommendations, which were necessary in order to find a job. It was also called *bhansun.*
3. Pettigrew (2003) has agreed that participation in the Maoist movement enabled Nepali rural youth to participate in a new type of modernity.

References

Adhikari, Jagannath. 2001. "Mobility and Agrarian Change in Central Nepal." *Contributions to Nepalese Studies* 28:247–267.

Adhikari, Kamal R. 1993. "The Participation of the Magars in Nepalese Development." Ph.D. diss., University of Austin.

Adhikari, Radha. 2013. "Empowered Wives and Frustrated Husbands: Nursing, Gender and Migrant Nepali in the UK." *Journal of International Migration* 51 (6): 168–179.

Ahearn, Laura M. 2004. *Invitations to Love: Literacy, Love Letters and Social Change in Nepal.* New Delhi: Adarsh Books.

Allen, Michael. 1994. *Anthropology of Nepal: Peoples, Problems and Process.* Kathmandu: Mandala Book Point.

Alvarez, Robert R. 1995. "The Mexican-US Border: The Making of an Anthropology of Borderland." *Annual Review of Anthropology* 24:447–470.

Baud, Michiel, and Willem Van Schendel. 1997. "Towards a Comparative History of Borderlands." *Journal of World History* 8 (2): 211–242.

Bebbington, Anthony. 1999. "Capitals and Capabilities: A Framework for Analyzing Peasant Viability, Rural Livelihoods and Poverty." *World Development* 27:2021–2044.

Beine, Dave. 1998. "Nepal—Then and Now: A Critical Appraisal of the Ethnography of Nepal." *Contributions to Nepalese Studies* 25:163–190.

Berreman, Gerald. D. 1972. *Hindus of the Himalayas: Ethnography and Change.* Berkeley: University of California Press.

Besky, Sarah. 2014. *The Darjeeling Distinction: Labor and Justice on Fair-Trade Tea Plantations in India.* Berkeley: University of California Press.

Blaikie, Piers, John Cameron, and David Seddon. 1979. *The Struggle for Basic Needs in Nepal.* Paris: OECD.

———. 1980. *Nepal in Crisis: Growth and Stagnation at the Periphery.* Delhi: Oxford University Press.

———. 2002. "Understanding 20 Years of Change in West-Central Nepal: Continuity and Change in Lives and Ideas." *World Development* 30:1255–1270.

Boehm, Deborah A. 2008. "Now I Am a Man and a Woman! Gendered Moves and Migrations in a Transnational Mexican Community." *Latin American Perspectives* 35 (1): 16–30.

Bourdieu, Pierre. 1977. *Outline of a Theory of Practice.* Cambridge: Cambridge University Press.

———. 2001. *Masculine Domination.* Cambridge, UK: Polity Press.

Breman, John. 1985. *Of Peasants, Migrants and Paupers: Rural Labour Circulation and Capitalist Production in West India.* Delhi: Oxford University Press.

Bretell, Caroline B. 2000. "Theorizing Migration in Anthropology: The Social Construction of Network, Identities, Communities and Globalscapes." In *Migration Theory: Talking across Disciplines,* edited by Caroline B. Brettell and James F. Hollifield, 97–135. New York: Routledge.

Burawoy, Michael. 1976. "The Functions and Reproduction of Migrant Labour: Comparative Material from Southern Africa and the United States." *American Journal of Sociology* 82 (5): 1050–1087.

Caplan, Leone. 1991. "'Bravest of the Brave': Representations of 'the Gurkha' in British Military Writings." *Modern Asian Studies* 25:571–597.

CBS. 2002. *Population Census 2001.* Kathmandu: CBS.

———. 2011. *Nepal Living Standard Survey 2011.* Kathmandu: CBS.

Charsley, Katharine. 2005. "Unhappy Husbands: Masculinity and Migration in Transnational Pakistani Marriages." *Journal of Royal Anthropological Institute* 11:85–105.

Clifford, James. 1997. *Routes: Travel and Translation in the Late Twentieth Century.* Cambridge, MA: Harvard University Press.

Cohen, Deborah. 2006. "From Peasant to Worker: Migration, Masculinity, and the Making of Mexican Workers in the US." *International Labour and Working Class History* 69:81–103.

Cohen, Jeffery. 2004. *The Culture of Migration in Southern Mexico.* Austin: University of Texas Press.

Connell, Raewyn W. 1987. *Gender and Power: Society, the Person and Sexual Politics.* Oxford: University of California Press.

———. 1995. *Masculinities.* Cambridge, UK: Polity Press.

Conway, Denis, Keshav Bhattarai, and Nanda R. Shrestha. 2000. "Population-Environment Relations at the Forested Frontier of Nepal: Tharu and Pahari Survival Strategies in Bardiya." *Applied Geography* 20:221–242.

Cornwall, Andrea, and Nancy Lindisfarne. 1994. "Introduction." In *Dislocating Masculinity: Comparative Ethnographies,* edited by Andrea Cornwall and Nancy Lindisfarne, 1–10. London: Routledge.

Cresswell, Tim. 2000. "Mobility, Syphilis, and Democracy: Pathologizing Mobile Body." In *Pathologies of Travel*, edited by Richard Wrigley and George Revill, 261–278. Amsterdam: Rodopi.

———. 2003. "Introduction: Theorising Place." In *Mobilizing Place, Placing Mobility: The Politics of Representation in a Globalized World*, edited by Tim Cresswell and Ginette Vertsraete, 11–32. Amsterdam: Rodopi.

Cross, Jamie. 2009. "From Dreams to Discontent: Educated Men and the Everyday Politics of Labour in a Special Economic Zone in South India." *Contributions to Indian Sociology* 43 (3): 351–379.

Das, Pushpita. 2008. "Towards a Regulated Indo-Nepal Border." *Strategic Analysis* 32 (5): 879–900.

DDC. 2000. *District Profile of Palpa*. Palpa: District Development Committee.

De Haan, Arjan. 1997. "Unsettled Settlers: Migrant Workers and Industrial Capitalism in Calcutta." *Modern Asian Studies* 31:919–949.

———. 1999. "Livelihoods and Poverty: The Role of Migration. A Critical Review of Literature." *Journal of Development Studies* 36:1–47.

De Haan, Arjan, and Ben Rogaly. 2002. "Introduction: Migrant Workers and Their Role in Social Change." *Journal of Development Studies* 38:1–14.

Des Chene, Mary K. 1991. "Relics of Empire: A Cultural History of the Gurkhas 1815–1987." Ph.D. diss., Stanford University.

———. 1995. "Locating the Past." In *Anthropological Locations*, edited by Akhil Gupta and James Ferguson, 66–85. Berkeley: University of California Press.

Eckholm, Erik P. 1976. *Losing Ground: Environmental Stress and World Food Prospects*. New York: W. W. Norton.

Farmer, Paul. 2004. "An Anthropology of Structural Violence." *Current Anthropology* 45 (3): 305–325.

Fisher, William F. 2001. *Fluid Boundaries*. New York: Columbia University Press.

Furer-Haimendorf, Christoph V. 1964. *The Sherpas of Nepal*. London: John Murray.

———. 1975. *Himalayan Traders: Life in Highland Nepal*. London: John Murray.

Galtung, Johan. 1975. *Peace: Research, Education, Action*. Copenhagen: Christian Ejlers.

Gellner, David N. 2013a. "Northern South Asia's Diverse Borders." In *Borderland Lives in Northern South Asia*, edited by David N. Gellner, 1–23. Durham, NC: Duke University Press.

———. 2013b. "Warriors, Workers, Traders, and Peasants: The Nepali/Gorkhali Diaspora since the Nineteenth Century." In *Routledge Handbook of South Asian Diasporas*, edited by David Washbrook and Joya Chatterjee, 136–150. Abingdon, UK: Routledge.

Government of Nepal. 2010. *Economic Survey for Fiscal Year 2009–2010*. Kathmandu: Ministry of Finance.

Gupta, Akhil. 1999. *Postcolonial Developments*. New Delhi: Oxford University Press.

Gupta, Akhil, and James Ferguson, eds. 1997. *Anthropological Locations: Boundaries and Grounds of a Field Science.* Berkeley: University of California Press.

Harper, Ian. 2014. *Development and Public Health in the Himalaya: Reflections on healing in Contemporary Nepal.* London: Routledge.

Hausner, Sondra L. 2005. *Migration, Trafficking and Prostitution in the Context of Nepal's Armed Conflict.* Kathmandu: Save the Children—USA.

Hausner, Sondra L., and Jeevan Raj Sharma. 2013. "On the Way to India: Nepali Rituals of Border Crossing." In *Borderland Lives in Northern South Asia,* edited by David N. Gellner, 94–116. Durham, NC: Duke University Press.

Hitchcock, John T. 1961. "A Nepalese Hill Village and Indian Employment." *Asian Survey* 1 (9): 15–20.

———. 1966. *The Magars of Banyan Hill.* New York: Holt, Rinehart and Winston.

Hodgson, Brian H. 1874. *Essays on the Languages, Literature, and Religion of Nepál and Tibet.* London: Trübner and Co.

Hutt, Michael. 1989. "A Hero or a Traitor? The Gurkha Soldier in Nepali Literature." *South Asia Research* 9:21–32.

———. 1997. "Being Nepali without Nepal: Reflections on a South Asian Diaspora." In *Nationalism and Ethnicity in a Hindu Kingdom: The Politics of Culture in Contemporary Nepal,* edited by David N. Gellner, Joanna Pfaff-Czarnecka, and John Whelpton, 101–144. Amsterdam: Harwood Academic Publishers.

———. 1998. "Going to Muglan: Nepali Literary Representations of Migration to India and Bhutan." *South Asia Research* 18:195–214.

Inden, Ronald. 1990. *Imagining India.* Oxford: Blackwell.

Ives, Jack, and Bruno Messerli. 1989. *The Himalayan Dilemma: Reconciling Development and Conservation.* New York: Routledge.

Jackson, Cecilia, ed. 2001. "Men at Work." In *Men at Work: Labour, Masculinities and Development,* edited by Cecilia Jackson, 1–22. London: Frank Cass.

Jeffrey, Craig. 2010. *Timepass: Youth, Class and the Politics of Waiting in India.* Stanford, CA: Stanford University Press.

Jeffrey, Craig, Patricia Jeffery, and Roger Jeffery. 2007. *Degrees without Freedom: Education, Masculinities and Unemployment in North India.* Stanford, CA: Stanford University Press.

Jest, Cornelle, Jean Galode, Marie Lecomte-Tilouine, and Philippe Ramirez. 2000. "The Population of Gulmi and Argha-Khanci." In *Resunga: The Mountain of the Horned Sage,* edited by Philippe Ramirez, 51–74. Kathmandu: Himal Books.

Jones, Adam. 2006. "Introduction: Worlding Men." In *Men of the Global South,* edited by Adam Jones, xii–xxii. London: Zed Books.

Joshi, Sushm. 2001. "'Cheli-Beti' Discourses of Trafficking and Constructions of Gender, Citizenship and Nation in Modern Nepal (Prostitution, Sex Workers)." *South Asia—Journal of South Asian Studies* 24:157–175.

Kearney, Michael. 1996. *Reconceptualising the Peasantry.* Oxford, UK: Westview.

——. 2004a. *Changing Fields of Anthropology.* Oxford, UK: Rowman and Littlefield.

——. 2004b. "The Classifying and Value-Filtering Missions of Borders." *Anthropological Theory* 4 (2): 131–156.

Kirkpatrick, William. 1969. "1754–1812: An Account of the Kingdom of Nepaul: Being the Substance of Observations Made during a Mission to That Country in the Year 1793." New Delhi: Mañjuśrī Publishing House.

Liechty, Mark. 2003. *Suitably Modern: Making Middle-Class Culture in a New Consumer Society.* Princeton, NJ: Princeton University Press.

Macfarlane, Alan. 1976. *Resources and Population: A Study of Gurungs of Nepal.* London: Cambridge University Press.

——. 2001. "Sliding Downhill: Some Reflections on Thirty Years of Change in a Himalayan Village." *European Bulletin for Himalayan Research* 20:105–110.

MacInnes, John. 1998. *The End of Masculinity: The Confusion of Sexual Genesis and Sexual Difference in Modern Society.* Buckingham, UK: Open University Press.

Malkki, Lisa. 1992. "National Geographic: The Rooting of Peoples and the Territorialization of National Identity among Scholars and Refugees." *Cultural Anthropology* 7:24–44.

——. 1995. *Purity and Exile: Violence, Memory, and National Cosmology among Hutu Refugees in Tanzania.* Chicago: University of Chicago Press.

Marcus, George E. 1995. "Ethnography in/of the World System: The Emergence of Multi-sited Ethnography." *Annual Review of Anthropology* 24:95–117.

——. 1998. *Ethnography through Thick and Thin.* Princeton, NJ: Princeton University Press.

Martínez, Oscar. 1994. *Border People: Life and Society in the U.S.-Mexico Borderlands.* Tucson: University of Arizona Press.

Mathema, Kedar B., and Min Bahadur Bista. 2006. *Study on Student Performance in SLC (Main Report).* Kathmandu: Ministry of Education and Sports.

McDowell, Linda. 2003. *Redundant Masculinities? Employment Change and White Working Class Youth.* Oxford, UK: Blackwell.

Mead, Margaret. 1930. *Growing Up in New Guinea.* New York: Mentor Books.

Mikesell, Stephan. 2006. "Thoughts on Why Children of Nepal Would Join the Revolution." In *People's Power in Nepal,* edited by R. K. Vishwakarma, 53–58. New Delhi: Manak Publishing.

Miller, Casper, J. 2002. *Decision Making in Village Nepal.* Kathmandu: Pilgrims.

Mills, Mary B. 1999. *Thai Women in the Global Labour Force: Consuming Desires, Contested Selves.* London: Rutgers University Press.

Monsutti, Alessandro. 2007. "Migration as a Rite of Passage: Young Afghans

Building Masculinity and Adulthood in Iran." *Iranian Studies* 20 (2): 167–185.

Nath, Lopita. 2006. "Migration, Insecurity and Identity: The Nepali Dairymen in India's Northeast." *Asian Ethnicity* 7 (2): 129–148.

NCASC. 2002. *Nepal's National HIV/AIDS Strategy.* Kathmandu: NCASC/UNAIDS.

Newman, David. 2006. "Borders and Bordering: Towards an Interdisciplinary Dialogue." *European Journal of Social Theory* 9 (2): 171–186.

Onta, Pratyoush. 1994. "Rich Possibilities: Notes on Social History in Nepal." *Contribution to Nepalese Studies* 21:1–43.

Osella, Filippo, and Caroline Osella. 2000. "Migration, Money and Masculinity in Kerala." *Journal of Royal Anthropological Institute (N.S.)* 6:117–133.

———. 2006. *Men and Masculinities in South India.* London: Anthem Press.

Pageni, Bhageshwor. 1991. *Palpama prajatantric andolanka saya deen.* Kathmandu: Neema Pageni.

Pettigrew, Judith. 2003. "Guns, Kinship, and Fear: Maoists among the Tamumai (Gurungs)." In *Resistance and the State: Nepalese Experiences,* edited by David N. Gellner, 305–325. New Delhi: Social Science Press.

Pfaff-Czarnecka, Joanna. 1995. "Migration under Marginality Conditions: The Case of Bajhang." In *Rural-Urban Interlinkages: A Challenge for Swiss Development Cooperation,* edited by I. A. Ida, 97–108. Zurich/Kathmandu: INFRAS.

Pigg, Stacey L. 1992. "Inventing Social Categories through Place—Social Representations and Development in Nepal." *Comparative Studies in Society and History* 34:491–513.

———. 2001. "Languages of Sex and AIDS in Nepal: Notes on the Social Production of Commensurability." *Cultural Anthropology* 16:481–541.

———. 2002. "Expecting the Epidemic: A Social History of the Representation of Sexual Risk in Nepal." *Feminist Media Studies* 2:97–125.

Poudel, Krishna. 1999. *Migration Pattern in Doti.* Kathmandu: UNDP/Participatory Planning and Management of HIV/AIDS.

———. 2001. *HIV/STIs Risk Behaviour among Migrants in Doti District.* Kathmandu: JICA.

Poudel, Krishna C., Masamine Jimba, Junko Okumura, Anand B. Joshi, and Susumu Wakai. 2004a. "Migrants' Risky Sexual Behaviours in India and at Home in Far Western Nepal." *Tropical Medicine and International Health* 9:897–903.

Poudel, Krishna C., Masamine Jimba, Junko Okumura, Mahesh Sharma, Kalpana Poudel Tandukar, and Susumu Wakai. 2004b. "Migration in Far Western Nepal: A Time Bomb for a Future HIV/AIDS Epidemic?" *Tropical Doctor* 34:30–31.

Poudel, Krishna C., Junko Okumura, Jeevan B. Sherchand, Masamine Jimba, Izumi Murakami, and Susumu Wakai. 2003. "Mumbai Disease in Far Western Nepal: HIV Infection and Syphilis among Male Migrant-

Returnees and Nonmigrants." *Tropical Medicine and International Health* 8:933–939.

Raithelhuber, Martin. 2003. "The Significance of Towns for Rural Livelihood in Nepal." In *Translating Development: The Case of Nepal,* edited by Manfred Domroes, 195–206. New Delhi: Social Science Press.

Ramirez, Philippe, ed. 2000. *Resunga: The Mountain of the Horned Sage.* Kathmandu: Himal Books.

Regmi, Mahesh C. 1971. *A Study in Nepali Economic History 1768–1846.* New Delhi: Mañjuśrī Publishing House.

———. 1976. *Land Ownership in Nepal.* Berkeley: University of California Press.

———. 1978. *Thatched Huts and Stucco Palaces: Peasants and Landlords in 19th Century Nepal.* New Delhi: Vikas.

———. 1988. *An Economic History of Nepal, 1846–1901.* Varanasi, India: Nath.

Seddon, David. 1998. "HIV-AIDS in Nepal: The Coming Crisis." *Bulletin of Concerned Asian Scholars* 30:35–45.

Seddon, David, Jagannath Adhikari, and Ganesh Gurung. 2001. *The New Lahures: Foreign Employment and Remittance Economy of Nepal.* Kathmandu: NIDS.

———. 2002. "Foreign Labour Migration and the Remittance Economy of Nepal." *Critical Asian Studies* 34:19–40.

Shah, Alpa. 2006. "The Labour of Love: Seasonal Migration from Jharkhand to the Brick Kilns of Other States in India." *Contributions to Indian Sociology* 40:91–118.

Shrestha, Nanda R. 1989. "Frontier Settlement and Landlessness among Hill Migrants in Nepal Tarai." *Annals of the Association of American Geographers* 79:370–389.

———. 1990. *Landlessness and Migration in Nepal.* Boulder, CO: Westview.

———. 2001. *The Political Economy of Land, Landlessness and Migration in Nepal.* New Delhi: Nirala.

Smadja, Joelle. (1922–1932) 1999. "A Journey towards Palpa." *European Bulletin for Himalayan Research* 15–16:41–49.

———. 2000. "Landscape Diversity and Water Availability." In *Resunga: The Mountain of the Horned Sage,* edited by Philippe Ramirez, 1–50. Kathmandu: Himal Books.

Stark, Oded. 1991. *The Migration of Labour.* Cambridge, MA: Harvard University Press.

Stone, Linda. 1989. "Cultural Crossroads of Community Participation in Development—a Case from Nepal." *Human Organisation* 48:206–213.

Subba, Tanka, and A. C. Sinha. 2003. *Nepalis in North East India: A Community in Search of Indian Identity.* New Delhi: Indus.

Thieme, Susan. 2006. *Social Networks and Migration: Far West Nepalese Labour Migrants in Delhi.* Münster, Germany: LIT Publishing House.

Thieme, Susan, and Ulrike Müller-Böker. 2004. "Financial Self-Help Associations among Far-West Nepalese Labour Migrants in Delhi, India." *Asian and Pacific Migration Journal* 13:339–361.

Thieme, Susan, and Simone Wyss. 2005. "Migration Patterns and Remittance Transfer in Nepal: A Case Study of Sainik Basti in Western Nepal." *International Migration* 43:59–98.

Todaro, Michael P. 1976. *Internal Migration in Developing Countries.* Geneva: ILO.

Turner, Ralph L. (1931) 1990. *A Comparative and Etymological Dictionary of the Nepali Language.* London: K. Paul, Trench, Trübner.

UNAIDS/NCASC. 2004. *The HIV/AIDS/STI Situation and the National Response in Nepal.* Kathmandu: UNAIDS/NCASC.

USAID. 2005. *Health Profile Nepal: NEPAL-HIV/AIDS.* Washington, DC: USAID.

Whelpton, John. 2005. *History of Nepal.* Cambridge: Cambridge University Press.

Whitehead, Ann. 2002. "Tracking Livelihood Change: Theoretical, Methodological and Empirical Perspectives from North-Ghana." *Journal of South African Studies* 28:575–598.

Wilmore, Michael. 2002. "Indigenous Media and the Anthropology of Development in Nepal: A Case Study of Local Media Use in Tansen, Palpa District, Nepal." Ph.D. diss., University of London.

World Bank. 1989. *Nepal: Poverty Alleviation Policies.* New York: World Bank.

———. 1998. *Nepal: Poverty at the Turn of the Twenty First Century.* Washington, DC: World Bank.

———. 2010. *Large-Scale Migration and Remittances in Nepal: Issues and Challenges.* Kathmandu: World Bank.

Index

Jeevan R. Sharma is a Professor of South Asia and International Development at the University of Edinburgh.